Guerrillas in the Industrial Jungle

Guerrillas in the Industrial Jungle

Radicalism's Primitive and Industrial Rhetoric

Ursula McTaggart

Cover art courtesy of Carni Klirs

Published by State University of New York Press, Albany

For information, contact State University of New York Press, Albany, NY
www.sunypress.edu

Production by Kelli Williams-LeRoux
Marketing by Anne M. Valentine

Library of Congress Cataloging-in-Publication Data

McTaggart, Ursula.
  Guerrillas in the industrial jungle : radicalism's primitive and industrial rhetoric /
Ursula McTaggart.
       p. cm.
  Includes bibliographical references and index.
  ISBN 978-1-4384-3904-4 (pbk. : alk. paper)
  ISBN 978-1-4384-3903-7 (hardcover : alk. paper)
  1. African American labor union members. 2. Black power—United States.
3. Civil rights movements—United States. 4. Labor movement—United States.
5. United States—Race relations. I. Title.

  HD6490.R2M38 2011
  305.896'073—dc22   2011004293

                 10   9   8   7   6   5   4   3   2   1

Contents

Illustrations

Acknowledgments

The project was inspired by the work of political activists, and I am grateful to those who donated their time for interviews: General Baker, David Finkel, Dianne Feeley, Wendy Thompson, Debby Pope, Kate Stacy, Frank Thompson, Elissa Karg, and Paul Le Blanc. Milton Fisk and David Finkel deserve special thanks for being "on call" to answer questions about socialist history and to track down old friends, and Dan La Botz generously allowed me to use his unpublished memoirs. I want to acknowledge Lisa Lyons, the Shrine of the Black Madonna Church, Emily Porter, Emory Douglas, and Peter Bauer, aka "Urban Scout," for permitting me to reprint their illustrations and photographs. Luke Tripp and Ernie Allen offered help in my attempts to contact former members of the League of Revolutionary Black Workers.

Special thanks go to Purnima Bose and Margo Crawford for acting as mentors and friends in the research and writing process. De Witt Kilgore, Robert Terrill, Anne Delgado, Chia-Li Kao, Laila Amine, and Karen Dillon shaped the text in its early stages, while Larin McLaughlin, Andrew Kenyon, Kelli Williams-LeRoux, Lauren Pacifico, readers from SUNY Press, and my colleague Ed Agran helped transform it into its final state.

It was my dad who took me to the University of Michigan library to pursue my first large-scale research project at the age of nine. Today, he and my mother, Fred McTaggart and Donna Carroll, have been endlessly willing to tackle thankless proofreading and provide commentary, while the political convictions of my brother Ted guided my choice of a valuable topic. Finally, my husband Steve Sharpe has helped me talk out the puzzles of this project. His work as a legal aid attorney looks very different from the activism discussed in this book, but it is yet another example of rhetoric in political action.

Key to Abbreviations

BAM	Black Arts Movement
BPP	Black Panther Party
COINTELPRO	Counterintelligence program
Comintern	Communist International (aka Third International)
CP	Communist Party
CPUSA	Communist Party-USA
USACWA	Communications Workers of America
diy	do-it-yourself
DRUM	Dodge Revolutionary Union Movement
DRUM	Newsletter of DRUM
ELRUM	Eldon Revolutionary Union Movement
ELRUM	Newsletter of ELRUM
GM	General Motors
ICV	*Inner-City Voice* (newspaper of LRBW)
IS	International Socialists (US)
ISO	International Socialist Organization
LCFO	Lowndes County Freedom Organization
LRBW	League of Revolutionary Black Workers
SDS	Students for a Democratic Society

sf	speculative fiction
SNCC	Student Nonviolent Coordinating Committee
SP	Socialist Party
SWP	Socialist Workers Party (US)
TTU	Telephone Traffic Union
UAW	United Auto Workers (officially United Automobile, Aerospace and Agricultural Implement Workers of America International Union)

Introduction

Visitors come to Trackers Northwest in Portland to gain "primitive" skills for the new millennium. The most dedicated can sign up for "immersion" classes in hunter-gathering, in which they learn to identify edible plants, build basic shelters, tan hides, and survive in the wilderness. Some of those who teach and take such lessons are anarcho-primitivists who believe that civilization is fundamentally doomed. They look forward to a collapse that will force humans back to their roots in small nomadic tribes. By making clothes out of roadkill and cultivating skills like boat-building and pottery, they are preparing for a better future. An early slogan of the anarchist environmentalist group Earth First! sums up the attitude perfectly with the exhortation "Back to the Pleistocene!" (Manes 235). Technological progress will not save us, they insist. The past holds the keys to sustainable human life.

Members of the small socialist organization Solidarity, on the other hand, still see industry as the focal point for revolutionary change. Radical union democracy, they believe, can give real power to the working class. In a revolutionary situation, they hope that democratic unions would take over the means of production and construct a nonabusive form of democratic socialism. Based on this "rank-and-file strategy," Solidarity recruits in union workplaces and encourages its young members to take jobs in the union sector. Once there, they can advocate for increased union democracy in often bureaucratic, corrupt international unions. Even in the post–Cold War era, when information technology dominates the social landscape and American manufacturing continues to migrate abroad, socialists see the factory as the site of resistance. In a socialist future, industry will provide for all.

As these competing ideologies demonstrate, advocates for radical change use some very basic conceptions of envisioning utopian—or at least more just—futures, invoking nostalgia for a lost past or the promise of technology helping people to construct a better world. The "primitive" and the "industrial," as metaphors and ideological concepts, have often driven leftist notions of a better world. They suggest that we are living in a state of either progress—which will lead to socialism, or degeneration—which requires that we return to the past for our solutions.

Perhaps it's natural to understand change by looking at other time periods—temporal distance allows us to imagine radical social differences. In America, however, the "primitive" and the industrial[1] are also steeped in the history of race. In fact, in this country, it's hard to speak about political change without also speaking about race. Colonial exploration, national expansion, the Civil War, the history of immigration, conflicts with indigenous peoples, and the Civil Rights Movement all involved conflicts about race as well as economic or social change. In 2008, in the throes of an economic crisis and two wars, the voting public wanted "change" after eight years under George W. Bush—and the best way to achieve symbolic change, at least, was through the issue of race. For a nation that associates economic and social change with race, the first black President brought both hope and fear that a new era was on the horizon.

As my investigation of radical leftist organizations will demonstrate, the imagery of race and radical change does not limit itself to the "primitive." Likewise, radical organizations do not simply choose one model—either primitive or industrial utopias. Rather, the "primitive" and industrial frequently coexist, and both can engage with issues of race politics, labor rights, or environmental activism. Contemporary anarchists not only romanticize hunter-gatherers—they also "hunt and gather" in city dumpsters and establish "tribal" communities in abandoned industrial buildings. Today's socialists may not rely on invocations of the "primitive," but their socialist and black nationalist predecessors in the 1960s and '70s sometimes did. The League of Revolutionary Black Workers, for instance, used images of African spears and drums while organizing within auto factories, and socialists of the 1970s spoke of "colonizing" workplaces, subtly suggesting that they were educators converting "natives" to radical beliefs.

The language of the "primitive" and the industrial allows activists to draw on unspoken cultural connotations that they hope will evoke emotion in their audience. And these metaphors for change can sometimes exist as mere propaganda, manipulating audiences emotionally without engaging them intellectually. However, political language is not merely propagandistic, even if it does employ abstract concepts like the industrial and the "primitive." Typically, the distinction between political speech and literature relies on perceived differences between the subtlety and complexity of their messages. Political language often resembles advertising, with simplistic or abstract rhetoric, while literature acknowledges the complexities of language, identity, and ethics and may or may not make a political statement. The varied rhetorical and visual projects of activists, however, often break these distinctions down.

Even the worst examples of manipulative propaganda get their force by evoking cultural, historical, or literary references. As a result, studies of social movements should focus not only on historical and sociological factors but also on rhetorical and literary analysis. T. V. Reed has begun this process by arguing that social movements can learn from literary theory, while literary theory can gain something from the pragmatism of social movements. He insists that we must study the "poetics of social movements," including "the underlying rhetorical figures that shape them" and the "movements themselves as forms of cultural and political expression" (*Fifteen Jugglers* 16). Reed begins this project by employing literary analysis and cultural studies methods in his work on music in the Civil Rights Movement, murals in the Chicano Movement, and popular film about the American Indian Movement, to name a few (*The Art of Protest*). The rhetoric and imagery of these movements, he argues, have shaped contemporary American culture.

Reed's scholarship is a large-scale undertaking that deserves to be built upon. While he takes on a wide range of social movements and their cultural impacts, I will narrow in on the "primitive" and the industrial as guiding concepts for twentieth-century American radicals. Four of the organizations I will examine, the Black Panther Party, the League of Revolutionary Black Workers, the International

Socialists, and the Socialist Workers Party, are broadly socialist, and all belong to the 1960s and '70s era of the "New Left." Contemporary anarchists are the final type of activist I examine, and they break the mold because they are not socialists and they rarely belong to formal or stable anarchist organizations. As the dominant strain in radical youth communities today, anarchists illustrate how primitive and industrial themes have evolved since the radical upsurge of the New Left. While they differ from socialists in their tactics and their understanding of the state, they share a fundamental critique of capitalism and a belief in revolution rather than reform. Many anarchists view themselves as cultural ancestors of socialist black nationalists from the 1960s and early 1970s, and several former Black Panthers have even announced their new anarchist affiliations in the last decade. Although the ideological label has changed, then, anarchists are the most prominent inheritors of the New Left movements.

The language these movements use to mobilize can best be understood in conjunction with literature of their time periods. While literary texts are not necessarily more complex than activist metaphors, they often provide necessary theoretical critiques, especially by using fiction to investigate the implications of radical ideas. For American activists, African-American literature has been an especially important source of commentary because it often wrestles with the social problems and potential solutions to racism, freedom, and social change. Black writers act as both cheerleaders and critics of their activist contemporaries, and they often model better strategies of political language or highlight important ethical questions for radicals to consider. Activists, on the other hand, face the pragmatic political decisions that literature can sidestep, and their language reflects this. African-American literature and activist language may not always speak directly to one another, but by looking at them together, we can test the validity of rhetorical strategies and the ethics of political ideologies.

Industrial Metaphors and the Labor Rights Tradition

The *primitive* and the *industrial* are abstract terms with no authoritative definitions, and this is exactly why they are so appealing to radicals who want to provoke emotional responses in listeners. This makes them slippery terms for analysis, however, and my use of them will necessarily be fluid. Nonetheless, some history of each term will offer context for understanding their role in activist discourse.

Because the industrial revolution began in England, American understandings of the industrial grew out of trans-Atlantic relationships. The growth of British factory production sparked dissent even before the seminal 1848 publication of Marx's *Communist Manifesto*. In the early nineteenth century, Luddites resisted new industrial machinery, and some of Britain's first railroad openings attracted protesters who were angry about the introduction of new machinery (Nye 54; *Opening of the Liverpool and Manchester Railroad*). Conservative and wealthy Britons also worried that industry could be a corrupting force. British writer Harriet Martineau, for instance, might have argued fervently against union movements, but she nonetheless used her 1832 story "A Manchester Strike" to depict factories as inhumane institutions plagued by the problems of brutal child labor, severe underpayment, and unhealthy working conditions.

Attitudes about industrial development were far more positive in the United States, as historical studies of technology by David Nye and John Kasson reveal. Although Kasson concedes that Americans were unsure about industrial development in the late eighteenth century because of their desire to establish a democratic republic based an agricultural production, these sentiments changed dramatically by the early nineteenth century. During this period, Americans began to see industry as a way to prove their worth in comparison to England (Kasson 3). With this more positive outlook, Americans also began to describe industrial development in dramatic, emotional ways—what Nye terms the "technological sublime." Just as natural phenomena like the Niagara Falls represented the "natural sublime," railroads, bridges, and factories generated a sense of awe in onlookers impressed by their scale, aesthetics, and productive capacity. Industry's enormous, intricate machines symbolized human dominance over the environment.

Sometimes this dominance appeared in the form of precise and ordered productivity. The identical white dresses of female workers lining the neat rows of machines in Lowell, Massachusetts's nineteenth-century textile mills, for instance, made visitors proud of American technological rationality and economic success (Nye 112–16). At other times, machines created sublime fear in observers, exemplified by Walt Whitman's reference to the locomotive as a "fierce-throated beauty" taking over the landscape. This mix of wonder and fear appeared in descriptions of industry well into the twentieth century (Nye 56; Whitman 358). In a 1923 biography of Henry Ford, William Stidger portrayed the massive River Rouge auto plant as "white waters of flame and fire, awe-inspiring, soul-subduing romance! Romance! Romance of Power!" (Nye 131; Stidger 115).

Even as industry evoked wonder in many Americans, industrial nay-sayers began to gain ground in the final decades of the nineteenth century. The Panic of 1873 sparked economic fears, and railroad strikes in 1877 and 1885 suggested that American laborers were not as enamored with the industrial system as the literary community and the press had been. By the 1890s, a paralyzing depression had deepened anti-industrial sentiments in a larger segment of the American public (Kasson 186–87). Journalists and novelists expressed such doubts through industrial accounts and dystopian literature. From 1900 to 1910, popular magazines published damning exposés of the beef, oil, and coal industries, the railroads, and the drug business, while Upton Sinclair's 1906 novel *The Jungle* and Margaret Byington's 1910 sociological study *Homestead: The Households of a Mill Town*, among others, drew attention to industry's abuses (Marchand 42). Through Byington and Sinclair, smoke, dirt, and underpaid labor replaced depictions of shiny machines and well-groomed workers in American imaginations.

Corporations struck back with the new field of public relations, which took hold between 1890 and 1910 (Marchand 42). In the 1890s, the H. J. Heinz Company in Pittsburgh, and the National Cash Register Company in Dayton, Ohio, began opening their factories to the public, displaying production as a tourist attraction. The factory tour soon became a staple of American industry, and factories shaped manufacturing processes into dramas for visitors. Owners often installed glass, overhead walkways, and partitions to separate visitors from the shop floor, and guides impressed tourists with statistics detailing the vast scale of production. Enormous machines, massive quantities of raw materials, and rows of interchangeable workers contributed to the factory spectacle. Viewers took pride in American wealth and ingenuity while the tour guide demonstrated the safety and cleanliness of the operation (Littmann). Eager to supplement these tours, public relations firms and corporations themselves advertised the factory as a positive feature of the landscape, publishing postcards or print ads displaying factories as part of the local scenery (Marchand 31).

Although we might associate positive representations of factories largely with such public relations projects, even socialists and labor rights advocates sometimes adopted optimistic representations of the industrial space. For these groups, the factory was not only a source of danger and exploitation but also the site of potential revolutionary sentiment and, thus, a symbol of hope. In Marx's conception of the socialist future, industry, under the control of its workers, would be responsible for using its advanced technologies to feed, house, and clothe the people. As a result, radical images of the industrial accommodated both exploitation and the possibility of a utopian future. For example, Diego Rivera's 1932 mural, *Detroit Industry*, which appears in the Detroit Institute of Arts, depicts the strong hands and arms of auto workers intertwined to mimic a maze of industrial piping. In Rivera's art, the worker transforms the metal into something more human, but in doing so he becomes intimately linked to it, taking on the characteristics of the machinery as he transforms it into a tool for liberation. This side of industry held particular resonance for African Americans in the early decades of the twentieth century. Jim Crow laws in southern states and industrial jobs in the North led many African Americans from the rural South to associate the North with the promise of economic opportunity and less virulent racism. Although participants in the Great Migration learned quickly that northern industrial spaces were not free of racism or exploitation, many African Americans saw a source of resistant power in their new industrial roles.

After the 1930s, however, when factories seemed to be the key place for resistance, American unions failed to adopt increased militancy, and the relatively high wages that workers had won made "industry" a symbol of conservative financial stability throughout the middle of the twentieth century. As a result, when students began to revolt in the 1960s, they often viewed industrial workers as unlikely dissenters. And in 1973, Daniel Bell added a new layer to this perceived working-class impotence when he predicted that the United States was transitioning into a "post-industrial" society. The rise of the information age and the shift from manufacturing to service-sector production challenged both industrial models of dissent and American understandings of the industrial.

These shifts did not, however, herald the disappearance of the industrial as either a cultural signifier or a site of resistance. While the factory tour is relatively rare among major corporations today, and few public relations departments would advertise factories as beauties of the natural landscape, the spectacle of industrial production remains an element of twenty-first-century advertising. In place of factory tours, many corporations now build stand-alone tourist attractions that they market as "museums." If traditional museums document human achievement and natural history, corporate "museums" argue that products and profits are cultural achievements and wonders of the natural world. Atlanta's "World of Coca-Cola" makes this claim explicit when it refers to Coke products as "artifacts." The history of its branding strategies, Coca-Cola tells us, is the history of American culture.

These new corporate "museums" sometimes feature worker-less industrial utopias, as Coca-Cola does in its fully automated bottling plant within the Atlanta museum. At other times, corporations continue to value the worker as a character in industrial success, as in Post's 2008 ad campaign for Honey Bunches of Oats breakfast cereal, which depicts uniformed factory workers in helmets and hairnets on a national tour promoting their product. Post and Coca-Cola demonstrate that the industrial metaphor remains a key component of the American cultural vocabulary, despite the fact that environmentalism has changed the public attitude toward smokestacks and the loss of union jobs has shifted the aspirations of many American youth away from industrial jobs. John Kerry still felt the need to don a hard hat to garner working-class votes in the 2004 elections, and the auto industry made daily national news during a United Auto Workers strike in 2007 and again during the financial crisis of 2009. The industrial worker continues to hold a large metaphorical share, if an increasingly diminished economic interest, in the notion of what it means to be an American, and the factory remains a symbol of lost prosperity and industrious virtue.

The Anthropological, Aesthetic, and Racialized Primitive

Few would doubt the centrality of industrial metaphors to leftist projects, as the factory is the site of Marx's revolutionary vision, but primitive imagery's role in radicalism has been less frequently examined. This oversight may be partially due to the fact that many activists have rightly rejected the term *primitive* as a marker of lesser development that has been associated with racism and imperialism. Nonetheless, metaphors of the "primitive" have frequently crept into radical organizations, and I use the term not because it is inherently accurate or appropriate but because it best conveys the problems with generic visions of an idealized past.

The "primitive" has a history in popular culture as well as anthropological and artistic communities. In all of these cases, assumptions about race have guided its definition. Explorers and colonists understood the "primitives" of Africa, the Pacific, and the Americas as remnants of an earlier period in human history, and they ascribed "natural" traits to both "primitive" and "civilized" peoples. While colonists defined whites as rational, civilized, hierarchical, and situated in history, they viewed "primitive" peoples as emotional, sexual, irrational, violent, communal, and mired in one moment of time.[2] People of the West were seen as fully human, but "primitives" were viewed as animalistic, and these stereotypes justified colonization and slavery. At the same time, Europeans were fascinated with "primitives," whom they both derided and desired as sexual objects and sources of entertainment.[3]

In the United States, such classifications erased the distinctions between tribal Africans and African Americans by suggesting that race rather than culture could make one "primitive." Stereotypes of blackness in the United States consequently merged ideas about American slavery and African colonial history. Minstrel shows offered a prime example, where blackface performers combined depictions of African Americans as plantation slaves with references to their "savage" behavior.

Such stereotypes persisted with the continued use of the term *primitive* in academic anthropology late into the twentieth century. Even in the 1980s, anthropologists studying hunter-gatherer cultures often viewed their subjects as the legacy of an ancient human experience. By observing the tools and social relationships of these cultures, researchers believed, we could learn about our former selves. Only in the last two decades has this notion been discredited, as many scholars have put contemporary hunter-gatherers back into the historical narrative, noting that their cultures are modern and changing rather than static and ancient.[4]

The term *primitive* is likewise common in the visual arts. It originally described art produced by nonprofessionals or pre-Renaissance artists, but around the turn of the twentieth century, it was attached to art by or about African and Oceanic peoples (Knapp 366; Rhodes 628). Beginning in the 1890s, Paul Gauguin infused Tahitian themes into his painting, and European artists Pablo Picasso, Henri Matisse, and André Derain became interested in African sculpture a decade later. The "primitive" helped define modernism in European visual arts, and it inspired narrower trends such as Cubism, Fauvism, and Dadaism. For artists in these traditions, "primitive" cultures appeared interchangeable rather than geographically or historically specific. According to Sieglinde Lemke, artists "indiscriminately referred to African, Oceanic, and Native American art as art nègre. They did not differentiate among contemporary African art, 'primitive art,' and 'Negro art' " (39).

The "primitive" attracted artists for both formal and anthropological reasons. Gauguin used striking colors and two-dimensional figures to challenge naturalistic representations in European art but also to present his Tahitian subjects as romantic, sensual, and mysterious. Picasso likewise embraced the geometric, abstract forms of African masks in his 1907 painting *Les Demoiselles d'Avignon*, yet he was also fascinated by the role of the mask in tribal life: "the masks weren't like other kinds of sculpture," he commented in a 1937 discussion with André Malraux. "Not at all. They were magical things. [. . .] To help people stop being dominated by spirits" (Flam and Deutch 33).[5] Picasso believed that Africans employed art as a form of mysticism, and this made it exotic for him. His anthropological ideas about "primitives," in other words, influenced him as much as the new geometric forms.

Art historians identify Picasso and his cohort as "primitivist modernists" or "modernist primitivists," and the movement spread from painters living in France to other regions and art forms in the ensuing decades. German Expressionists took the movement beyond France; Dadaists incorporated the "primitive" into performance art with their mock-"Negro" poems and African masks; and according to critic Michael North, Gertrude Stein's 1909 short story "Melanctha" brought primitivism to American literature (Flam and Deutch 12). With this text, Stein translated anthropological definitions of the tribal "primitive" into a racial "primitive" that she applied to African Americans (North). Stein's inclusion warrants mention because scholars often exclude the United States from primitivist modernism. African art objects had a particular impact on European artists because colonial expeditions delivered artifacts to European museums. Paris's *Musée d'ethnographie du Trocadéro*, for instance, sparked the interests of Picasso and others in African art. The United States, on the other hand, had no colonial relationships to Africa (though it did occupy the Philippines, Guam, Samoa, Hawaii, and a host of Central American and Caribbean nations in the early twentieth century). As a result, the American link to primitivism came largely through its history of African slavery and its population of African Americans. Scholars have rarely seen this connection as a reason to put American artists in the same category as Europe's primitivist modernists.[6] Sieglinde Lemke's study *Primitivist Modernism*, however, argues otherwise. Citing writers and visual artists like Alain Locke, Zora Neale Hurston, and Loïs Mailou Jones, Lemke observes that European interest in African art led African Americans to celebrate Africa and the "primitive" as symbols of their own identity. Poet Helene Johnson, for instance, identified with the "primitive" in her 1927 "Poem" while acknowledging the disjuncture between the African "primitive" and African Americans: "What do I know / About tom-toms?" she asked, "But I like the word, sort of, / Don't you? It belongs to us" (38). Jones grappled with the relationship between contemporary

Africa, African ancestors, and stereotypes of Africa, claiming modernist art's key inspiration as her own while remaining uncomfortable about the artistic white gaze that had assumed knowledge of and power over diverse African and tribal cultures.

As Johnson indicates, primitivism became a source of conflict for many African Americans. It recognized black creations as art, but it also brought problematic race relations to the surface. White artists in the Harlem Renaissance like Vachel Lindsay, wealthy patrons like Charlotte Osgood Mason, or combinations of the two like Carl Van Vechten often inspired anger among black artists even if they did value black art. Langston Hughes's poetry, for instance, represents African Americans as spiritually linked to Africa. As he writes in "The Negro Speaks of Rivers," "I've known rivers ancient as the world and older than the flow of human blood in human veins. / My soul has grown deep like the rivers. / I bathed in the Euphrates when dawns were young. / I built my hut near the Congo and it lulled me to sleep. / I looked upon the Nile and raised pyramids above it" (Rampersad 73). In these lines, Hughes links African Americans to Egypt, the Congo, and the Middle Eastern Euphrates, suggesting that the speaker is spiritually connected to these disparate sites by his dark skin. His romantic sentiments evaporate, however, when his white patron makes the same connections. As Hughes writes in his autobiography:

> She [Mason] wanted me to be primitive and know and feel the intuitions of the primitive. But, unfortunately, I did not feel the rhythms of the primitive surging through me, and so I could not live and write as though I did. I was only an American Negro—who had loved the surface of Africa and the rhythms of Africa—but I was not Africa. I was Chicago and Kansas City and Broadway and Harlem. And I was not what she wanted me to be. (326)

Here, Hughes denies the links that were crucial to "The Negro Speaks of Rivers." Although a spiritual association to Africa is liberating in his own hands, it becomes tainted when Mason expects it. His African-

American status, Hughes insists, does not give him access to "the rhythms of Africa." Instead, he identifies with American cities—not a generalized vision of "urban America," but a collection of cities that are familiar to him. Hughes grew up in Lawrence, Kansas, not far from Kansas City; his mother lived in Chicago while he was in high school, and as an adult he wrote for the *Chicago Defender*; and he spent much of his adult life in Broadway and Harlem. By naming these cities, Hughes insists on the particularity of *his* identity rather than the universality of black identity.

Hughes was uncomfortable with white appropriation of "primitive" imagery and culture, and it wasn't only artists who were participating in this trend. Many young whites in the 1920s were fascinated by Harlem and its culture of black music and arts, and they flocked to "safe" opportunities for slumming, such as Harlem's segregated Cotton Club, where Duke Ellington played "jungle music" surrounded by a décor that mixed depictions of an African jungle and a Southern plantation: "You go sort of primitive up there," white musician and actor Jimmy Durante remarked (Lawrence 106, 117–119; Durante and Kofoed 114). Racial stereotypes of black primitivism had sparked artistic interest in African art objects, and modernist primitivism bounced back into American popular culture to confirm original stereotypes of black difference.

These racist primitivist notions persisted throughout most of the twentieth century. As chapters one and two will examine, black radicals of the 1960s and '70s confronted the stereotypes just as Hughes and Johnson had in an earlier generation, both using and challenging primitive metaphors to fight for racial equality. In the last two decades, however, the term *primitive* has largely disappeared from polite conversation and academic discussions of art or anthropology. A 2009 exhibition at New York's Metropolitan Museum of Art adopted the title "African and Oceanic Art from the Barbier-Mueller Museum" for a collection that would have been labeled "primitive" as late as the 1980s. This title, as *New York Times* reviewer Holland Cotter notes, reflects the frighteningly recent understanding that African and Oceanic tribal cultures are historically and socially different—they do not fit into one capacious myth of the "primitive."

Primitive Meets Industrial

The fact that mainstream American culture is rejecting the industrial and the primitive as descriptors of the twenty-first-century world at approximately the same time is notable because, although the two concepts are distinct, they have never been far apart in cultural representations, and each has historically helped define the other. This interdependence became apparent in the second half of the nineteenth century with the popularity of international exhibitions, which displayed the progression from "savage" to "civilized" lifestyles for visitors in the world's urban centers. London's Great Exhibition of 1851 celebrated imperial English progress in public displays of industry, art, science, and architecture from around the world. Britain and other industrialized nations appeared as the epitome of progress, whereas the colonial exhibits displayed raw materials for industrial production (Auerbach and Hoffenberg). Many Britons automatically linked displays of global industry with voyeuristic examinations of "primitive" peoples, as Paul Young notes. In a humorous fictional account of the Exhibition, for instance, Henry Mayhew imagined the Hottentot Venus and other "primitive" indigenous peoples from around the world taking their place in the ranks of progress with Chinese, German, and British visitors (P. Young 23; Mayhew and Cruikshank 3). International industrial displays, he indicated, necessarily brought the "primitive" and the "industrial" together.

This trend continued throughout the century in both Europe and America in much more obvious forms: the 1889 French Exhibition encouraged visitors to see the colonies as exotic parallels to industrial development with reconstructions of "primitive" Tahitian villages, while the Philadelphia Centennial Exhibition of 1876 allowed viewers to experience both the "industrial sublime" of the Corliss steam engine and the "primitive" habits of Native American life, displayed in a full-scale replica of a teepee and wax statues of Native Americans (Çelik and Kinney; Barkan and Bush 8; Rydell 22–27). By the Chicago World's Columbian Exposition of 1893, coordinators had expanded the Native American exhibit to include actual Native American people, and in 1904 the St. Louis World's Fair advertised America's own colonial adventures by creating a mock Filipino village (63; Rydell 63; Barkan and Bush 3). The industrial urban centers that held these exhibitions built pride and wonder in their own culture's industrial achievements by examining the equally wondrous but inferior experiences of "primitive" others.

In the United States, the clash of industrial and primitive concepts helped define the national identity, as Leo Marx argues in his 1964 monograph *The Machine in the Garden*, which examines the pastoral tradition in American literature. Marx focuses on pastoralism rather than primitivism, though he makes only one distinction between the two: pastoralism depicts nature that has been *improved*—the pastoral includes tamed gardens and pastures—while the primitive connotes wilderness or jungle. American literature, Marx held, was sometimes wary of the "machine" that threatened to destroy the pristine landscape, but writers were also willing to accept industry as a supplement to the landscape and a means of maintaining it with less labor. Marx's positive vision of the pastoral, then, is actually a mix of the "primitive" and the industrial that rejects the "primitive's" untamed elements. The pastoral was America's reconciliation between the exciting, frightening "primitive" and the benefits of cultivation and industry.

While Marx saw the pastoral as a positive combination of "primitive" and industrial worlds, Eugene O'Neill's 1922 play *The Hairy Ape* envisions this merger more negatively. O'Neill's steel heiress heroine, Mildred Douglas, originally imagines industry as powerful, and she wants to experience it: "I'm a waste product in the Bessemer process—like the millions. Or rather, I inherit the acquired trait of the by-product, wealth, but none of the energy, none of the strength of the steel that made it" (O'Neill 21). When she enters the stoke hole of a ship, however, where protagonist Yank and his fellow workers shovel coal into furnaces, Mildred finds that industry resembles the menacing "primitive." The workers, bare-chested and covered in coal, assume the "crouching, inhuman attitudes of chained gorillas," and Yank shouts with abandon at the bosses (29). The flaming furnace and clanging shovels transform the industrial machine into a frightening, lifelike object, and the men are racially marked by the coal dust, appearing both black and gorilla-like. Yank's masculine aggression, punctuated by his link to the gorilla when he pounds his chest, signals to Mildred that she has left "civilized" society, and she faints in fear. The stereotypical, racialized "primitive" and the horrifying foreignness of industrial production join, generating an animalistic, working-class "primitive" in opposition to feminized, intellectual civilization.

For O'Neill and Leo Marx, the combination of the "primitive" and the industrial represents either progress into a tame, integrated future of the pastoral or regression into anarchic, animalistic relations. Radicals shared these writers' interests in the question of social development, but they viewed images of the "primitive" and the industrial through different eyes, and they were much more likely to see the "primitive" as an inspiration rather than a source of contempt or fear.

"Primitive" and Industrial as Activist Utopias

Just as Western civilization valued an Enlightenment concept of progress, most radicals developed their ideologies based on what Afrocentrism scholar Wilson Jeremiah Moses labels the historiographies of progress and decline. Marxists, in the Enlightenment tradition, believed in a progressive view of humanity. Although Friedrich Engels notes that "primitive communism" existed among tribal peoples, he does not view this as an ideal to be imitated (Engels, "On Social Relations in Russia" 666). Instead, he posits that the socialist future will use industrial technology to provide affluence for all. Anarchists, on the other hand, have more varied views on the value of progress. While some envision utopia as an equitable industrial society much like Marx and Engels's socialism, others do aspire to return to "primitive" social structures.

To examine the interaction of these two activist models, I will begin in the 1960s, when anticolonial revolutions raged around the globe and segregation had come to a breaking point at home. Based in the "land without socialism," American activists sought validation from international movements, and many attempted to imitate industrial revolutionaries, guerrilla fighters, or peasant insurgents because of their interest in recent revolutions in Eastern Europe, Africa, Cuba, and Asia. Some took factory jobs while others adopted the militarist look of Third World guerrillas by donning berets, rifles, and guerrilla-inspired clothing. Anxiety about the American potential for revolution led US activists to write and perform the role of the ideal revolutionary—a character, they suggested, that is not an organic national product.

Socialists in this period were forced to question teleological understandings of the industrial, the "primitive," and socialist development. Contrary to Marx and Engels's expectations, revolutions had emerged not from the most developed industrial countries but from underdeveloped and colonized nations such as Russia and Vietnam, and activists began to wonder whether industrial progress was the key to socialism. What did it mean that the Soviet revolution did not precipitate a socialist revolution in Western Europe, as Lenin and Trotsky predicted? Why had socialist revolutions spawned corruption and human rights abuses in the Soviet Union, China, and Cuba?

Primitive metaphors gained steam in 1966, when the Black Power Movement sparked popular interest in generic, often romanticized forms of African dress or tradition among African Americans. Similar phenomena occurred in other communities. Members of the American Indian Movement reclaimed the racist identification of Native Americans as "red" people when they declared "Red Power" (a parallel term to Black Power that also expressed interethnic solidarity) and revived community interest in traditional religious ceremonies, dress, and hairstyles. Mexican Americans in the Chicano Movement declared themselves the indigenous people of California and the Southwest, which they named Aztlán after the legendary birthplace of the Aztec people. For Chicanos and Native Americans as well as African Americans, claiming pride in one's ethnic identity meant embracing a mythic time and space of ethnic unity. In other words, members of these movements viewed their ethnic identities through metaphors of the primitive, *including* tropes with racist histories.[7]

While ethnic nationalist groups of the 1960s and '70s had many ideological differences, they shared a broadly defined socialist perspective. After this era came to a close, however, anarchists began to replace socialists as the key figures in American radicalism. The fall of the Eastern Bloc and the Soviet Union confirmed the suspicions of young radicals that state socialism was a lost cause, and anarchism seemed to be a viable alternative to the generation of activists who were angry about free trade policies and loan repayment plans that imposed rigid "austerity programs" on Third World nations. Many embraced anarchist federations as an alternative to the nation-state. Unlike their socialist predecessors, few anarchists today view industry as a key to future affluence and justice. Rather, some envision a technological future that incorporates environmentalist and egalitarian values while others imagine that civilization is destined to collapse, forcing humans into small hunter-gatherer societies.

As I trace the history of industrial and primitive metaphors in political organizations from the 1960s to the present, African-American literary texts will provide aesthetic and theoretical critiques of activist language, serving as an analytical tool and an aesthetic model for complex political language. And even as creative writers pinpoint the ethical or theoretical problems in political projects, activist texts bring political substance and pragmatism to literary metaphors. At the juncture of literature and activist language, we might find politics that is more than propaganda and literature that offers concrete theories of political change.

CHAPTER ONE

How the Panther Lost Its Spots

Primitivism, Marxism, and the Black Panther Party

Nineteenth-century understandings of race identified people of African ancestry as animalistic. Some researchers viewed Africans and Europeans as different species, and because the public was struggling to absorb Darwin's claim that humans may be related to apes, many whites—members of the public and the scientific community alike—saw Africans as the obvious connection between the two (McClintock 49). During this time period and well into the twentieth century, cartoon imagery of African Americans capitalized on such links, depicting blacks as bestial or ape-like. In many racist drawings, animal characteristics were applied broadly, and although apes and monkeys were the most common choices, other animals sometimes took their place. Elephants, frogs, panthers, and tigers, among others, purveyed racist stereotypes. Often, black cartoon characters were not even identifiable as any specific animal—they simply didn't look human. Such depictions reinforced scientific explanations of racial difference and bolstered rationales for segregation: separate lunch counters, drinking fountains, and bathrooms made sense when the public associated African Americans with animals.

Why, then, would black radicals intent on eliminating racial inequality identify with an animal, no matter how fierce? In 1965, the Lowndes County Freedom Organization (LCFO), which mobilized black voters in Alabama around registration and black candidates, did just that when it claimed the black panther as a mascot (Austin 12). This set off a wave of interest in the panther as a symbol of black national- ism that would culminate in the most famous example: Huey Newton and Bobby Seale's Black Panther Party (BPP), founded in Oakland, California, in 1966. By choosing the panther insignia, the LCFO and the Black Panther Party revised definitions of black Americans as animals, using sensational depictions of themselves to gain currency in the mass media and creating a new association of the panther with Black Power. Ultimately, the panther and its connections to primitivism would allow the Panthers to critique both the racist Western binary between civilization and "primitive" life and the Marxist notion that the industrial working class was the key to socialist revolution. They created a new urban "primitive" fraught with racist history but essential to defining a new vision of black radicalism.

Seale and Newton devised the Party in response to what they perceived as the ineffectiveness of black nationalist groups that they had worked with as students at Oakland's Merritt College (Austin 29). When they took the panther name and logo, they defined the organization with ten demands and accompanying political analyses, titled "What We Want/What We Believe" (Newton with Blake 115, 121). The demands, which included adequate housing, food, employ- ment, education, an end to police brutality and unfair treatment in the justice system, and black exemption from military service, combined Newton and Seale's interests in Marxism, black nationalism, and the pan-Africanism that had inspired Malcolm X in his last days.[1]

While distributing this document in the black community, New- ton, Seale, and their first recruit Bobby Hutton instituted an armed citizen patrol against police brutality. Permitted by California law to carry loaded rifles in the open, they trailed Oakland police on duty, observing their behavior at traffic stops or arrests, while Newton, who was taking courses at San Francisco Law School, cited law books to convince officers of the patrol's legality (Seale 64–77; Newton 115, 121). These tense confrontations sparked local interest and white concern, and the party recruited a core of members. Local notoriety turned into national fame in May 1967, when Bobby Seale and a group of fellow

Panthers carried rifles into the California legislature to protest a bill banning loaded guns in public. The bill was intended to quell the Panthers' patrols, but instead it provoked nationwide interest in the group. Soon, Newton and Seale were establishing branches all over the country (Austin xi–xviii). Organized into a hierarchical structure beneath Oakland's Central Committee, members wore the Panther uniform of a black jacket, blue shirt, and black beret. Many were full-time activists who lived collectively and survived off the meager proceeds of their *Black Panther* newspaper sales. In addition to selling the paper, they learned military skills, attended political education classes, organized protests, and built community service programs (215).

Between 1966 and 1971, the Black Panther Party was a cultural force, inspiring other radical groups and challenging white activists to address racism in new ways. In these years, the group earned national fame, had showdowns with the police, fought a host of government charges against its members, and built community programs all over the country that offered free food, medical care, and other local needs. And although a 1971 factional split destroyed its national prominence, a remaining core of members continued activist work until 1982 (Joseph 299). Its wild, if temporary, success was based in part on the BPP's skillful "branding" of itself with the panther name and logo. By choosing the panther as a subtle racial symbol that could be revised, the BPP capitalized on stereotypes to bind together its members and attract white interest.

Panthers: Spotted, Black, Pink, and Brown

The panther, unlike the gorilla or the chimpanzee, is not a self-evident racial symbol, and the association is even less clear because of the BPP's success in recoding the term. Before Newton and Seale emerged on the political scene, however, panther imagery *was* often problematically linked to race. In a biological sense, *Panthera* is a genus of large cat that includes the lion, tiger, jaguar, and leopard. The common name "panther" is applied to African or Asian leopards, North American cougars, or South American jaguars. The term can describe spotted, tawny, white, or black animals, but while spotted and tawny animals frequently go by other names, black animals are nearly always given the label "black panther" (Kure 157). In other words, the black panther earns its name for its blackness, not its species, and this sets the animal up as a potential racial signifier.[2]

In nineteenth-century American poetry, panther imagery often served as a code for racial or ethnic difference. Henry Wadsworth Longfellow's epic poem "The Song of Hiawatha," for instance, describes Native American Hiawatha "treading softly like a panther," while his poem "Kambalu," a part of "The Spanish Jew's Tale" in the series "Tales of a Wayside Inn," links Jews and panthers indirectly by describing the "miser's" gold like "the eyes of a panther in the dark" (306, 546). Ralph Waldo Emerson likewise associates the panther with gypsies in his poem "The Romany Girl" (227). In these cases, the panther symbolized a connection between ethnic difference and nature and evoked such traits as sneakiness, a potential for violence, and a desire to be free of civilization's constraints. Being pantherlike meant having animal characteristics that could not be tamed, and this was often associated with nonwhite people.

The *black* panther emerged in representations of black Americans in the twentieth century, frequently in reference to boxing. During the 1910s and '20s, interracial boxing matches drew national press, and both white and black newspapers identified African-American boxers such as Harry Wills, Jack Johnson, Joe Louis, and Senegalese French boxer Louis Fall as black or brown panthers. White newspapers used the name to identify black contenders, while African-American publications used it as a nickname. Wills, then, remained the "black panther" in African-American newspapers even if his opponent was also black. Although white boxers were sometimes given animal characteristics as well, at least one black sportswriter, Roscoe Simmons of the *Chicago Defender*, saw the black panther nickname as evidence of racial animalization: "Hope that [Harry Wills] will be more of a bulldog than a panther," Simmons wrote, "since the name of some animal will be given him. A panther springs at you. A bulldog takes hold and stays" (Simmons A1). Despite Simmons's dissent, the title black panther stuck to an array of African-American boxers, signifying fearlessness, stealth, fierce beauty, and black skin. The nickname also reflected white fears of black violence, as the black newspaper the *Pittsburgh Courier* pointed out in 1926, when it recorded that a man accused of murdering three whites was referred to publicly as a "black panther" killer ("Panther Is Executed" 12).

The panther evoked not only ferocity and strength but also "primitive" spaces and feminine "cattiness." While spotted or tawny panthers could be American animals, black panthers inhabited African and Asian landscapes, making them exotic and linking them in the white imagination to tribal regions that Western explorers had seen as "primitive." In the 1920s, when references to black panther boxers were popular, artists and writers were simultaneously embracing the "primitive" as a source of inspiration. Pablo Picasso, Alberto Giacometti, Paul Gauguin, and other "primitivist modernists" saw tribal art and "primitive" people as keys to new ideas about abstract art and to more abandoned emotional expressions. Although they focused on African and Oceanic tribal cultures rather than African-American culture, these artists relied on stereotypes that had also haunted African Americans. In the years that followed, black Americans would participate, reluctantly or enthusiastically, in confusing black skin, tribal cultures, and "primitive" imagery.

Josephine Baker exemplified this crossover and its relationship to panther imagery. As a black American performer, she was ushered into vaudeville roles that presented her as a bumbling blackface caricature like those in nineteenth-century minstrel shows. And although French audiences were first drawn to her in this role when she toured with *La Revue Nègre*, she eventually traded in an American slave caricature for the tribal African "savage"—even as she continued to incorporate American dances like the Charleston (Jules-Rosette 56–61). For her French audience, she was "savage" or "primitive" because she had dark skin, not because she came from a tribal culture, and she was saddled with the same animalistic nicknames that her boxing contemporaries faced. In an inscription to Baker reprinted in *Josephine Baker vue par la Presse Française*, the novelist Colette referred to Baker as "la plus belle panthére," and Baker wrote in 1931 that "I had a mascot—a panther—Ancestral superstition" (Abatino 51; Rose 157). The panther was not simply an idea for Baker—in fact, she appeared on stage with a live panther and even adopted the animal as a pet, becoming famous for walking it down Parisian streets on a leash.[3]

Like the sportswriter who was uncomfortable with the descriptor "black panther," Baker felt ambivalent. She acquiesced in the label and even embraced it when she adopted the panther as a pet, but she subtly presented herself as the *owner* of a panther rather than a panther herself. In the 1931 poem stating, "I had a mascot—a panther," Baker distances herself from the association by placing the panther in the past tense. Elsewhere in the poem she refers to her current state: "I do not drink—I am an American / I have a religion / I adore children" (Rose 157). In this list, she separates her identity as an African *American*, a woman, and a mother from the past tense panther—the eroticized and racialized animal that once identified her. Like Harlem Renaissance writers and artists who took pride in the "primitive" as a sign of their African-American heritage, Baker both accepted and challenged white uses of racial imagery.

By the time the Black Panther Party was founded in October 1966, forty years and a continent away from Josephine Baker's Paris, the panther had marched through a variety of cultural forms, from Nazi Panther tanks and the US Navy's F9F Panther airplane of the Korean War to Pink Panther cartoons (Seale 62). In its relationship to planes and tanks, the panther connoted strength, masculinity, virility, and sometimes race. For the 761st "Black Panther" Tank Battalion in World War II, the term signaled a segregated unit of black soldiers, while the 66th "Black Panther" Infantry Division of white soldiers used the concept simply to evoke masculinity.

The Pink Panther cartoon figure, on the other hand, introduced the panther as a wily villain, and although the character was not a clear symbol of race relations, the focus on color in the original cartoon reminds viewers of the panther's ties to racial symbolism. The first Pink Panther animation, *The Pink Phink*, ran before the 1964 movie *The Pink Panther* (a detective movie about a "pink panther" diamond that included no actual panthers). In this short, the blundering human hero attempts to paint his house blue while the panther repeatedly tricks him into painting it pink. The panther is both effeminate in his obsession with pink and a masculine hipster, accompanied by jazzy music and smoking a cigarette as he saunters through the frame. The emphasis on color wars in 1964, when America was in the throes of the civil rights debate, allows race to lurk in the background. The paper-white hero finds that, no matter what he does to protect his work, the Pink Panther succeeds in painting the world his own color.

Other panther references during this era were much more explicit about their connection to race. Between 1964 and 1966, three directly racialized versions of the panther entered pop culture. In Alex Haley's 1965 *Autobiography of Malcolm X*, M. S. Handler's introduction describes his wife's first meeting with Malcolm X: "it was like having tea with a black panther," she remarks. Handler expands on her metaphor: "The black panther is an aristocrat in the animal kingdom. He is beautiful. He is dangerous. As a man, Malcolm X had the physical bearing and the inner self-confidence of a born aristocrat. And he was potentially dangerous" (ix). Handler invokes the primitivist stereotype: X was dangerous but beautiful and exotic. As a white liberal supporter of civil rights, he argues that X is appealing because he was half-"tamed": a genial guest for tea who remains a threat to the liberal civil rights project. Newton and Seale, admirers and readers of *The Autobiography of Malcolm X* who rejected the liberal dream of integration into capitalist society, would soon speak back to Handler's introduction in a way that the martyred X could not.

Months later, in July 1966, a similar panther debuted in Marvel's *Fantastic Four* comic series (Ture 106; S. Lee, et al.). Although it appeared in the midst of national discussions about race, Marvel's Black Panther character is a traditional African caricature. He inhabits the mythical village of Wakanda, where tribal villagers wear "togas" and garments resembling ancient Egyptian kilts, and he evolves from foe to friend of the Fantastic Four as he avenges the death of his tribal chieftain father (S. Lee, et al.). The Black Panther propagates stereotypes while reflecting the combination of urban unrest and primitivist imagery that was surfacing in the black community at the time. Marvel's Black Panther is as much an urban figure as a tribal one—he lives not in a tropical jungle but in a high-tech "industrial jungle": "The very branches about us," the heroes observe, "are composed of delicately constructed wires . . . while the flowers which abound here are highly complex buttons and dials!" (#52: 9). By depicting the Black Panther as a technological sophisticate, Marvel hoped that it would resist racial stereotypes. However, the comic succeeded in conveying white fear about black Americans claiming urban spaces of power. The combination of "primitive" culture and industrial know-how was the Black Panther's most threatening trait, and the Fantastic Four needed to be rescued by the traditional skills of their Native American ally Wyatt Wingfoot. In Marvel's worldview, people of color who stick to their "primitive" skills make safer allies for the white heroes than those who attempt to gain technological prowess.

As examples from nineteenth-century poetry to Josephine Baker to Marvel's Black Panther suggest, the panther had a primitivist history. It evoked the erotic and sensational power of the jungle. But civil rights and emergent Black Power activists were nonetheless attracted to the image. In 1965, national activists associated with the Student Non-Violent Coordinating Committee (SNCC) joined locals in Lowndes County, Alabama, to form an independent political party, the Lowndes County Freedom Organization. Because Lowndes was a majority-black county, activists reasoned, the black community should be able to claim political power by registering voters—if it could overcome white intimidation (Austin; Joseph). Only two black voters were registered in the entire county as of 1965, but by May 1966, the organization had earned a place on the ballot for the local elections (Joseph 127–30).

The origin of the LCFO's panther insignia remains uncertain, and historian Jeffrey Ogbar cites three stories about it. In the first, former SNCC member Willie Mukasa Ricks claimed that it was a reference to a local woman, Mrs. Moore, who was "strong and powerful like a panther" (*Black Power* 76). In his interpretation, the panther connects national SNCC organizers to the "essential" black community, represented by Mrs. Moore, whom he describes as a "peasant" and part of "the people." Mrs. Moore was strong like a black panther because she was a "peasant woman" who had stepped outside her social status to resist. Here, the panther evokes a primal connection to the land and a belief in the natural strength of "natives." SNCC activists appear in this reading like colonial explorers celebrating the innate skills of local people.

The second and third origin stories associate the panther with generic "toughness." SNCC member Ruth Howard Chambers links the image to Clark College's panther mascot, while James Forman claims that it was chosen as a strong native animal of Alabama. The panther, like all animals known for ferocity, was a common sports mascot, and tawny colored "panthers," also known as mountain lions, cougars, or pumas, were native to Alabama. Consequently, we could read these two histories of the panther mascot as expressions of local pride. *Black* panthers existed only in local myth, however, and many sports mascots capitalize on racial and cultural difference, as Native American, Viking, and Fighting Irish mascots demonstrate. Racial connotations, then, may lurk even in apparently generic uses of the panther.

The white media's enthusiasm for LCFO's mascot indicates that the name did in fact spark racial connotations beyond toughness. Stokely Carmichael, who helped organize the group, expressed frustration with the racialized interpretation of the panther in a June 1966 appearance on *Face the Nation*. When reporter James Dole referred to the LCFO as the "Black Panther Party," Carmichael responded:

> The name of the organization in Lowndes County is not the Black Panther Party. The symbol happens to be a black panther. The name is the Lowndes County Freedom Organization. I am very concerned about that, you see, because Americans—particularly white America—have been referring to it as the Black Panther Party, and that is their problem with sex and color. They do not refer to the Alabama Democratic Party as the White Rooster Party, and that happens to be the emblem of that party. (CBS News 160–61)

Carmichael's anger demonstrates his belief that the panther did reflect primitivist black stereotypes. Few took heed of his point, however, either in the mass media, radical organizations, or the black community. Black organizations around the country began adopting the panther symbol, and white viewers persisted in identifying the LCFO as the "Black Panther Party." The Socialist Workers Party's Young Socialist Alliance, for instance, published a 1966 pamphlet supporting the LCFO but referring to the organization *solely* as the Black Panther

Party despite the fact that the LCFO members interviewed never used this name (*The Black Panther Party*). African Americans also exploited the panther symbol, regardless of its history of racial connotations. In the year between the LCFO's appearance and the founding of Newton and Seale's organization, Black Panther Parties emerged in New York City, Los Angeles, San Francisco, Oakland, Detroit, Chicago, and St. Louis, suggesting that there was something about the panther *name* that had currency in 1966 (Austin 15).[4] Seale and Newton traced the name of their organization solely to the LCFO, even adopting the same drawing of a leaping panther that it had used (Newton with Blake 113). Although they allowed the panther to resonate with Marvel and Handler's panthers and the Pink Panther, they narrated a simple radical trajectory that ignored the existence of other Black Panther Parties and posited themselves as the sole child of the new Black Power movement. Their panther, they insisted, grew out of black radicalism rather than a history of racism.

The BPP brought new layers of meaning to the panther. While racists identified black Americans as animalistic, the BPP used its animal mascot to guide rather than define its members' behavior. According to organizational lore, panthers did not initiate violence—they attacked only in self-defense (Newton with Blake 120). This supposed panther quality helped control group behavior and public perceptions. Black Americans were not innately *like* panthers, but they could choose to behave in disciplined ways like panthers. Likewise, the Panthers challenged animalistic depictions of black Americans by turning the tradition on its head. In their literature, Black Panther men and women looked fully human, and individual Party members were often recognizable. The panther itself was always an animal on the masthead, never a human-animal mix. Police, judges, and a personified US empire, on the other hand, appeared in the *Black Panther* cartoons and articles as grotesque pigs and rats. In response to white culture's association between "exotic" animals and African-American people, the Panthers saddled whites with notoriously filthy domestic animals. The panther could be pulled out of its mire of racialization, they suggested—but the pig would be much more difficult to rehabilitate.[5]

As James Doyle acknowledged when he referred to LCFO as a "Black Panther Party," the panther image captured both white and black imaginations, and the BPP capitalized on this. "Positive" stereotypes can strengthen a sense of collective identity, making members feel more powerful than the oppressors. Moreover, because the panther already had cultural meaning, it attracted media attention in a way that a political program could not. The BPP appealed to existing American understandings of race, and only after drawing public attention did it challenge those notions with political actions and theory. The name, of course, was only one element of the BBP's sensationalism. Its guns, uniforms, and aggressive rhetoric drew new members in, and once they were admitted, the Party employed a rigid structure to educate them on black history, literature, and revolutionary politics. The BPP aimed to rewrite the panther image with activists who would defend the community and articulate antiracist and anticapitalist positions. By some counts, they were extremely successful. In April 1970, a poll revealed that 64% of black Americans claimed that the Black Panther Party gave them a sense of pride ("The Black Mood").

With the BPP's propaganda in full swing, the media continued to use panther metaphors in derisive ways, but it could no longer rely on simple primitivist definitions of panthers. Between 1968 and 1976, *Time* and *Newsweek* combined standard descriptors of virile, threatening panthers (exemplified by terms like "snarling," "pack," or "pounce") with more domestic images such as "pussycat," "purring," and "Tame Panthers" to describe the Black Panther Party (Morgan). These references no longer reflected a perverse white enjoyment of black virility and potential danger. The threat was now more immediate, and the media responded to a new, black definition of the panther. The words "tame," "purring," and "pussycat" suggest that the media felt genuinely threatened by the metaphor of black primitivist violence and now wanted to dampen it.

The BPP slowly lost public prominence after a 1971 factional split between groups led by Huey Newton and Eldridge Cleaver that concerned, among other issues, the relative importance of violent revolutionary actions and community programs. The faction led by

Huey Newton, which promoted community programs over revolutionary action and dominated on the West Coast, maintained the Party name, newspaper, and community programs until the early 1980s, but the organization had lost its dominant position in national politics. In 1980, the newspaper printed its final issues, and by 1982, when the Party's Oakland Community School shut its doors, it became clear that the BPP was defunct (LeBlanc-Ernest 325). While the Party did not survive, its interpretation of the panther image did. Today, the animal is no longer linked to primitivism and racist assumptions. Instead, it evokes black power and radicalism. When Mos Def and Talib Kweli rap in a 1998 album about "a black cat—a panther," they expect listeners to know that they allude to the Black Panther Party, not to racialized links between panthers and African Americans (Mos Def and Kweli "Astronomy").

Black Panthers Meet Black Arts Movement

By transforming the panther from a primitivist image into a symbol of Black Power, the Black Panthers made a substantial contribution to American culture as well as politics. This is an important point because the Panthers and many who have studied them make clear distinctions between cultural and political change. In the 1960s and '70s, cultural trends often accompanied political sentiments, whether it was long hair and ripped jeans for white radicals or Afros and dashikis for black activists. But the political work of sitting in meetings, waking up in the early morning to serve breakfast to children, or risking one's life in confrontations with police was much more difficult than growing an Afro or buying a dashiki. As a result, committed activists of all ethnicities sometimes distanced themselves from what they identified as "cultural nationalism"—a belief that cultural changes, including dress, hairstyle, and communal traditions, were essential to changing society. As Panther Linda Harrison explained in a 1969 issue of the *Black Panther*, "cultural nationalism ignores the political and concrete, and concentrates on a myth and fantasy." As a result, she derided those who believed that "there is dignity inherent in wearing naturals;

that a buba makes a slave a man" (Harrison 151).[6] Like many of her Panther comrades, Harrison wanted to emphasize her political work rather than her dress or hairstyle.

Personal disputes between the Panthers and Maulana Ron Karenga's cultural nationalist Us organization exacerbated these negative associations. Us was an LA-based group that developed independent black cultural traditions while fighting for racial equality, and Karenga is best known for founding Kwanzaa (Ngozi-Brown). His local competition with the Panthers caught the attention of the FBI, which sought to aggravate the conflict until a 1969 confrontation left two Panthers dead (Churchill and Vander Wall, *COINTELPRO Papers* 130–35; Swearingen 82–83).[7] The severity of the dispute with Us may have contributed to the Panthers' negative view of cultural nationalism in general, and their animosity spread to poets, dramatists, and others associated with the Black Arts Movement (BAM).

The Black Arts Movement describes a group of black writers and visual artists who were inspired by the activism of the 1960s and hoped to make their work politically relevant. Artists like Amiri Baraka, Ed Bullins, and Sonia Sanchez targeted the black community with accessible, politically radical literature. Black Arts poems were handed out as broadsides or flyers, while visual art was painted on the walls of abandoned buildings in black communities. Because many espoused black nationalism, Black Arts participants had initially been friendly with the Black Panthers. In 1967, San Francisco's artists and Panthers had lived together in a collective known as Black House and had joined forces for local events. A May 1967 "Black Experience" conference at Merritt College, for instance, combined art and politics when it featured a lecture by Huey Newton and poetry readings by Sonia Sanchez, LeRoi Jones (the future Amiri Baraka), Marvin Jackmon, and Ed Bullins (Bay Area Black Panther Party Collection, box 1, folder 26). Such interactions were short-lived, however. While Baraka briefly used Black House as a rehearsal space during his tenure as a professor at San Francisco State College, Eldridge Cleaver and his Panther comrades soon ousted artists from the building, deeming them counterrevolutionaries (Baraka, *Autobiography* 351–60). Later, Baraka was vilified in the *Black Panther* newspaper for his affiliations with the Us organization, which he maintained for approximately two years until he, too, moved away from Karenga and Us around 1969 (353).

When Black Arts writer Larry Neal famously claimed that the BAM was the "aesthetic and spiritual sister of the Black Power concept," he glossed over the strained relationships between the Panthers and their artistic contemporaries (Neal 272). Nonetheless, Neal's statement remains instructive. As scholars continue to define the parameters of the Black Arts Movement, we should recognize disagreements but also look beyond factional fights to see political and aesthetic continuities. Just because the Panthers distanced themselves from cultural nationalism and the Black Arts Movement does not mean that critics should do the same. In fact, I think it is useful to use the critical tools and aesthetic themes of the Black Arts Movement to analyze the Black Panther Party. James Smethurst has already begun the project of breaking down the barriers between "cultural nationalism" and what the Panthers identified as their own "revolutionary nationalism" in his study *The Black Arts Movement.* He notes that Black Arts writers were influenced by political traditions of Marxism, black nationalism, the Nation of Islam, and the Civil Rights Movement, and many of them were activists. Smethurst's claims can be expanded and reversed as we look from the perspective of the Panthers toward the Black Arts Movement. The Black Arts Movement contributed to the Black Power movement materially, by building black cultural institutions and radically revising aesthetic forms, but they also brought aesthetic and political strategies to the Black Panthers. Their investigations of revolutionary ethics and their vision of participatory, community-based art influenced the way the Black Panthers produced their propaganda and the way it was received. Moreover, while Black Arts Movement participants aimed to create a black aesthetic, the Panthers built on this by contributing a Black Power cultural aesthetic.

Even taking ideological disagreements into account, there are many reasons to see continuities between the Black Panthers and the Black Arts Movement. If Baraka's 1965 founding of the Black Arts Repertory Theatre/School (BART/S) in Harlem was an informal starting point for the BAM, it predated the Panthers by little over a year, and both movements thrived in the late 1960s and began to decline in the early to mid-1970s (Baraka, *Autobiography* 293–95).

Their contemporaneous rise and fall, coupled with their shared desire for Black Power and leftist change, made even adamantly conflicting movements somewhat porous. Before the split between the Panthers and the Us Organization, Bobby Seale performed in plays by Ed Bullins and Marvin X (the former Marvin Jackmon), and even after tensions developed, some direct relationships remained (Smethurst, *The Black Arts Movement* 170). Visual artist Fundi, who collaborated with Baraka on his illustrated book-length poem *In Our Terribleness*, contributed a celebratory drawing of Black Panther Eldridge Cleaver to the journal *Black Politics* in 1969; Sonia Sanchez published numerous poems in *The Black Panther* in 1968; and BPP artist Emory Douglas returned the favor by illustrating the cover of her 1969 collection *Home Coming* (Bay Area BPP Collection, box 2, folder 4). For people entering the movement, moreover, artistic expressions of black nationalism seemed to confirm the Black Panthers' perspective rather than negate it. Black Panther and later Black Liberation Movement member Assata Shakur remembers that the plays of Amiri Baraka and Ed Bullins helped inspire her political activism (Shakur 175).

Realizing the influential power of literature, the BPP emphasized the importance of black literary history in its member education process even as it denounced cultural nationalism. The Party's reading list, published in early issues of *The Black Panther*, highlighted political theory and African/African-American history, but it also included Arna Bontemps's *American Negro Poetry* collection and Richard Wright's novel *Native Son*. Bontemps's collection, published in 1963, grounded Panther readers in two important eras of black American poetry before the Black Arts Movement. Bontemps included the Harlem Renaissance work of Langston Hughes, Claude McKay, and Helene Johnson, and he also introduced readers to poetry by writers who would later ally themselves with the Black Arts Movement (Dudley Randall, Margaret Walker, Margaret Danner, Gwendolyn Brooks, Ted Joans, LeRoi Jones, and Mari Evans). Even if the Panthers couldn't get along with living artists, they recognized the role of African-American arts in political and cultural education.

As Smethurst observes, the BAM reciprocated by insisting on the crucial juncture between art and radical politics. Participants in the BAM believed that the construction of black institutions was just as important as the production of African-American art. Many helped forge long-lasting political and artistic organizations, and they saw their art as a form of *movement*, both physical and political.

Amiri Baraka's 1966 poem "Black Art" expresses this sentiment, elevating political movements and people into art forms. His poem, controversial for its anti-Semitic references and exhortations to violence, remains a seminal text of the Black Arts Movement. Baraka famously writes that:

> Poems are bullshit unless they are
> teeth or trees or lemons piled
> on a step. Or black ladies dying
> of men leaving nickel hearts
> beating them down.

Most critics have read this poem as a manifesto to politicize aesthetics. I suggest, however, that Baraka is defining political action *as* an aesthetic. The active, political poems in "Black Art" appear as people, whether "black ladies," "wrestlers," or "assassins." "Let Black People understand," Baraka says, "that they / [. . .] / Are poems & poets & / all the loveliness here in the world" (*The LeRoi Jones/Amiri Baraka Reader* 219–20). People, in this text, are not simply artists but poems—they are pieces of art and the creators of that art. As poems and poets, they must take action to avoid being "bullshit." Baraka says that the best poetry appears in the political actions of people, and in doing so he permits us to see the Black Panther Party as a *poem*.

This reading illuminates how the Black Panther Party benefited from its simultaneously political and cultural status. With the Black Arts Movement producing violent rhetoric as poetry, the Black Panthers could claim refuge from accusations of real violence by associating their behavior and language with poetry. The Party used metaphorical language and imagery not only to recruit members but also to limit its culpability for violent rhetoric. Although the FBI was targeting many radical groups in this period through its Counterintelligence Program (COINTELPRO), the Panthers singled themselves out for special attention with phrases like "off the pigs," cartoon images of Panthers shooting police officers, and language about armed revolution.

Violent rhetoric attracted media attention and potential members, but it also drew police repression. The FBI employed informants, *agents provocateurs*, wiretapping, burglary, and frame-ups to investigate and destroy the Panthers. In the most egregious example, police murdered Chicago Black Panther leader Fred Hampton while he was asleep (or drugged) in his bed during a 1969 raid orchestrated by COINTELPRO.[8]

The BPP used the hazy line between metaphorical and intentional speech in ways that both attracted and deflected such attacks. When the US House's Committee on Internal Security investigated the Kansas City Chapter of the Panthers in 1970, for instance, attorneys and witnesses fought over the interpretations of Panther expressions. Were they metaphors or proof of illegal action? The committee's attorney Donald G. Sanders devoted several questions to the phrase "off the pigs" while examining Kansas City pastor Phillip Lawson:

> Mr. Lawson. [The term] is symbolic of the desire of young people in the black community and young adults in other communities to remove from the community those kinds of law enforcement officers who are brutalizing the people, so "off" is within that context. Shouting "off the pig," as I understand it, is to get off, to get away, to leave.
>
> Mr. Sanders. [. . .] We have had a number of witnesses before this committee in previous hearings who have testified that "off the pig" means "kill the cops" or in perhaps one larger context, "kill any officer of the Establishment." Is this not your understanding of the meaning of that term?
>
> Mr. Lawson. It is not my understanding of the meaning of that term. "Off the pigs" is a symbolic kind of a chant, like "right on" has a symbolic kind of meaning in our society, "so be it." It is not necessarily saying that everyone who says "off the pigs" is going to go out and start killing somebody. (United States, *Black Panther Party, Part One* 2637)

In this case, Lawson attempted to interpret "off the pigs" as a metaphor, and his semantics were central to the Panthers' project of generating uncertainty around their rhetoric. While many Panther members did see the phrase "off the pig" as figurative, others construed it as a literal call to assault police. Former Panthers Eddie Thibideaux and Masai Hewitt claim that Panthers sometimes attacked officers and stole their weapons, and members Elbert "Big Man" Howard and Emory Douglas maintain that the Party's April 6, 1968 shootout with police began after Oakland Panthers ambushed a police cruiser with gunfire (Austin 91, 166–68; Joseph 228).

Some members would have rejected such offensive measures, using "off the pigs" as a metaphor at all times, but even those who supported literal interpretations retreated to literary readings of the term when they faced legal challenges. For example, the Panthers insisted that Huey Newton had not fired any shots during the infamous encounter between him and two Oakland policemen that left Officer John Frey dead in October 1967 (Austin 86). The "Free Huey" campaign, which coincided with Newton's imprisonment and trial, relied on the notion of police aggression and Panther victimization. The officers, Panthers implied, had shot one another in their eagerness to kill Newton. In Panther autobiographies like Newton's or Assata Shakur's, moments of Panther-police confrontation and, in Shakur's case, escape from prison, remain shrouded in unconsciousness or authorial silence. After witnessing an officer shoot him, Newton says that "there were some shots, a rapid volley, but I have no idea where they came from. They seemed to be all around me" (171). Somewhere in this haze of shots, Frey is killed. Shakur describes an encounter with police that leaves Panther Zayd Shakur and New Jersey State Trooper Werner Foerster dead in a similar manner (Sullivan 89):

> There were lights and sirens. Zayd was dead. My mind knew that Zayd was dead. The air was like cold glass. Huge bubbles rose and burst. Each one felt like an explosion in my chest. My mouth tasted like blood and dirt. The car spun around me and then something like sleep overtook me. In the background i could hear what sounded like gunfire. But i was fading and dreaming. (Assata Shakur 3)

Police bullets did severely wound both Shakur and Newton in these battles, so their vague memories may be the result of physical injury. But the absence of more specific information about their confrontations, combined with Shakur's and Newton's insistence that readers believe in their innocence, asks readers to accept on faith that "off the pigs" is simply a metaphor. To this day, the lines between metaphorical and literal readings of Panther actions are unclear, largely because many former members may still be subject to prosecution if they admit to any illegal action.

The BPP was able to rely on artistic readings of their images and phrases because Black Arts writers were producing work with similarly violent themes. And although Black Arts writing also forced the audience to wonder how serious the authors' calls to violence were, within the space and time of the performance the threat of violence was clearly artistic and not real. A play, then, acted less as a call to violence and more as a meditation on the ethics of violence. Amiri Baraka's 1964 play *The Slave*, for instance, which depicts a black revolutionary who confronts his white ex-wife and her new husband to claim his children, illustrates the Black Arts attempt to parse out the relationships between metaphor, action, and personal ethics. First performed in 1964 after Baraka's break with white Greenwich Village bohemians but before his full shift to Black Power, this play is somewhat early for a Black Arts piece, but it initiates themes that emerged in the work of Ed Bullins and Jimmy Garrett in the following years.[9] During the revolutionary moment, the black revolutionary hero stages a fight between himself and his ex-wife. Eventually, he kills her new husband, she is killed by the bombs of the revolutionary war, and the children die mysteriously, perhaps at the protagonist's hand. By presenting characters in ethically fraught situations, Baraka confronted the problems of revolutionary violence, often more successfully than the Panthers did.

In *The Slave*, Baraka employs the field slave as a stand-in for the role of metaphor in political action. The protagonist, Walker Vessels, appears in the prologue as a field slave about to tell the story of his revolutionary youth. At the time *The Slave* was written, Malcolm X was motivating audiences by making a distinction between the passive house slave and the rebellious field slave, and the twentieth-century Walker Vessels, an educated man and a poet, adopts the field slave persona when he becomes a black revolutionary. In the postrevolutionary moment of the play's prologue, however, Vessels is still a slave.

Although we don't know whether the revolution has succeeded, we do know that Vessels has not escaped the slave's role: he is ragged, old, and pessimistic. By taking on the persona of the field slave, he has locked himself into the status of a slave rather than opening up a space for liberation.

Throughout the rest of the text, which describes Vessels's encounter with his white ex-wife during the revolution, dramatic roles like that of the field slave continue to guide and distort political decisions. Easley, the wife's new husband and a professor of literature, accuses Vessels of adopting tired metaphors and recycling clichéd dramatic themes. Claiming that Vessels performs "flashy doggerel" and "ritual drama," Easley insists that "you're not going to make one of those embrace the weeping ex-wife dramas" (55–56). His ex-wife Grace, in turn, declares that Vessels is "playing the mad scene from *Native Son*," and she downplays a threatening comment Vessels makes by responding that "He was making a metaphor . . . one of those ritual drama metaphors" (70). By deriding Vessels's political project as a metaphor, Grace and Easley view him only as a stock figure in a racial drama. They refuse to interpret him as a real political threat or a skilled writer of his own metaphors. Vessels himself seems to do no better. He accepts the roles of Othello and the field slave and loses himself in those characters, succumbing to destructive violent impulses that leave the entire family dead.

Here, Baraka highlights the problems of using racialized stereotypes as political tropes. As Vessels comments in the prologue, "I am much older than I look . . . or maybe much younger. Whatever I am or seem . . . to you, then let that rest. But figure, still, that you might not be right. Figure, still, that you might be lying . . . to save yourself. Or myself's image" (44). The character presents himself as the metaphor of the field slave rather than an actual person. When he says "I am much older than I look . . . or maybe much younger," he suggests that this character evolves over time. Is the field slave, he wonders, a product of the nineteenth century or of Malcolm X's 1960s rhetoric? The field slave persona, in other words, morphs in the hands of those who invoke it: "Whatever I am or seem . . . to you, then let that rest." But the metaphor sometimes overwhelms those who use it, guiding them to make bad political decisions simply to maintain the persona: "you might be lying . . . to save yourself. Or myself's image." The reader may deny personal or political realities to save his romanticized notion of the revolutionary field slave. As this passage indicates, the characters' obsessions with metaphors of black rebellion ultimately have concrete and tragic consequences for the interracial family. At the end of the play, only the *metaphor* survives: the field slave remains, but the family is dead, and even Vessels himself seems to have been absorbed into the persona.

Baraka's play reveals misgivings about the transition between violent metaphors and political action. Metaphors, he suggests, sometimes lock political actors into stock roles and ill-considered decisions. The Panthers allowed themselves to be trapped in this kind of role-playing game. They saw the hazy line between action and art as a tool that could provide a cover for members who chose to participate in illegal activity, but they became overwhelmed by the violent revolutionary persona—they found that they could not put it aside. As a result, Panther rhetoric and drama became a liability for members who pursued more legal means of protest. Aboveground activities such as the free breakfast program probably attracted more government repression because of the violent rhetoric. Even as they struggled with the violent persona they had created, however, the Panthers continued to find tactical benefits in their dramatic, metaphorical behavior and rhetoric. While the free breakfast program may have suffered persecution because of violent Panther rhetoric, it also gave moral authority to the BPP. The existence of the free breakfast program softened the Panthers' media image to the extent that Newton and Seale were able to escape serious convictions by raising funds for legal services through mass protest and arousing at least some doubt about their guilt in the public at large. Metaphor, for the Panthers, was simultaneously a liability and a political tool.

The tension between metaphorical and literal meanings, and the constant need for ideological interpretation that came with it, led to internal strife in the BPP. In 1971, when Eldridge Cleaver and his faction split from the organization, they did so over the interpretation of "off the pigs" (Joseph 265). While Cleaver argued that the Panthers should adopt guerrilla warfare within the United States, Newton preferred to focus on the group's "survival programs" (free breakfast, free medical care, free groceries, etc.). He wanted "off the pigs" to remain largely figurative, and the split was based on a difference in political and artistic interpretations.

Black Arts Primitivism

The Panthers did not simply use the Black Arts Movement as a cover for political action. Just as the two groups shared an interest in violent metaphors, they also had a common focus on metaphors of the primitive and the industrial that have long been part of the African-American literary tradition. The Black Panthers employed the "primitive" both in their use of the panther logo and in their most widely circulated image of Huey Newton, which positioned him amid an array of African signifiers: a zebra-skin rug lay at his feet, shields sat in the background, and he held a spear. The leaping panther that adorned their buttons and newspaper headline coupled with the image of Newton as a faux African chieftain played into primitivist notions that black Americans could channel the "jungle" or tribal Africa. And although the Panthers disavowed cultural nationalism, many members wore African garments.

Like the Panthers, who attempted to reframe the panther outside the primitivist tradition, Larry Neal claims in the afterword to the BAM anthology *Black Fire* that BAM artists "have not been talking about a return to some glorious African past," but spears, magic, and African warriors nonetheless appear in celebratory passages throughout this text and its Black Arts cohorts (639). In his 1968 poem "The Primitive," Haki Madhubuti glorifies "the / shores of Mother Africa" that he envisions filled with "our happiness, our love, each other?" (Madhubuti 26); Amiri Baraka and Fundi Abernathy's *In Our Terribleness* refers to its black photographic subjects as "the magic people" and intones: "Do not despair Ancient People / We are your children / and We have conquered" (60, 66); Lethonia Gee's "Black Music Man" compares "The epitome of man / BLACK MUSIC MAN" to "a Masai warrior / With his Burning Spear / Blessed by the Gods" (Jones and Neal 222); Lebert Bethune's "Harlem Freeze Frame" depicts an "old sweet-daddy" on 116th and Lenox as a "gaudy warrior / spear planted, patient eyes searching the veldt" (Jones and Neal 382); and Norman Jordan's poem "Black Warrior" declares that "the heat of a / thousand African fires / burns across my chest // I hear the beat / of a war drum / dancing from a distant / land" (Jones and Neal 389).

All of these artists revel in primitivist metaphors, seeing them as part of African-American identity, but they are also influenced by the American industrial world. The question mark at the end of Madhubuti's "our happiness, our love, each other?" leaves the "primitive" utopia in doubt, and Fundi's photography for Baraka's *In Our Terribleness* depicts the author's "magic people" inhabiting the economically depressed streets of Chicago. Jordan's poem likewise ends with the speaker breaking an urban shop window with a rock, and Lethonia Gee and Lebert Bethune place their speakers on American inner-city streets.

As these examples demonstrate, the Black Arts Movement toyed with the interaction between American urban life and depictions of an abstract, timeless Africa. The Panthers wrestled with the same questions, and they were often successful in using abstract concepts to make useful political points. Just as the Party changed the cultural meaning of the panther image, it also used primitive metaphors to critique both Western racism and Marxist definitions of revolution. Its urban, industrial, primitive aesthetic genuinely contributed to Black Arts musings on black identity and its relationship to "primitive" stereotypes. Lebert Bethune's "gaudy warrior" on Lenox and 116th came to life in the figure of Huey Newton, and I think that we can't fully understand Black Arts combinations of urban and primitive metaphors without the context of the Panthers' popular use of similar imagery. For the Panthers, the urban and the primitive met at the juncture of the contemporary African experience, Third World[10] colonialism, and the black American ghetto.

Huey Newton as the Panthers' Primitive Fetish

We can see this layered aesthetic in the two most iconic images of Huey Newton, one depicting him in a wide-backed rattan chair, armed with a spear and a rifle (fig. 1), and the other presenting him standing with a gun, wearing a bandolier across his chest (fig. 2). The second image derives from fig. 2, a photograph of Seale and Newton together, but it was more frequently cropped to exclude Seale in Panther publications. Both photos depict Newton wearing the Panther uniform of black pants, black beret, and black leather jacket. The two images were mass produced as posters, and they appeared compulsively in the *Black Panther* newspaper. Numerous issues feature one of these photos on the cover, and nearly every copy includes one or both on an inner fold. The January 4, 1969 edition illustrates the ritual nature

Figure 1. Huey Newton as a tribal chieftain in a photo conceptualized and staged by Eldridge Cleaver. Courtesy of Picture History

Figure 2. Bobby Seale and Huey Newton. Courtesy of AP/Wide World Photos/*San Francisco Examiner*

of this repetition by printing a vertical row of rattan chair photos, each a slightly different take from the same photo shoot (*The Black Panther* 4 January 1969: 3).

Through these images, the Panthers exploited white fears of the fantastical African "primitive" and the communist revolutionary. In both photos, Newton imitates the swagger of the armed guerrilla. The beret aligns him with armed revolt, and although it was chosen to commemorate the French resistance in World War II, it also suggests a contemporary reference to the Cuban Revolution (Ogbar, *Black Power* 118). Together, the beret and gun convey solidarity with international revolutionary movements. The leather jacket, on the other hand, celebrates black *American* urban culture. According to Elbert Howard, the Panthers chose the black leather jacket as a uniform because "it seemed that everybody had one anyway" (Austin 61). It was designed not to set the Panthers apart from their community but to mark them as part of it.

The sitting pose, on the other hand, in which Newton surrounds himself with African art objects and rests his feet on a zebra-skin rug, could as easily portray Marvel's Black Panther as a radical internationalist. His upright posture and wide-backed chair recall the Black Panther superhero's caricatured position as tribal chieftain, and the juxtaposition of spear and sword mimic the cartoon's threat of hand-to-hand combat complemented by modern technology. In fact, Newton's stance strikingly resembles Marvel's twenty-first-century Black Panther (fig. 3). In Liam Sharp's 2003 drawing for Marvel Comics, replicated in figure

Figure 3. Marvel's Black Panther in 2003. Courtesy of Marvel Entertainment, LLC

3, the Black Panther appears with masks in the background, a spear in his hand, a "superhero" uniform, and a circular ray of light behind his head, all of which mimic Newton's famous photograph. While Marvel probably echoed Newton intentionally in an attempt to insert antiracist politics into today's Black Panther superhero, the missing beret and gun remind the viewer that *this* Black Panther emerges out of the tradition of racial stereotypes and not out of the history of Black Power. And the slippage between the two images demonstrates how closely Newton's photograph resembles Western images of "primitive" tribal power.

This photo of Newton in the rattan chair was staged by Eldridge Cleaver, a Party member famous for his work of cultural criticism *Soul on Ice*, written while he served time for marijuana possession and rape (Austin 71–75). Several months after Cleaver's 1966 release from prison, he joined the BPP, and in the following years he played the roles of Party theorist during Newton's imprisonment, leader of the Party's International Section in Algeria when he fled legal charges in the United States, and head of Newton's opposition (Lazerow and Williams 1). When he constructed the photo of Newton, he capitalized on and attempted to reverse the stereotype of the "hypermasculine menial" black man that he had identified in *Soul on Ice*. Cleaver argues that this figure, in addition to the black female "Amazon," the white male "omnipotent administrator," and the white female "superfeminine elite," allows white culture to desire and consume black bodies, denying their intellect and blocking them from healthy sexual relations. In the rattan chair photo, Cleaver and the Panthers cling to the hypermasculine element of the black male stereotype, but they present Newton as a political leader rather than a menial figure. This photo appeared in the *Black Panther* alongside theoretical tracts, making him a threatening black body for public consumption but also an intellectual. The BPP took advantage of white fears of black masculinity, yet it disturbed the stereotype by inserting intellect and revolutionary strategy into the mix, highlighting stereotypes without simply repeating them.

Robert Reid-Pharr insists that the prominence of Newton's body cannot be easily discounted, however, as a site of beauty and desire. By combining a hypermasculine role with a primitivist image of generic

African identification, Reid-Pharr argues, Newton employs stereotypes of the "savage" that position blackness outside of civilized modernity. Reid-Pharr sees this as a problem not only because it replicates racist notions but also because it presents black identity as politically *innocent*. While whites have exploited others, "premodern" blacks are victimized and potentially heroic because they exist outside real political relations. Reid-Pharr criticizes the Panthers for propagating these ideas but insists that Newton eventually became uncomfortable with them, retreating from generic depictions of the African heterosexual male in favor of political and social complexity. By distancing himself from hypermasculine, sexualized definitions of black power, he began to accept modern, imperfect versions of blackness: "He wanted, that is, to put his clothes back on" (143). Reid-Pharr helps us understand why the Panthers would choose the primitive, a set of stereotypes based in a racist history: it offered them access to political innocence. He also provides a way of periodizing the Panthers' shift from misogynist and antigay practices into vocal support of the women's and gay rights movements.

His periodizing of ideology on women's rights and gay rights is certainly correct. The Party originally recruited men, appealing to their desires to protect black women and children, and even when women entered the Party, they were deemed "Pantherettes" and separated from male cadre (Jennings; LeBlanc-Ernest). By 1968 the Party eliminated this term and consolidated men and women together in the ranks. In 1969, Ericka Huggins founded and became the leader of the New Haven BPP chapter, and in 1974 Elaine Brown took charge of the entire national organization (LeBlanc-Ernest 310–21). Party ideology likewise began to change. In a September 1968 edition of the *Black Panther*, two articles written by Panther women stressed that women should maintain subordinate roles. Linda Greene argued that a Panther woman "is what her man, and what her people, need her to be, when they need her. [. . .] In her work, she does not distract the men with whom she works when it is the time for work" (11). Gloria Bartholomew similarly argued that "the black women must drop the white ways of trying to be equal to the Black man" (11). A year later, in August 1969, Candi Robinson insisted in the *Black Panther* that "for far too long we have been double oppressed, not only by capitalist society, but also by our men" (9). Seale likewise commented in a 1970 interview with the *Guardian* that "the idea of saying 'keep a woman in her place' is only a short step away from saying 'keep a nigger in his place'" (Foner, *The Black Panthers Speak* 86).

Similarly, despite rampant homophobia in the Party (and in society at large), especially in public comments by Newton and Cleaver, Newton led the BPP in supporting gay liberation by 1970, and Jeffrey Ogbar cites an openly gay Panther who earned the respect of the Jamaica Queens, New York branch. While these new stances in favor of gay rights and women's rights certainly didn't translate into a perfect atmosphere for women and gays in the Party, it did reflect a step forward.

Reid-Pharr is right, then, that the Panthers shifted their vision of hypermasculinity over time to incorporate the needs of women and gay members. But Newton and the Panthers never wholly gave up either their vision of hypermasculinity or their romantic definitions of the African "primitive." Instead, they allowed their vision of modern, complex, African *Americans* to coexist with the timeless, "primitive" vision of the premodern African hero. After all, even in the image of Newton in the wicker chair, he wears a black leather jacket that signals his rebellious, cool status within black *American* culture. The leather jacket itself, often associated with those outside of the American mainstream, connotes dangerous social rebellion rather than innocence. The gun and beret that set off the spear and masks indicate that the "timeless African" *does* belong to a modern era of anticolonial revolution. And although anticolonial revolution may be ethically justified, it cannot claim moral innocence. The geographical incongruities between the American leather jacket, the African spears, and the Cuban beret asked viewers to build associations between black Americans and international allies, and Newton's combination of styles acted as a declaration of future solidarity rather than a shared past.

The Panthers confirmed this international political realism both rhetorically and concretely. In their newspaper the *Black Panther*, they published reports on African and other Third World revolutionary struggles, and they also established relationships with many international radical movements. Eldridge Cleaver fled to Algeria in 1970 to escape legal charges and founded the International Section of the Black Panther Party. In the Western hemisphere, Cuba served as a stopping point for Cleaver and Panther fugitives like Assata Shakur; and to make Asian connections, Cleaver headed a group of radicals to China, North Korea, and North Vietnam in 1970 (K. Cleaver, "Back to Africa"; Assata Shakur). He even negotiated with the National Front for the Liberation of South Vietnam to offer an exchange of American war prisoners for Black Panthers in American prisons (K. Cleaver, "Back to Africa" 232–34). By 1971, the Panthers' international links had grown so substantially that they had contact information for major leftist political figures in such disparate places as Albania and Laos (Kenner).

The pseudo-diplomatic connections between the BPP and international revolutionary governments or movements reoriented the Panthers' primitivist image of Newton toward specific nations. Just as their violent rhetoric sometimes overwhelmed their real ideological questions, however, the Panthers' vision of an international identity for people of color did not always take into account the ethical realities of revolution around the world. These realities quickly confronted Panthers who participated in international work. When the Cleavers moved to Algeria, they found themselves shunned by the Algerian government, and although they eventually received some government funding and office space, tension remained, and many international Panthers moved elsewhere. Although these Panthers quickly determined that Algeria was not a socialist paradise, average readers of the *Black Panther* continued to understand it through the lens of Newton's celebratory photos of Third World solidarity. Twice in 1972, black Americans hijacked planes and ordered them to Algeria, where the Algerian government delivered them to the Party's International Section (K. Cleaver, "Back to Africa" 245; Lindsey 1). These hijackings suggest that the Panthers successfully marked Algeria as a site of identification for black Americans, but this identification remained abstract for most readers. Although their international references did not rely simply on political *innocence*, the Panthers did sometimes produce romantic, unrealistic notions of international solidarity and socialist revolution.

As Reid-Pharr usefully reminds us, we don't need to limit ourselves to either recuperating or renouncing the Panthers for their tactics. Their embrace of sexualized embodiment in concert with concrete political discussions of the American moment produced conflicting results. While disrupting traditional stereotypes, the Panthers also became trapped in their sexualized imagery, and Newton became a Freudian fetish of masculine leadership for the Panthers. The Party was still young in October 1967, when an encounter between Newton and police left officer John Frey dead and Huey Newton on trial for murder, so the burgeoning group of members knew him only through photos and the disembodied words of his written addresses. At a 1968 birthday party held in his honor, the rattan chair stood empty at center stage to mark the leader's absence. As Panther Elaine Brown remarked, "Thousands had joined the Black Panther Party while Huey was behind bars. To them he was a mythical figure, a godly photograph of a man" (251). The organization's reliance on Newton's symbolic, mythical status initially enhanced recruitment efforts and group cohesion. But if Freud's fetish is a psychological compensation for a lack or absence, then Newton was a literal fetish for the Panthers: he was missing, imprisoned by the American government. Because the notion of the fetish arose out of Freud's understanding of "primitive" religious practice, the Panthers symbolically challenged the irrationality of such behavior when they made a fetish out of a missing person. Their "primitive" fetish symbolized real absences in the black community—not only Newton but safety, good jobs, and affordable food and housing. The Newton fetish could not survive its subject's return, however. After the Court of Appeals overturned his conviction for voluntary manslaughter and released him in May 1970, Newton's leadership decisions clashed with Cleaver's perspective, and his real-life persona disappointed many. His small stature and high-pitched voice didn't fit the hypermasculine image, and his awkward public speaking style, new "Supreme Commander" title, and luxury penthouse at the Party's expense brought him under fire from the rank and file (Joseph 250–61; E. Brown 258–66). The absence behind the fetish was black liberation, and the return of Newton's body to the Black Panther Party was a poor substitute.

Newton's Other Half: The Figure of the Oppressed

Just as Newton's vision of the premodern African savage coexisted with the historically grounded anticolonial guerrilla, Newton's hypermasculine hero merged with images of the oppressed, helpless black male figure, often depicted in the person of Bobby Seale. While Newton was imprisoned, Seale took a backseat in Party imagery even as he acted as an organizational leader. It wasn't until after the October 1968 Democratic National Convention and the 1969 murder of Panther Alex Rackley that he took center stage because of his indictments in two trials: first as a member of the "Chicago Eight" for conspiracy and inciting to riot at the Chicago Convention and then for allegedly ordering Rackley's murder as a suspected FBI informer in New Haven, Connecticut.

Seale's trials became a focus of Black Panther imagery in the first months of 1970, when the Panther leader was battling presiding judge Julius Hoffman over his right to legal counsel. The judge ordered Seale to share an attorney with his seven codefendants because his lawyer, Charles Garry, was unavailable (Seale 296; Hoffman).[11] When Seale protested, the judge eventually resorted to gagging him and handcuffing him to a chair. Court and media artists' renditions of the sole black defendant bound and gagged circulated widely in the activist community and the mass media, and the *Black Panther* adopted both this image and one nearly identical to it as a complementary set of icons to Newton's guerrilla warrior photos. Seale's images were illustrations, one signed by B. Jones and the other created by Emory Douglas for a March 1970 cover of the *Black Panther*.[12] The courtroom drawing depicted Seale bound to a chair, while Douglas rendered the defendant strapped into the electric chair, as seen in figure 4.

Unlike Newton, who was presented as the picture of machismo, Seale appeared as an all-too-human figure enmeshed in America's racist structure. the *Black Panther* separated Seale's oppressed humanity from Newton's mythic masculinity, just as he was frequently omitted from the photo in figure 2 to highlight Newton's armed leadership. As the imprisoned Newton spoke in published articles and wielded weapons in accompanying photos, the similarly jailed Seale was metaphorically

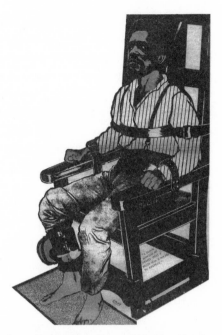

Figure 4. Emory's Douglas's depiction of Bobby Seale on the cover of the *Black Panther*, March 15, 1970. Courtesy of Emory Douglas/Artists Rights Society (ARS), New York

silenced. The two images of him were factual, as they reflected real punishment that Judge Hoffman had meted out and the threat of the death penalty that he could have faced in his trial for the murder of Rackley. But Newton, too, could have faced the death penalty, and his experience was interpreted differently than Seale's.

Paired as Seale and Newton were as Party founders, these images identified them as symbols for black Americans in their dual roles as the resistant and the oppressed. Newton took on the part of the hero and Seale that of the vulnerable black body. The *Black Panther* needed both images to present its ideological perspective, and despite Newton's dominant position, the Panthers did not simply demean Seale. The Panther uniform presented not only Newton but *any* member as a threat to white America, and it was Seale who led the Party during the BPP's first action at the Sacramento legislature and later when Newton was imprisoned. Although the rattan throne that stood empty at Newton's birthday highlighted the leader's absence, it also anticipated the emergence of new Panther leaders to take Newton's position. The dueling images were self-conscious fictions about the two individuals that expressed the BPP's political stance. Newton's image refused political innocence with its anticolonial undertones, and Seale's helplessness countered Newton's hypermasculinity. Their layered imagery of blackness called on viewers to identify simultaneously with the oppression of the black experience, the power of anticolonial responses, and the countercultural strength of black street-style. These images indicate that the Panthers were not simply saviors of a helpless community. Rather, they were part of that community—helpless as well as heroic.

The American "Primitive"

These layered visions of black masculinity and "primitive" identity were not simply evident in these few images. The *Black Panther* newspaper reinforced the Panther vision of the industrial, urban primitive with its combination of illustrations, photos, and stories. After its 1967 beginnings in a police brutality case, the *Black Panther* evolved into a weekly newspaper and a central focus of Panther life. The BPP put substantial resources into it, assigning many of its most talented recruits like Eldridge Cleaver and Emory Douglas to writing, editing, and illustrating, while the Panther rank and file spent the greater part of their days selling issues (Seale 179; Austin 277). Even though the FBI interfered with shipping routes, surveillance records from March 1969 indicate a printing of 40,000, and former editor JoNina Abron reports that weekly distribution was as high as 125,000 in 1970 (Seale 180; Huey P. Newton Collection Series 4, box 1, folder 5; Abron 182; Ogbar, *Black Power* 121; Clegg 160). It trailed only the Nation of Islam's *Muhammad Speaks* in national distribution for African-American newspapers (Ogbar, *Black Power* 121).

As chapters spread across the country, the newspaper consolidated national ideology and created a sense of solidarity among branches—

although it was also a venue for the national office to exert control over its members by publicly expelling or denouncing dissenters, informants, or "jackanapes." The *Black Panther*'s content included cartoons, poetry, photos, reading lists, reports on branch activity, ideological tracts, and syndicated articles from the radical Liberation News Service on international events (*Black Panther* 17 February 1970; 19 May 1970). When Newton, Seale, or members such as the "New York 21" were imprisoned, the paper printed appeals, legal complaints, and trial summaries. Reports of local police brutality or poor housing conditions stressed a direct connection to local communities, while stories about Communist Party activity in China or strikes in Mexico put these injustices into a global perspective. Nearly every issue also reprinted stock items: the Party's "Ten-Point Platform," its organizational rules, and "A Pocket Lawyer of Legal First Aid." These standards were supplemented by specific photos, illustrations, and articles that appeared frequently as reprints. The paper was a ritual for readers that affirmed their identification with the Panthers and their dissociation from the "pigs."

The ritual of the *Black Panther* newspaper again reveals the Panthers' participation in the aesthetic innovations of the Black Arts Movement. Dramatists like Amiri Baraka and Ed Bullins were interested in ritualizing black theater, making it into a space for black community participation rather than detached viewing. Kimberly Benston notes that their drama operated by methexis, or cooperative production, rather than representative mimesis (28). And Mike Sell stresses that Ed Bullins's *We Righteous Bombers*, a controversially plagiarized version of Albert Camus's *Les Justes*, modified Camus's original by forcing the audience to see the performative, constructed nature of the play (272). In both cases, the dramatist invites the audience to participate in meaning production. It would be easy to argue that the Panthers rejected this strategy. After all, as "revolutionary nationalists" from the Marxist tradition, they wanted to win members of the black community to their side through propaganda. And although the *Black Panther* did employ traditional Marxist rhetoric that might have been tiresome or pushy, it also altered the traditional journalistic process to create a more participatory, more community-based newspaper. Just as poet Sonia Sanchez lifted the black vernacular to the status of poetry, the Panthers mixed Marxist jargon with the language of street gossip, referring to "brothers," "sisters," and "punks" while publishing small stories of inner-city poverty in intimate ways. A 1970 issue, for instance, told the short but moving story of nine-year-old Rose Marie Smith being harassed by a white store manager for trying to purchase black pepper with food stamps: "this PIG said that he would buy the pepper for her if she would stand before him and eat it" (Kent 12). As this illustrates, *Black Panther* journalism was local, emotional, and community-focused. Members from throughout the country could submit articles, and community members could attract publicity for complaints against landlords or local business owners. Articles were not objective, and they often included grammatical or spelling errors. This was a newspaper where art, opinion, and reporting merged seamlessly. It was not a "paper of record," charged to deliver objective world news with authority. Rather, the *Black Panther* invited its audience to join the rituals of storytelling, complaining, analyzing political events, and planning for resistance.

The newspaper exhibited a constant tension between abstract, romantic imagery and specific instances of solidarity, for better and for worse. Abstractions encouraged ideological commitment, while specifics built concrete activist realities. When abstractions and specifics coexisted in articles or images, the Panthers were at their most successful. Where abstractions ruled, the Panthers sometimes failed to achieve the necessary level of complexity. The newspaper was at its best in analyses of "primitive" conditions within the United States. By using racialized primitive metaphors to describe the American urban environment, they tied American and Third World abuses together, generating international bonds of solidarity while redefining the "primitive" as the *product* of industrial civilization. And just as the Panthers specified particular nations in their definition of the revolutionary "primitive," they likewise used details of African-American life to define "primitive" America.

A July 1970 issue of the newspaper, which printed a "Letter Written by a Racist to Sister Frances Carter of the Conn. 9, Recently Released from Prison," illustrates this strategy. The letter began with the exhortation to "Do us a favor and go back to Harlem or Africa, where you belong," equating Harlem and black Americans with Africa—an association that might have appeared in the poetry of Madhubuti or Sonia Sanchez. In this case, however, the link didn't call for a discussion about the relationship between black Americans and Africa or the possibility of a black aesthetic. It was simply racist. With this in mind, the Panthers moved beyond abstractions. On this page, the newspaper didn't locate people simply in "Africa" or "Harlem." Instead, names, occupations, and addresses became the stuff of the Panther aesthetic as editors detailed the "inhuman living conditions" of Mary Williams at 615-619 Ocean Avenue in Jersey City; the failure of the Winston-Salem jail to repay the widow of Henry Martin Foy for his bond; and a police attack on Flozell Johnson of the Mission Hill projects in Boston. These stories trace the origins of black community members—not the tropes of Harlem or Africa, but 615 Ocean Avenue in Jersey City or the Mission Hill projects in Boston.

While "primitive" traditionally describes a historical or developmental point that will progress into civilization, the BPP presented it as an inevitable byproduct of capitalism. Industry, the Panthers suggested, did not replace the "primitive" as a civilization advanced. Instead, it was generated by civilization, specifically industrial capitalism. The Party's political theory gave meaning to its primitive aesthetics. Unlike traditional socialists (though like many of its New Left cohorts), the BPP did not see the working class as the primary revolutionary actors. The Russian and Chinese revolutions had already questioned the notion that revolution would emerge first in the industrial center, and Mao had modified Marx by validating the peasantry as a revolutionary class. The Panthers, inspired by Mao (the *Little Red Book* was required reading in political education classes), *did* inhabit the world's industrial core, and they aimed to make a revolution out of the materials they had. In urban North America, this meant working with an impoverished urban population struggling with unemployment. Their setting was, in the Panther aesthetic, an American "primitive."

Marxist terminology, especially as interpreted by Mao and Frantz Fanon, remained basic to Panther vocabulary, but they posited the *lumpenproletariat* instead of the working class as the key revolutionary class. The lumpenproletariat includes figures like prostitutes, criminals,

and the homeless who exist outside the wage labor system. While Marx
had dismissed them as counterrevolutionary, Fanon celebrated their
potential but cautioned that, due to lack of education, they could be
swayed by either revolutionary or counterrevolutionary forces (Marx,
The Eighteenth Brumaire 75–78; Fanon, *The Wretched of the Earth*
81–87). Although Fanon's reading of society's bottom layer was not
wholly sanguine, the Panthers nonetheless declared themselves a party
of the "Lumpen."

In part, their enthusiasm for the lumpenproletariat grew out of the
black urban population's struggles with unemployment. Between 1966
and 1972, when the Panthers were at their height, the unemployment
rate for whites in the United States ranged from a low of 3.1% in 1969
to a high of 5.4% in 1971, while for nonwhites it fluctuated between
6.4% in 1969 and 10% in 1972 (Carter). The situation was worse in
Oakland, where unemployment was 11% for all workers and 20% for
African Americans in 1964. The city's manufacturing sector was also
in decline, forcing many blue-collar workers to commute as plants
moved into the suburbs (Self 170–71; Nicholls and Babbie 104–06).
New white suburbanites built what historian Robert Self refers to as
"industrial gardens" in the suburbs—locations that offered green spaces
for leisure and industry for economic stability, leaving Oakland's black
residents with the dregs of industrial development. Explicit segregation
was rampant in real estate development, making homes in the suburbs
off limits. Meanwhile, new highways and public transportation tore
through black neighborhoods to make way for suburban commuters,
and urban "redevelopment" destroyed areas that city councils deemed
undesirable.[13] For many blacks, factory jobs were inaccessible, so the
factory—whose labor unions had often been dominated by white workers[14]—seemed like the wrong place for a black revolution.

In response to these developments, the Panthers painted industry
as a threat to black America. It didn't offer jobs, and it didn't even
promise worker solidarity in hopes of a socialist future. The *Black
Panther* portrayed this bleak outlook on industry with particular
eloquence on June 6, 1970, when the cover photo portrayed three
children approaching the camera amid industrial rubble. A building
behind them, missing all its windows, bears the marks of smoke and

fire, and a pile of debris stands in front. Although one of the children smiles and gestures toward the camera, another, wearing a black leather jacket, stares coldly ahead, one hand at his side formed into a fist. Two stories on the next page illustrate the photo by reading the urban landscape as an example of the "primitive" that industrial capitalism has generated. On these pages, the "primitive" is both damaging to the black community and potentially threatening to white power. The children, meanwhile, appear as victims and possible future Panthers, as indicated by the boy who wears a leather jacket and forms a nascent Black Power fist.

Afeni Shakur, member of the Panther 21 and future mother of rapper Tupac Shakur, composed the first of the articles, which is flanked by three photos: the cover shot, a photo of four children jumping on a box spring amid the urban trash, and a photo of a woman holding an emaciated baby captioned "Brownsville, U.S.A. or Capetown South Africa [sic]." Paired with Shakur's text, these images present children as the victims and inhabitants of a postindustrial city that is indistinguishable from Africa. Brownsville's economy had been based on garment manufacturing (a sweatshop industry that didn't connote upward mobility) and construction work. This page, however, shows no trace of industrial production.[15] No longer a center of capitalist accumulation, the landscape becomes a warped playground barren of workers. Only children remain to march through the rotting industrial framework of the neighborhood. This decimation benefits industry, according to Shakur: "Brooklyn, like Harlem, is being prepared for an industrial takeover. The filthy businessmen cannot do this until the people have been either burned out, bombed out, or shot out." In Shakur's reading, industrial capitalism resembles colonialism, claiming land for profit while ignoring the needs of its people.

Brooklyn Panther D. Jenkins expands this analysis by making references to the "primitive" explicit. Her article "Brooklyn" begins by describing how the "roar of the Panther" has awakened the black "colony" to the abuses of the police and the capitalist structure. The people of the "Black jungle," Jenkins insists, will only get "complete satisfaction [by] chopping that head [of the power structure] off and throwing the remains into a huge pot to be bar-be-qued." She invokes cartoon images of "primitive" cannibalism in which an African or Polynesian native monitors a huge pot containing a dismembered colonialist, but Jenkins morphs the primitivist fantasy of Western colonists into a revolutionary fantasy for black Americans. Just as Marx's alienating workplace can become the scene of solidarity, the Panthers insist that racist primitivism can become the metaphorical setting for black revolution.

If Shakur and Jenkins redefine the "primitive" as an oppressed space generated by colonial or capitalist systems, they likewise rework Marxist notions of the "industrial" by replacing the industrial worker with the lumpenproletariat. Marx argued that the lumpenproletariat did not share the interests of the working class because their fate was not tied up in relations of production. Jenkins rejects this assessment, however, when she suggests that the "Lumpen," too, have political interests and economic power. Although they might not be able to attack production by going on strike, they can target the capitalist system indirectly through urban landlords. "Tell that fool landlord responsible for all of those scattered vacant lots throughout Brownsville," Jenkins says, "that he no longer owns that land, that in fact he stole it from you and you are taking it back as an overdue payment of the 40 acres and two mules his grandfather promised yours." Jenkins's rhetoric again mixes the history of racism with that of colonialism, suggesting that blacks are the rightful owners and original inhabitants of Brooklyn—the "natives" being exploited by colonists/landlords.

For Jenkins, rent strikes (a form of political action that the Communist Party used regularly) emerge as the point of influence between the "Lumpen" and the capitalist structure just as, in other Panther texts, attacks on the petit bourgeois police force are revolutionary moments. These strategies were not ultimately successful, in part because they attracted repression and reduced public sympathy and in part because they affected only small numbers of landlords or police. Nonetheless, the Panthers did attempt to give real social purpose to the "Lumpen," whom they defined not only as the urban unemployed or underemployed but also as black prisoners and military personnel.[16] If the "Lumpen" did not take part in the traditional capitalist economy, the BPP attempted to initiate them into an alternative economic structure within the black community. Most Panthers "worked" as full-time activists, transforming their "unemployed" status into the work of community building. In doing so, they questioned human dependence on alienating industrial labor.[17] While some members took on militaristic roles, others adopted "civilian" roles in the community structure. Family, home, and community were crucial components of Panther imagery *and* action, and this is often glossed over in favor of their more aggressive rhetoric. In the images described above, children and the need for urban play spaces take center stage. Likewise, stories detailing landlord/tenant disputes or photos of Huey Newton interacting with children (which appeared frequently after Newton's release from prison) tempered the militaristic images in the newspaper. On the streets, Panthers acted out these family-friendly images with their survival programs, which, by providing basic needs, began to construct a new set of economic relations for the urban black community.

Aesthetics and Ethics: Finding the Right Level of Abstraction

When they used industrial and primitive metaphors together, the Black Panther Party expressed its modified Marxist ideology in a decidedly literary way, and neither its politics nor its metaphors were simple, as debate about the chant "off the pigs" suggests. By seeing the Panthers' complicated rhetoric and imagery through the lens of the Black Arts Movement's literary history, we can understand not only the political complexity of the Panthers but also the intricacy of political art. Although political art is often criticized for adopting social realist or allegorical models, BAM poet and essayist A. B. Spellman reminds us that Black Arts was *not* simply mimetic:

> Some called it the new mimesis because it made a mirror that affirmed us. But I thought that it was an anti-mimetic art, for it was art beyond the probable, beyond talking, beat down reality, beyond the oppressive "is." Why do art if you can't make worlds and populate them with perfectible brethren? (53)

Spellman directs us to widen our perspective of the Black Arts Movement beyond realism. In fact, Black Arts work often incorporated fantastical, utopian, dystopian, or abstract elements even as it engaged Black Power politics. Primitivist images, for example, were not simply realist depictions of a unitary black identity but meditations on the interaction of fractured, multiple black identities with racist history and radical politics. The tribal chieftain was not a realist representation but a revolutionary fantasy based on the history of racist stereotypes.

The Black Panthers, with their images of jungle panthers, barnyard pigs, and urban warriors, likewise employed political metaphors that were not always realistic. Nikhil Pal Singh notes that this disjuncture from the "real" may be inevitable for an oppressed group first trying to break out of hegemonic identities and repressive social structures. But the level of fantasy was both an expression of oppression and a kind of theoretical political musing. Like Black Arts writers and visual artists, the Panthers imagined a variety of improbable political futures, questioned them, modified them, and attempted to create them. When Eldridge Cleaver posed the shot of Huey Newton in his rattan chair, or when Emory Douglas imagined Bobby Seale as a field slave in the electric chair, they asked viewers to remember the history of racialized metaphors. They required the public to make a link between the electric chair and the rattan chair or between the spear and the gun, and they offered no easy answers. But while artistic representations of the "primitive" and the "industrial" can revel in complexity and open-endedness, the Panthers combined antimimetic metaphors with strategies for political change.

Today, Panther imagery and rhetoric continue to have cultural currency even though the organization is long dead. For twenty-first-century artists like Dead Prez, Mos Def, Talib Kweli, Common, Aaron McGruder, Game, and Kanye West, the "panther" and "Huey" are so commonly used to describe radicalism that they have become clichés. These terms, like the phrases "off the pigs" and "power to the people" or the image of Newton in his rattan chair, can sometimes lose their political force when detached from their historical context. Although artists like Mos Def and Aaron McGruder employ Panther metaphors to give young listeners and readers access to a radical black history that rarely appears in their textbooks, the political moment of the early twenty-first-century threatens to flatten Panther references to simple celebrations of revolution. Hip-hop artist Game (formerly The Game), for instance, associates Newton with a generic "gangsta" figure that has only a vague antiracist political position when he raps about "Huey P. Newton with Air Force Ones On" (Snoop Dogg featuring The Game).[18] Game grasps at the masculinity and violence of the Panther image without engaging its complexities, producing a commodified version of the Panthers for the new millennium.

Yet even as Game employs the Panthers as a symbol of violence, he cannot empty them of their radical connotations. In fact, he uses them to invoke a radical authenticity. Just as the Panthers could not adopt the panther or the spear without engaging racist primitivism, today's artists cannot invoke the panther or Newton without referencing black radicalism. The fame of the Black Panthers, in fact, has distanced the term *panther* from race and attached it instead to radical politics. In the years immediately following the BPP's emergence, this trend appeared in the guise of organizations like the Gray Panthers, who took the panther as a sign of retiree radicalism rather than race ("Gray Panthers' History"). Even Marvel has revised its racist panther caricature into a figure who fights racism and discusses Malcolm X.

The Black Panther Party recognized that it could not erase associations between black Americans and animalism or "primitive" depictions of tribal life. Instead, it chose to work through the "primitive," inhabiting it and revising it for an American location. The term *panther*" then, comes to twenty-first-century activists fraught with a racist history yet engraved by revolutionaries not just with guns and spears but with political analyses. Black Americans today might repeat Josephine Baker's "I had a mascot—a panther" in a different tone of voice.

CHAPTER TWO

The League of Revolutionary Black Workers Brings Back the Industrial Jungle

"We can hang bullets around our necks and wear all kinds of dashikis, but that's not going to bring about an ultimate end to oppression," declared Ken Cockrel at a 1970 antirepression conference (Cockrel 89). A lawyer and a central figure in Detroit's League of Revolutionary Black Workers (LRBW), Cockrel was distancing himself from the other panelists, Emory Douglas of the Black Panther Party and Robert Williams of the Republic of New Afrika. Just as the BPP's Linda Harrison had rejected cultural nationalists for believing "that a buba makes a slave a man," Cockrel now used the same tactic to denounce the Panthers (Harrison 151). The ritual of dissociating oneself from style was a way of insisting on the real content of activist work. But many Panthers wore bubas, and many LRBW members wore dashikis and hung bullets around their necks. Although the LRBW attracted less media attention than the Panthers, it, too, depended on performance and metaphor.

By stressing the rhetoric of workers and factories, the League insisted that the United States was *not* a postindustrial world, as the Panther lumpenproletariat model seemed to suggest. In 1968, 39.9% of Detroit's laborers worked in manufacturing, and African Americans were a major source of that industrial labor (Widick 211; Geschwender,

Class, Race 58). Unlike the Panthers, who saw black Americans as a colony within the United States, the League believed that African Americans were at the center of capitalist production. If the Panthers joined primitive and industrial metaphors when they envisioned the inner city as a postindustrial colony, the LRBW identified the factory as a site of a different kind of "jungle" warfare.

The League of Revolutionary Black Workers led alternative union movements in Detroit's auto plants during the late 1960s and early 1970s. Beginning with the Detroit Revolutionary Union Movement (DRUM) in Dodge's Hamtramck Assembly Plant in 1968, a group of black activists and auto workers organized against plant management and union bureaucracy. They claimed that the United Auto Workers protected white workers, leaving blacks with the most miserable and low-paying jobs. By starting black nationalist union movements in factories across Detroit and supplementing this work with community organizations, bookstores, and publishing outfits, the League of Revolutionary Black Workers hoped to build a revolutionary base among workers that would spread to the larger community. Facing internal strife, the organization suffered a split in 1971, and by January of 1972 it had collapsed (Georgakas and Surkin 164).

Just as many whites and blacks were fascinated by the "primitive," attributing both frightening and romantic traits to it, the League viewed the "industrial" as a site of both beauty and fear. Diego Rivera's mural *Detroit Industry* in the Detroit Institute of Arts, which depicted 1930s Ford workers producing automobiles amid a tangle of machinery and contrasting symbols of natural life, had allowed Detroiters to see the auto factory as a work of art. Like the League after him, Rivera portrayed auto production as fiery and hazardous, but he knew that the worker would overcome this alienation. For Detroit radicals, this ability to endure the danger and exploitation of industrial production gave the auto worker a privileged social position.

The League's fascination with the factory emerged in the same primitivist metaphors that guided the Panthers and cultural nationalists. Through these images, the LRBW distinguished its black union movement from organized labor's often racist past while welcoming the aggression and confrontation that the "primitive" permitted. Moreover, the League envisioned a broad African-American movement extending through factories, communities, and schools. Thus, although members saw the *worker* as the central revolutionary actor, under League direction the term *worker* became slippery. Just as the whole city of Detroit associated itself with auto production, the League often identified auto workers with Detroit's entire black community.

DRUM and the Little RUMs

The League of Revolutionary Black Workers was not one organization but many. Founded in June 1969 to manage several existing black nationalist workers' groups in Detroit, its central committee eventually governed a slew of related organizations (Georgakas and Surkin 84). Ironically, the initial cell, the Dodge Revolutionary Union Movement, emerged from a wildcat strike[1] led primarily by white workers. On May 2, 1968, a speed-up in the assembly line at Hamtramck Assembly Plant (known as Dodge Main) angered workers on the afternoon shift (24).[2] According to General Baker, a future leader of the LRBW who was working in the plant, a set of mostly white workers responded to the speed-up by declaring that they wouldn't return to work after lunch. Eager to take action, Baker and some African-American friends joined in, and they successfully shut down the plant for four days, gaining the support of approximately 4,000 workers (Baker; Geschwender, "The League" 6). Although the action was initiated by whites, management came down harder on black participants. Seven workers were fired, five of them black. Five eventually regained their jobs, but General Baker and Bennie Tate, both African Americans and radicals, remained blacklisted (Geschwender, *Class, Race* 89).

Angry about the distribution of punishment, Baker and nine others formed the Dodge Revolutionary Union Movement, which at first did little more than a weekly newsletter handed out to black workers (H. A. Thompson 110; Baker). Bent on exposing poor working conditions in addition to management and union racism, the newsletter alienated some whites and older African Americans but mobilized a sector of young black workers. Because auto plants in the 1960s had hired many black workers to replace retiring whites, it was a propitious time for such activism, especially because the low seniority of young African Americans meant that they were grouped together on the afternoon shift, increasing their ability to act as a unified force.[3]

DRUM's first step after printing the newsletter, focused more on race relations than working conditions, was to boycott the bars outside factory gates with the demand that they hire African Americans. The protesters quickly won the battle, and as a result members turned to the factory, leading a second wildcat in July that kept about 70% of black workers out of the plant (Georgakas and Surkin 46; Ahmad, *The League* 8; Foner, *Organized Labor* 414). Although picketers did not recruit white workers, some whites honored the strike, and the walk-out lasted two days. Both Chrysler and UAW Local 3, DRUM argued, were responsible for the plight of black workers, and the organization demanded concessions from each. From the corporation it requested an exhaustive list of black foremen, managers, and executives, in addition to equal wages for whites and blacks and amnesty for fired workers. From the union it requested more blacks on staff, especially at the executive levels, a revision of the grievance procedure, better safety protections, guards against speed-ups, recognition of DRUM as the official voice of black workers, a decrease in union dues, UAW investment but not interference in the black community, an end to the check-off system of union dues, and a general strike against the Vietnam War ("DRUM Demands"; "DRUM's Program").

These demands, which included manageable local tasks and large utopian ones, earned some press, and a host of other "RUMs" emerged in the following years. ELRUM, the Eldon Revolutionary Union Move-ment, also located in Detroit, started a newsletter in November 1968, and the organization quickly surpassed DRUM. As the only gear and axle plant in Chrysler's assembly, the Eldon Avenue factory had leverage over the entire production process. Sensing the power of the overall movement, smaller RUMs multiplied around Detroit: Ford's River Rouge produced the organization FRUM, Jefferson Avenue formed a JARUM, Mack Avenue a MARUM, Cadillac's Fleetwood plant a CADRUM, the Dodge Truck factory a DRUM II (or DTRUM), and the Mound Road Engine Plant a MERUM. Outside the auto industry, black workers at

United Parcel Service established an UPRUM, health workers created an HRUM, and the Detroit News boasted a NEWRUM (Georgakas and Surkin 82–85).

Such proliferation prompted the original DRUM organizers to form the League of Revolutionary Black Workers as an umbrella organization in 1969, installing a seven-man executive board of Luke Tripp, Chuck Wooten, General Baker, Mike Hamlin, Ken Cockrel, John Watson, and John Williams. Bound by common work experiences and a history in Detroit activism, the LRBW leaders had long anticipated the possibility of a radical union movement. In 1967, an enlarged version of the forthcoming LRBW executive board had begun the *Inner-City Voice* (*ICV*), a monthly radical newspaper directed at Detroit's black community (Georgakas and Surkin 84; Ahmad, *The League* 5).[4] Inspired by Robert F. Williams's and Malcolm X's critiques of the Civil Rights Movement and versed in Marxist ideology, *ICV* writers and editors envisioned a workers' movement before the 1968 wildcat that founded DRUM, and they were poised to grasp any opportunity for a worker-led movement that might arise. When DRUM appeared on the scene, *Inner-City Voice* editors quickly identified their paper as the "organ of the League of Revolutionary Black Workers."

Between the 1967 founding of the *Inner-City Voice* and the 1971 split that led to the League's demise, the executive board and a growing list of allies built a network of activist projects. In addition to the RUMs, the League oversaw high school organizing, a bookstore, a publishing outfit, a press, a filmmaking collective, and a fund-raising effort. Members also took part in unaffiliated organizations such as the West Central Organization (which promoted community control of schools), the North Woodward Interfaith Organization, and the Detroit branch of the Black Panther Party (Geschwender, "The League" 10). Nearly every League activity had its own publication. *ICV* served as a public mouthpiece for the League, each RUM produced a plant newsletter, and high school students published the *Black Student Voice* with the help of adult members (Ahmad, *The League* 14). This broad range of League activities demanded enormous financial and time commitments, and disputes arose on the executive body between those who wanted to maintain a broad community focus and those who prioritized factory work. This debate, which ultimately led to the 1971 resignation of the community-focused faction (Hamlin, Cockrel, and Watson), reflects the importance of the League's relationship to workers and the "industrial" (Georgakas and Surkin 164).

Civilizing the Industrial Jungle

The factory became a source of Black Power for the League by way of a cultural history that combined references to race, barbarism, and industrial settings in terms such as *industrial jungle*, *urban jungle*, and *concrete jungle*. The most common of the three is *urban jungle*, which the *Oxford English Dictionary* dates to a 1926 *New York Times* article that described, in a tongue-in-cheek manner, the dangers of the city for a country girl. At the height of the jazz age and the modernist primitivist moment in aesthetics, author Miriam Beard used the term to describe the city as mysterious, frightening, and full of strange machinery. She also referenced the ways that hip white youth were appropriating blackness and the "primitive." She refers to the "speed and jazz of modern life," limbs aching from the Charleston, and fashionable women who "wear the slave bracelets and the abbreviated skirts whose fashion was set by the Congo long before Paris ever heard of it." The phrase *urban jungle* arose out of the same complications between race, modernism, and urban chic that haunted modernist art. It reflected desire as well as fear, and it suggested that the city itself—not simply the urban ghetto—deserved the title *jungle*.

While this 1920s use of *urban jungle* elicited positive connotations of the jazz age for urban hipsters, the phrase has since descended into more negative associations. Today, *urban jungle* and *concrete jungle* refer to an oppressive urban condition, often an inner-city community populated largely by people of color. As early as 1973, Bob Marley's "Concrete Jungle" bemoaned the distinction between the "sweet life" and the "concrete jungle / where the living is harder" (the Wailers). As Marley's song indicates, the term had lost the romantic edge that Miriam Beard played on, invoking fear and mistrust on the part of whites and despair or defiance among those who live there. By the

1960s, both senses of the phrase had currency, and negative connotations were quickly winning the day.

Industrial jungle, on the other hand, a term that described the Black Panther's lair in Marvel's 1966 comic book, is less common. Like *urban jungle*, it sometimes refers to a ghetto. A 1962 fight in Westport over zoning, for instance, elicited this comment from a white Westport resident: "we commute and pay the premiums to escape the congested commercial industrial jungles that border major cities. [. . .] We all bought at a fancy price to get a nice home in a sophisticated community" (Parke). This speaker employs the industrial jungle as a descriptor of the inner city that white, middle-class homeowners want to avoid. It is undesirable and jungle-like because it mixes residential and commercial spaces, because it is poor, and, presumably, because it is not all white.

The other history of the phrase *industrial jungle* arises from the labor movement. In 1906, Upton Sinclair used the term *jungle* to describe the horrific conditions of Chicago's meatpacking industry, and by the 1930s, labor unions, especially garment worker unions in New York, had adopted the term as an organizing tool. It functioned in two ways: as an illustration of working conditions and as a reference to labor relations without union mediation. In the first case, it substituted for the word *sweatshop*, as a 1932 *New York Times* article illustrated: " 'think well before you permit a return of long hours of labor for a reduced number of workers . . . ; a return of competitive wage-cutting with 1933 sweatshop earnings as a goal; [. . .]; a return to the industrial jungle" ("Favorable Report"). This "industrial jungle" signified "primitive," abusive workplace conditions. The second meaning emerged when labor and management fought openly, without "civilized" grievance procedures. This connotation appears in a 1947 *New York Times* article that warns readers against decreasing funding to the National Labor Relations Board: "in the absence of peaceful procedures the unions would resort 'to the law of the industrial jungle'" (Stark). Similarly, in 1959, NLRB chairman Boyd Leedom praised the leaders of garment worker unions "as the architects of stability in what would otherwise be an industrial jungle" (Raskin). In these examples, the "industrial jungle" was a state of competitive chaos.

Unions were also guilty of invoking racist assumptions when they employed the phrase. In the early twentieth century, corporations had battled organized labor by employing African Americans as scabs. In union rhetoric, the phrase *industrial jungle* suggested that if majority-white unions did not manage employer-employee relations, factories would revert to dangerous working conditions—and they would also lose their white majority. The industrial jungle idiom signaled not only a threat to *worker* power but also a threat to white union power.

Already an Auto Worker

Just as the phrases *industrial jungle* and *urban jungle* often collapsed the distinction between urban and industrial locations, the League elided the roles of the urban African American and the auto worker. It claimed to be the League of Revolutionary Black *Workers*, but many of the executive board members had no connection to Detroit factories. Hamlin, Tripp, Wooten, and Baker had once been auto workers, but when DRUM held its first wildcat, only Wooten and Baker were auto workers, and after Baker's swift termination, Wooten was the only one.

The entire board came from working-class backgrounds. Their parents had worked as domestics, auto workers, janitors, and postal employees or struggled with unemployment, but the younger generation sought mobility (Geschwender, *Class, Race* 171–75). Watson, Williams, Baker, and Tripp attended college at Detroit's Wayne State University, where they absorbed literature and politics while founding the radical student group Uhuru. This connection as classmates, not coworkers, launched their activist careers. Some of the men did go on to hold working-class jobs. Watson met Cockrel and Hamlin, for example, when they all worked in the delivery department of the *Detroit News* (Geschwender, *Class, Race* 171). Cockrel did not stay in this role for long, however. He soon became one of Detroit's most prominent attorneys, while the other executive board members earned paychecks from the LRBW or held a variety of working-class and professional jobs (Mast 86).

We need not see this assortment of occupations as a reason to condemn the League as "inauthentic," composed of "outside agitators" who took advantage of auto workers. Such claims are often used to denounce labor activists or to scare working-class people away from radical politics. Instead, the relationship between League leadership and the factories underscores the complicated mix of identities in the LRBW. Members were students, working-class people, full-time activists, and professionals all at once. They shifted from one identity to another or claimed more than one simultaneously.

General Baker illustrated this status when asked whether he entered an auto plant expressly to organize workers:

> If you grew up in the city of Detroit in the '60s you were going to go to one of the auto plants, so we used to call it baptism. I got baptized at the Ford Rouge at the Dearborn Stamping Plant in 1963. So I was already in an auto factory as I was taking classes at Wayne State [. . .] I didn't go in there to organize, I went in there to live. (Baker)

When he says that he went into the auto plant to *live*, Baker disturbs the typical distinction between student and worker activism. His status as a student, Baker suggests, depended on his income as an auto worker. The two were intertwined, and just as the factory was essential to capitalist Detroit, so was it essential to his identity as a black Detroiter (Mast 305).

This complicated relationship between workers, the community, and students was prominent in LRBW language. Although Marxists have always privileged the industrial worker as the key to revolution, the League's fusion of Marxism and black nationalism celebrated workers as the center of an ideological program and insisted that to be black in America *was* to be a worker. This feeling grew out of a long tradition of radicalism and Marxism in the black community. Cedric Robinson outlines this history in *Black Marxism*, which traces a radical black history from feudal Europe to the present. Robinson argues that notions of racial difference developed in Europe before capitalism, thus determining the ways that capitalism developed. Because slavery coexisted with capitalism and worked within it for so long, Robinson notes, there is no reason to see the white working-class as the sole agent of revolutionary change. But Marxism nevertheless offered both a critical toolbox and, by the early twentieth century, an activist structure with which black radicals could align themselves. As Robinson notes, black radicals adapted Marxism to fit their own needs, forming a new tradition of Black Marxism rather than submitting to the often dogmatic views of majority-white socialist organizations.

Robin D. G. Kelley's history of black Communists in Depression-era Alabama continues Robinson's work, demonstrating how poor black workers saw the Communist Party as a means to combat black oppression even if they were not interested in pursuing the international aims of the Party as a whole. Alabama workers "became Communists," he says, "out of their concern for black people and thus had much in common with the black elite whose leadership they challenged" (116). Although he argues that the Communist Party brought to the surface some latent class conflict between working-class and middle-class African Americans, Kelley stresses that cross-class collaboration among blacks continued even when it was strained by physical attacks and anti-Communist propaganda. Racism was the first site of battle for most black Communists.

Even members of the Communist Party-USA (CPUSA) tacitly sponsored this perspective. Between 1928 and 1958, the CPUSA formally supported the interpretation of black Americans as a national minority with rights to self-determination. Thus, although being black did not *make* one working class, black liberation was a key focus of Communist Party (CP) campaigns, as Kelley usefully highlights. Despite the conflicts over the primacy of racial politics that arose in the CP, especially during World War II, Communist politics and black liberation were closely intertwined for much of the twentieth century (L. Young; Haywood).

When it broadened the definition of "worker" to embrace the entire black community, the League expressed and extended the Black Marxist tradition in just the way that Robinson and Kelley had seen in earlier generations. They were employing Marxist terminology and

history but manipulating it to accommodate the needs of *black* liberation. As Ken Cockrel emphasized:

> We do not simply define workers in the orthodox sense of
> those who toil laboriously with their hands over a lathe, or
> on the line, or in the trim shop, or in the frame plant, or
> in the foundry. We say that all people who don't own, rule
> and benefit from decisions which are made by those who
> own and rule are workers. (Cockrel 87)

Statements like this reminded black community members that their
labor, and that of their slave ancestors, had built American wealth
(Tripp 3). This was true, according to Cockrel, whether they worked
on plantations, in auto plants, in employers' homes, in service industries, or even if they worked in the home or struggled with unemployment. For women in the League, many of whom did not work in the
majority-male auto industry, this point bore particular weight. Former
League activist Marian Kramer recalls women reminding male comrades
that "all those men got to come back into the community; they live
somewhere. We've got to be organizing in both places" (Mast 104). In
her reading, "community" activism was a part of workplace activism
because it included the context of workers' families and social lives.

Students were among the community members that the League
included in its activism, though their role in relation to workers was
always controversial. In Detroit's high schools, the League advocated
for African-American Studies curricula and student power. Even outside school, students were important in factory organizing, as they,
too, would presumably be "baptized" into auto work one day. A 1969
League handbill specifically addressed black students as "pre-workers"
and asked them to identify with their elders (Detroit Revolutionary
Movements, box 1, folder 1-21). And because auto workers could be
fired for picketing during wildcat strikes or targeted as radicals for
distributing literature outside plant gates, these tasks often fell to high
school and college students (Geschwender and Jeffries 141). Performing
the role of strikers by walking the picket line, students made themselves
interchangeable with young workers. In an era when many students

distrusted "anyone over thirty," the League asked students to respect older workers as allies and future coworkers.

Despite such positive relationships, League language was not always so welcoming to students, as John Watson's takeover of Wayne State University's newspaper the *South End* demonstrates. Printers had become reluctant to print the *ICV* because of its political content, so editor John Watson signed up for classes at Wayne State and ran for editor of its paper, stacking the student committee assigned to fill the position with sympathetic faces. He won, and for his eight months as editor in 1968–69, the *South End* replaced *ICV* as the League's official publication (Georgakas and Surkin 55). During this time, LRBW members appropriated some of the paper's staff positions, distributed newspapers off campus at factories and in the black community, and printed a newspaper that carried the banner "One Class-Conscious Worker Is Worth 100 Students."

According to Baker, the *South End* takeover did not aim to influence Wayne State students one way or another—it was simply a way of obtaining a printer and funding (Georgakas and Surkin 55). But in fact the LRBW did influence the Wayne State community enormously, while students, faculty, and alumni also molded the paper. With the exception of Watson and a few League staffers, the majority of reporters were Wayne State students who honed their journalistic skills not only on League stories but also on an array of student and activist concerns. Sports and sorority/fraternity reports retained prominence in the paper, appearing alongside discussions of antiwar protests and wildcat strikes. And while the paper's masthead and its radical content certainly provoked controversy on campus, it did not prevent students, faculty, or alumni from reading it or participating in discussion about it. In a letter to the editor, for instance, a professor mocked the masthead for its "Marxematics," offering alternate equations such as "1S=1 C.C.W.," supposedly "submitted by a sizeable Marcusian minority" and "One of anything=100 students. Submitted by renegade rightist with 50 years of teaching experience" (*South End* 28 February 1969: 4). This writer deflated the self-importance of the masthead and, in doing so, unknowingly highlighted the League's real relationships to students, which were more complicated than the equation suggested.

In fact, the students who worked for the *South End*, distributed *DRUM* and *ELRUM*, or picketed at wildcats were key assets of the organization. Likewise, students and faculty gained something from increased exposure to their community's labor struggles. Many were no doubt angry about the banner's antistudent stance, but others saw it as an exhortation to continue their political work after college.

Panthers Invade the Shop Floor: Cultural Nationalism Meets Marxism

Although definitions of the worker were crucial for the LRBW, the group's literature also invoked the set of primitivist images that Panthers and cultural nationalist groups employed. The masthead of the *South End* and each issue of the plant newsletters depicted the same leaping panther that the BPP had borrowed from the Lowndes County Freedom Organization, and images of spears, African masks, and drums abounded throughout the publications. Even the acronym for the original workers' group, DRUM, evoked primitivist associations, as it was depicted on the newsletter with a conga drum and an African mask.

In one sense, these symbols reflected the fact that the League was a black nationalist group as well as a Marxist one. In 1968, physical expressions of solidarity with the black liberation movement in the form of Afros, Panther buttons, dashikis, or Africanized names, were widespread. General Baker verifies this when he argues that cultural nationalist expressions were the initial spark that drove the DRUM movement. He traces the beginning of radical African-American sentiment in the auto plant to the period immediately following the 1967 Great Rebellion. Baker was imprisoned during the riots, and when he returned to work, he remembers a change in style:

> We picked up all those empty fifty-caliber machine gun shells [that the National Guard had used] and took necklaces out of them. We put rawhide straps through them and everybody wore these fifty-caliber machine gun empty casings, you know, as a souvenir of the Rebellion, and everybody

started growing Afros, so you can imagine all these workers starting back up in the plant with their hair standing out on their head and these fifty-caliber machine guns. (Baker)

The bullet casing necklaces were a resistant style specific to urban rebellion, bearing witness to the firepower that the government had employed against the black community. Baker repeats the type of casings to emphasize their enormity, as they are nearly four inches long. Their size is a mark of bravado, a phallic symbol that allows the wearer to advertise his or her ability to live through a battle with the US military.[5] At the same time, the necklace threatens future combat by reminding onlookers of the wearer's propensity to *unleash* violence.

The enormous bullet roughly resembles the shape of an animal's tooth or claw, both traditional adornments in indigenous American and Pacific Islander societies. Many Western depictions of unspecified "natives" or "primitives" highlight such necklaces, especially on males, whom Western culture typically sanctions against wearing jewelry. By stringing their own necklaces from bullet casings, Baker's coworkers at Chrysler expressed solidarity with the national Black Power movement while replacing romantic images of the "primitive" with the threat—and the reminder—of urban rebellion.

Seeing that black workers were motivated by cultural signs of solidarity with the Black Power movement, the League accepted the widespread influence of the panther trope and, later, the Black Panther Party itself. In 1966, before Newton and Seale had established the BPP, the Revolutionary Action Movement (RAM), including future LRBW members Baker and Glanton Dowdell, founded a Detroit organization with the name Black Panther Party (Ahmad, *The League* 5).[6] Three years later, when Newton and Seale's BPP was famous, the League set up a meeting for John Watson to travel to Oakland and discuss a coalition (Ahmad, *The League* 18; Federal Bureau of Investigation 21 March 1969).[7] The *Black Panther* published several positive stories about the League that summer of 1969, and the two organizations cooperated for a time. Although the relationship deteriorated, partly because the LRBW disapproved of the Black Panthers' tactics, the League continued to use the panther logo, recognizing and validating the sway that

Panther imagery held over the minds of young black Americans. By adopting panthers, spears, and drums as symbols, the League presented black dissent as a vast project that united cultural nationalist and revolutionary nationalist groups. The Panthers and the League, despite their actual differences, merged visually in League pamphlets and even in the Detroit Panther organization, forging a bond between the industrial workplace and black radical thought outside factory gates.

For workers who wanted to make this leap from plant activism to the larger black liberation struggle, the *Inner-City Voice* offered political education, printing theoretical materials by Che Guevara or Robert F. Williams and articles on local and international political issues. In this newspaper, unlike the plant newsletters, primitivist imagery played a small role. *ICV* stories on national liberation movements in Africa typically included maps and historical overviews that detailed the area's colonial past, its economic structures, and its resistance movements. Although the articles usually supported liberation movements uncritically, they did offer readers enough context to understand the relationship between colonial oppression and the capitalist exploitation that auto workers faced in Detroit.

International solidarity wasn't the only thing at stake in the League's combination of industrial and cultural nationalist themes. These metaphors also portrayed the League's strategy for dealing with exploitation. If the union had transformed the auto plant from an "industrial jungle" characterized by extreme heat, dangerous machines, low wages, and labor-management warfare, into a "civilized" structure of negotiation, the League questioned the value of "civilization." Discomfort, danger, and low wages remained, so it seemed that the union had only succeeded in eliminating labor-management warfare. The UAW cooperated with Chrysler, according to the LRBW, by planning strikes when the company would suffer the least, and the check-off dues system prevented union members from holding leaders accountable by withholding dues money ("The Real Deal on the Special Conference"). Grievance systems existed, but many workers considered them inadequate. An ELRUM flyer claimed that, before the 1970 contract negotiations, Chrysler had 60,000 local grievances outstanding with the UAW, and although a dispute in a Dallas Ford plant finally sparked it to take action, it did so by settling grievances at "a rate of 1,837 per day" ("Attention Black Workers!"). The sheer number of grievances and the UAW's eagerness to solve them only under duress suggested to the League that the "civilized" relationship between union and corporation benefited union officials but not workers.

Fed up with the failures of union negotiation, the League chose to embrace the conflict, if not the bad working conditions, that characterized the "industrial jungle." Its tactic of choice, after all, was the *wildcat*, a term whose reference to unsanctioned strikes dates back to at least the 1930s and coincides roughly with the *industrial jungle* as a label for worker militancy. The unpredictability of the wildcat contrasted with the monotonous assembly line and staid grievance procedure. For black workers who felt they were treated like machines, jungle metaphors offered a sense of agency and spontaneity that originated not only in racist notions of the primitive but in antiracist movements that had employed the same metaphors. Moreover, jungle images presented the next step in union radicalism as an African-American one.

A July 12, 1968 DRUM rally described in League publications illustrates their particular strategy of merging black nationalism and Marxism. In the protest, participants revolted in ways that expressed their status as both black radicals and workers, and the League's articles capitalized on both identities. Writing for the *South End*, Luke Tripp at first highlighted the working-class status of the protesters when they confronted union leaders at Local 3 headquarters: "you had workers in their 'humping' blue coveralls, and their union 'representatives' laid to the bone in their mohair suits" (Tripp 66). Here, the LRBW suggests that working-class "authenticity" lies in sartorial expression. By noting the coveralls as a sign of hard work or "humping," Tripp juxtaposes the laborers with extravagant union officials in a "bourgy air conditioned room" and "mohair suits." As the protest moved from Local 3 headquarters to Chrysler headquarters, however, he remarks on a different subset of the same protesters, commenting that the sound of conga drummers "brought every Honky in the building to the windows," and "the sisters in their bubas and the brothers dashikied to the bone went for their thing" (68). While the confrontation with Local 3 officers had elicited a demonstration of working-class status, the move to corporate headquarters prompted a shift to cultural nationalist imagery.

At first, it seems that these moments use dress to evoke authentic revolutionary identity, demonstrating to UAW officials that this was *real* working-class revolt, convincing the corporation that it was a true threat, and persuading fellow blacks that it was the definition of radical blackness. But these forms of authenticity were not permanent or essential. While cultural nationalism is often criticized for embracing essential notions of blackness, the League's adoption of African dress in tandem with working-class dress rejects essentialism in favor of style and tactics. In some moments, one style expresses the League's political position, while another moment requires another style. The dashiki and the coveralls are tactical metaphors rather than permanent identities.

We can see how these tactics function in the disparity between the demonstration and its description. Within the protest itself, the two groups mixed, forming a visual picture of diverse working-class/black nationalist militancy. The textual narrative of the protest, on the other hand, separates the two styles into different confrontations. When marching into the union office, DRUM claims working-class status to highlight the distinction between the protesters and the union officials. The UAW had long struggled with black workers over racism and civil rights, and it denounced DRUM for "black separatist" behavior, so in this case the League insisted on pitching a battle against the UAW on its own turf of labor rights rather than relying on the discourse of race.

When confronting the corporation, on the other hand, Tripp stressed the presence of drummers and dashiki-wearers. Chrysler, unlike the UAW, already saw itself as labor's opponent. Historically, however, auto plants had employed black workers as strike-breakers and low-wage workers. Tripp destroys this vision of the black worker. As corporate "honkeys" look out the windows, they could see by the Afros, dashikis, and bullet necklaces that the black liberation movement on the streets would not skip the auto factories. Even if white and black workers were divided, management could no longer rely on black workers to fill miserable low-wage jobs.

Male Aggression as Black Radical Authenticity

These dueling metaphors of the primitive and the industrial were empowering for the League, but they also led to a problematic emphasis on masculinity and aggression. This reflected the rhetoric of the Black Arts and Black Power Movements, but it was also a response to the UAW's tone of moderation and union-management cooperation. The union's monthly publication, *UAW Solidarity*, tempered its presentation of labor rights issues with upbeat pieces such as reports on good camping locations or dressmaking patterns. Local workplace grievances rarely earned space in the newsletter, and national contract negotiations were described as great successes. Staff writer Ted Ogar, for example, described the 1969 contract's increased pension benefits as a "burst of sunshine that would light the worker's golden years of retirement" (Ogar 3). Moreover, the UAW actively distanced itself from the League by embracing civil rights in place of Black Power. In 1969, the UAW's International Headquarters, Solidarity House, sent a mailing to members denouncing the League and its affiliates. The text presents the UAW as a moral force against racism, citing its participation in Selma, Detroit, Washington, DC, Jackson, and Memphis marches, while describing the League's tactics as "racist," laced with "hatred," "violence, fear and intimidation" (United Auto Workers International Executive Board).

DRUM and *ELRUM* newsletters countered the UAW with angry rhetoric. They valued masculine virility and black radical militancy over solidarity with workers who didn't conform to League expectations. In one particularly egregious instance, an ELRUM flyer referred to a woman coworker who was running for a steward position as "Marie Banks, Eldon Ave.'s No 1 WHORE," ("Let's Get Down"). Another flyer referred to a group of white secretaries as black Local 961 president Elroy Richardson's "prostitute service."[8]

The League used sexual metaphors about both black and white female coworkers to express its political positions, and these depictions reflected gender conflicts within the organization as well. Women had no role on the LRBW executive board and few leadership positions, and although many participated in League work, they were often relegated to tasks such as "cooking committee" or "clean-up committee." Marian Kramer remembers that LRBW women spent much of their time fighting the men against epithets that labeled women comrades "the IWW: Ignorant Women of the World" (Baker; H. A. Thompson 171). Today, General Baker regrets the League's gender politics, and some former members contend that it was a lack of respect for women that, in part, led to the 1971 split. According to Hamlin, a male member or aspiring member sexually assaulted a female League worker in one of the organization's offices. Angry over the organization's inability to curb or punish such violence (and frustrated with other political differences), Hamlin, Watson, and Cockrel left the League (Hamlin, Interview).

Just as vituperations against women confirmed male radical identity, expressions of heterosexual masculinity guided the League's relationships with nonradical African-American men in the plant, who often earned the labels of "Tom" or "Mollytom." While Tripp's description of dashikis and overalls as identities that could be taken on and off suggested a flexible attitude about black radical identity, many stories in *DRUM* and *ELRUM* were not so generous. Men who didn't live up to the League's notion of black radicalism were skewered as traitors to both blackness and heterosexuality. The cover story of a 1970 *DRUM* issue marked fellow worker Joe Davis as an Uncle Tom when he vied for a staff position with the UAW. The writers recycled racist white discourse in the title by referring to him as "Ole' black Joe," and the article wondered why Davis "refuse[s] to be black" (*DRUM* 3.3). In its nonplant publications, the League broadened the definition of "workers" to include the black community, but here it attempted to reverse the association, denying "authentic" blackness to workers who moved into positions of union or management leadership.

This was ironic, as the League stressed the importance of black leaders in both places, and the LRBW frequently ran candidates for union leadership. Perhaps because they had little success with their own candidates, they tended to reject the black foremen and union officials who were elected. What they wanted were *radical* black foremen and union officials, although they used "black" to signify "black radical." By confusing these terms, *DRUM* could claim that Joe Davis "refuse[d] to be black." His true allegiance, *DRUM* suggested, should lie with black radicals and not with white leaders who, regardless of his politics, would see him as "Ole' black Joe."

This vision of the ideal black radical candidate meant that, in League publications, any form of interracial cooperation appeared as weakness. This was a feature of the League's *texts* more than its actions, as the group did work regularly with white allies.[9] Within ELRUM, white worker and radical John Taylor was an organizing partner; the white radical group Eldon Wildcat often supported League actions; and the Eldon Workers' Safety Committee included whites as well as ELRUM members. From a rhetorical standpoint, however, any inter-racial association could deplete a black worker's radical status. The *DRUM* article about Joe Davis noted that:

> he was even seen down on his knees in the parking lot building a fire under the lock of the car door which was frozen for a group of old white women in his Dept. He was playing the role of a punk boy scout so that he could brown-nose upon a few votes.

For DRUM, Davis's kindness in helping fellow workers unlock a car (a decidedly nonpolitical act) marks him as a traitor to his race, bowing subserviently before the white master. The women appear as dominant figures whose presence demotes Davis to the status of a child—a "boy scout"—asking him to serve them.

Despite *DRUM*'s attack on Davis, the article concludes by calling him back to blackness and, by extension, to radicalism. Challenging him to answer DRUM's accusations, the author announces that "The black workers in 9150 would like to know Joe. The same workers who took up that 200 dollars to buy that watch for you for Christmas Joe. They thought quite highly of you THEN Joe. Say something Joe . . . Joe. JOIN DRUM." These final lines include Davis as a member of *DRUM*'s reading audience by speaking directly to him and opening the door for him to join the club. By framing Davis as a black traitor and an Uncle Tom, *DRUM* hoped to elicit emotional responses from readers and to intimidate Davis into changing his ways. Such aggressive performances of heterosexual masculinity were intended to bolster organizational morale. Instead, they probably kept many potential members away from the organization. White Eldon worker and ELRUM ally John Taylor observed that the tone of ELRUM leaflets alienated many older black workers, in addition to white workers. He maintained that, had the League not insulted fellow black workers with labels like "Tom" and "Mollytom," the black ELRUM-supported candidates for union leadership positions might have been able to carry the day (Taylor 4–5).

Art and the Auto Worker

The League's strident rhetoric was part of the organization's "poetics," which, like the Panthers' language and imagery, shared a great deal with the Black Arts Movement. Amiri Baraka produced similarly controversial depictions of women, conservative African Americans, and Jews in his Black Arts poetry, and the League's language, like Baraka's, disavowed conciliatory civil rights discourse. Although the LRBW rightly distinguished between civil rights and Black Power ideologies, it also left readers of League publications in the dark about the political nuances of daily LRBW activism. Potential members who read *DRUM* or *ELRUM*, for instance, may not have known that the LRBW built networks dependent on key women figures and white allies. By combining this rhetoric with poetry in its publications, however, the League mitigated the problem. It published poetry that exhibited the same kinds of aggression, and it aligned itself with the Black Arts Movement. Because poetry invited interpretation, the League hinted to readers that its political metaphors might also require analysis. Art, in other words, built a bridge between the League's aggressive metaphors and its ideological complexity.

Although the League could be critical of artists in the same way that the Black Panthers were, accusing them of merely performing politics, it did value radical art and envisioned the creation of a National Congress of Black Artists and Musicians ("Open Letter to Black Artists" 7). In an attempt to implement such ideas, it ran a bookstore and planned to use Black Star Publishing and Black Star

Productions to release black film and literature. "It is our intention," a 1971 *ICV* article stated, "to explore the Black arts (music, poetry, drama, etc.) and attempt to offer suggestions and concrete proposals to the developing revolutionary Black Arts movement" ("Open Letter to Black Artists" 6). The National Congress of Black Artists and Musicians never got off the ground, but the League built connections to the Black Arts Movement in other ways. Beginning in 1970, member Ernie Mkalimoto Allen served on the editorial board of the *Journal of Black Poetry*, a vehicle for Black Arts writers, and plant newsletters printed poetry and advertised BAM events. A 1969 issue of *DRUM*, for instance, publicized a local production of Jimmy Garrett's play *We Own the Night* and linked artistic and plant cultures by reserving July 19 as "black worker night" (*DRUM* 2.18).

The most famous piece of League art was the Shrine of the Black Madonna. This mural, seen in figure 5, was painted in 1967 by LRBW member Glanton Dowdell for Reverend Albert Cleage's Detroit church (Dillard 287). Cleage was a major figure in Detroit's black radical community, working in the Group on Advanced Leadership with local Marxists and black nationalists and attracting radicals to

Figure 5. Mural by Glanton Dowdell for the Shrine of the Black Madonna Church in Detroit. Credit: Shrine of the Black Madonna Church

church with a brand of theology that hailed Jesus as a black revolutionary (Ahmad, *The League* 2; Haskins 65–66). Cleage's black Jesus took second place, however, in Dowdell's mural. In this painting, the dark-skinned Madonna stands on a rocky surface with a town visible in the distance, holding her child so that his face is largely hidden. Unlike League texts, which tended to represent women negatively or ignore them altogether, Dowdell's piece positions Mary at the center of the scene. While traditional images of the Madonna and child usually guide the viewer's eyes to the child by depicting Mary gazing at him from a sitting position, Dowdell represents the child swaddled and facing sideways. Mary's standing pose and direct gaze make her, not Jesus, the symbol of Black Power.

Dowdell's mural offered a counterpoint to the League's often sexist texts. Although the LRBW failed to present its positive relationships with women and other allies in its publications, this lone instance of visual art illuminated the group's more conciliatory side. It also helped the League build a connection with Cleage's politicized version of the black church. As General Baker remarked years later, the church remained an important core for black community work even if many LRBW members did not accept religion as part of a Marxist ideology (Baker). Dowdell's painting, which remained in Cleage's church long after the League's relationship with its minister had broken down, made the links between disparate black radical organizations metaphorically permanent even when political tempers raged (Georgakas 146; Dillard 299; Haskins 65–66).

The *ICV* and the League's plant publications added to Dowdell's artistic project by printing original poetry on a regular basis. Poems were presumably collected from League members or sympathizers, as they were not typically the work of nationally renowned artists. Nonetheless, these poets imitated the performative, politically engaged structures of more famous Black Arts poets. They also capitalized on the Black Arts interest in accessible poetry written by and for the people. Black Arts writers wanted to produce a "black aesthetic" by rejecting white notions of poetic beauty and producing work both for and by the black community. The "black aesthetic" was intended to express the unique experience of black Americans through their

folk languages, musical styles, and vernacular expressions. The movement's theorists spent much of their time defining and redefining it,
but, as Julian Mayfield observes, it evades firm definition because it
is flexible, changing from person to person and from time to time: "I
cannot—will not—define my Black Aesthetic, nor will I allow it to be
defined for me," Mayfield insists (27). But many theorists, including
Hoyt Fuller and the Us organization's Maulana Ron Karenga, saw the
aesthetic as a set of criteria for judging black literature that differed
from the traditional set of Western aesthetic criteria: "The traditional
Western ideals," said Fuller, "are not only irrelevant but they must be
assiduously opposed" (Fuller 8).

     In devising this new set of criteria, adherents of the black aes-
thetic attacked the notion that formal education and training should
be necessary to understand literature. "We should not demand that
our people go to school to learn to appreciate art, but that an artist
go to school formally or informally to learn new and better techniques
of expressing his appreciation for the people and all they represent,"
Karenga argued (Karenga 34). His stress on the possibility of informal
education, in addition to the Black Arts emphasis on collective literary
production, vernacular, and art "for the people," demonstrated that
the BAM not only welcomed but also encouraged artists who came
through nontraditional educational routes. The key BAM anthology
Black Fire, which Amiri Baraka and Larry Neal edited, defined the
Black Arts Movement as a space that was welcoming to inexperienced
black writers. Although the volume included well-known writers, among
them Stokely Carmichael and Harold Cruse, it also published a host
of newcomers. This strategy was troubling to literary critics, many of
whom deemed *Black Fire* and the Black Arts Movement unprofes-
sional. A 1974 reviewer, for instance, remarked that the collection
"rang[ed] in quality from embarrassingly amateurish to profoundly
powerful" (Sackett 252). For the editors, however, it was a point of
pride. They were challenging traditional valuations of literary quality,
and some of the more traditionally educated authors, like Baraka, even
sought to throw away their links to the white literary establishment.
In reality, of course, avant-garde literary technique with roots in the

Western tradition remained a key component of Black Arts work, even as many Black Arts writers strived to open up the field to less experienced poets; but the desire for a black folk aesthetic made many BAM participants reluctant to acknowledge such links (Smethurst, *Black Arts Movement* 43).

Moreover, if Western literary forms like the sonnet, formal grammatical speech, or inverted syntax seemed counterrevolutionary, then formal training sometimes appeared less desirable than informal experience. Poets with college degrees and mainstream reputations like Gwendolyn Brooks or those who were enmeshed in the majority-white Beat movement like Baraka not only had to change their poetic style to become Black Arts writers—they also had to claim a different social status. As Don Lee (later Haki Madhubuti) suggests in his 1969 poem "Gwendolyn Brooks," the transition into the Black Arts Movement for Brooks meant rejecting the title "Negro poet" that the white literary establishment had offered: "the poets walked & as space filled the vacuum between / them & the / lady / 'negro poet' / u could hear one of the blackpoets say: / 'bro, they been callin that sister by the wrong name'" (37). Although BAM artists didn't reject intellectualism per se, they did reject its manifestation in American English departments and Western literature. As Kalamu Ya Salaam puts it:

> BAM opened literature to the unlettered and in so doing an entirely different set of views and values was introduced into Black literature, so different in fact that the work produced by these non-middle class writers seemed—well actually was—"unliterary." By conventional literary standards, much of the BAM literature was technically ordinary, even mediocre, albeit psychologically liberating.

Because the spirit of "the people" was central to the black aesthetic, black auto workers viewed themselves as ideal poets. They, too, might have attended college or been educated in literary history, but as workers they held an aura of "folk" authenticity. In LRBW publications, then, poems appeared both as imitations of Black Arts work and as contributors to it. The writers sometimes fell into the category that *Black Fire* reviewer Sackett identified as "embarrassingly amateurish," but they took a stab, like writers in *Black Fire*, at expressing black vernacular and black traditions of communication in verse.

By publishing poems that mimicked or attempted to participate in the Black Arts Movement, the LRBW refined its ideology through its literature. While most articles in the League's in-plant publications focused on issues of immediate concern within the plant, poems addressed larger problems of racism and international politics. They often employed the League's metaphors of black radical masculinity, but, transformed into poetry, these metaphors now begged for interpretation. The overlap between anti-intellectual and intellectual work simultaneously reassured readers that they could access poetry and encouraged them to think more deeply about political metaphors.

A poem by Slick Campbell titled "Let Freedom Ring"[10] demonstrates how art, especially when printed in the in-plant publications, introduced complexity where the League's rhetoric seemed overly simple. Appearing in both *DRUM* and *ELRUM* in late 1968, Campbell's poem opens with phrases that match the League's generic metaphors, using basic rhymes and a sing-song tone: "We've spent century after century / us black children / trying to find and give our / love // but all we have found is injustice / in the eyes of the peace loving dove." While platitudes dominate in the opening stanzas, the poem evolves. Simple rhymes become more oblique, sometimes disappearing altogether; the lines increase in length; and the language intensifies until the seventh stanza introduces raw, rapid-fire language that mimics Amiri Baraka's contemporaneous work: "while black martyr's [*sic*] walk down hot southern roads a greasy white finger twitches and the barrel of a shotgun roars." By beginning with a trite opening and progressing into more urgent language and complex content, Campbell joins the Black Arts project and maintains a safe distance from "bourgeois" literary culture.

As the poem continues, it shifts not only in style but also in content. Although it proceeds in its commentary on the Civil Rights Movement's inability to handle white violence, it also introduces a new location and a first-person speaker:

but I am not to fight standing here
in the Mekong Delta with a punji stick
in my groin

eyes bloodshot bulging with terror
as I watch them X slave master my enemy
dragging bloody bodies across
the living color horizon
instilling fear into young black minds
and courage to exploit bloody atrocities into sad youthful
    white souls.

Campbell moves from generalities about the black liberation movement to the speaker's experience in Vietnam. Although he is injured
by the Vietnamese *punji* stick, a sharp stick intended to produce small
but debilitating injuries, he identifies his "enemy" not as the North
Vietnamese but as the "X slave master [. . .] / dragging bloody bodies
across / the living color horizon." The bloody bodies are simultaneously black and Vietnamese, but even this realization doesn't lead the
author to completely demonize the white soldier, whose act of "cutting
out hearts and kissing / sex symbols at night" is conflicted. On the
one hand, he "cuts out hearts" in a ruthless way, while on the other
hand, he uses magazine cutouts to reminisce about more positive
relationships at home. The *X* in place of an *ex* produces a similarly
ambivalent effect. Nation of Islam members adopted the *X* as a last
name to signal the unknown African name behind the "slave name."
In this case, Campbell denies a name to the slave master with the *X*.
At the same time, the *X* could be read as a shared stain of slavery's
history on the names of *both* white and black Americans.

Meanwhile, the speaker suffers physically from a wound inflicted
by the Vietnamese and emotionally from the racism that has brought
him there. The phrase "I am not to fight standing here / in the Mekong
Delta" might be a sarcastic comment to whites who denounce blacks
for fighting back against racism—or it may refer to the soldier's real
inability to fight as a result of his injury. In these stanzas, Vietnam's

violence and US racism intertwine, and the poem moves from the Mekong Delta to the refrain of black martyrs shot on southern roads. As it draws to a close, Campbell lengthens the lines into run-on phrases, repeating "let freedom ring"—the same phrase that Martin Luther King, Jr. had repeated as a hopeful call at the March on Washington—but stripping it of King's hope, presenting it only as the empty promise of American society. "Let freedom ring," the poem closes, "to the rhythm of blond quivering hips while death sees angry loving black lips let freedom ring." These final phrases seem to reference black-white sexual encounters that leave black men susceptible to the lynch mob. In this case, white female "freedom" leads to black male death. "Freedom" has a salacious ring, suggesting that black deaths are as pleasurable and "freeing" for whites as sexual release. This warped notion of "freedom" urges the reader to question the goal of the black "freedom" struggle as well as its tactics.

The poem's final moments address some of the theoretical holes from the League's in-plant newsletters. Campbell inserts the international political landscape into the newsletter with his discussion of Vietnam, suggesting that international politics overlap with and influence local politics of race and class. Moreover, his final mingling of white sexual deviance and "freedom" calls into question the League's own rhetorically violent uses of sexuality in its newsletters. By suggesting that white culture links sexuality metaphorically (and literally) with violence against African Americans, Campbell warns the League that the rhetoric of sexuality can be used as a weapon. He reveals the problems, then, with the League's use of sexuality to demean and silence coworkers.

The League projected a similar message with "Our Thing Is DRUM,"[11] the signature verse of the Dodge Revolutionary Union Movement. The poem relies on a heavy meter and a generic rhyme scheme with melodramatic content: "Deep in the gloom / of the firefilled pit / Where the Dodge rolls down the line, / We challenge the doom / of dying in shit / While strangled by a swine." "Doom," "gloom," and the "firefilled pit" are clichés, though the "firefilled pit" is a literal description of the hottest auto industry jobs, which hints at something more interesting. Out of this hellish atmosphere, DRUM emerges as an outsized hero: "now we stand— / For DRUM's at hand / To lead our Freedom fight, / [. . .] / and damn the plantation / and the whole Dodge nation / For DRUM has dried our tears." Personified as a conquering champion, DRUM rescues the passive, teary-eyed workers. As the poem ends, however, the workers gain more power with the line "U.A.W. is scum / Our thing is DRUM!" This closing moment functions as a rallying cry for group cohesion, and it was often chanted at League rallies. Like a fight song for a sports team, it need not be sophisticated poetry.

But "Our Thing Is DRUM" may be more tied into African-American poetic traditions than its simple rhetoric suggests. It employs the ballad form, with a repeating structure of four beats followed by three. Simple rhymes are standard fare in a ballad, and the literary ballad has a history in African-American music and literature as a tool for eulogizing the victims of oppression or celebrating resistors. The ballad is a narrative poem that is by nature a folk form (something the Black Arts Movement celebrated), and it is common in both black and white cultures—including English, white American, Scottish, or African American. Ballads rarely end happily. They can be sad tales of woe, as the numerous stories of John Henry were: a strong black man tragically defeated by a machine. Or, as Jerry Bryant traces in his *"Born in a Mighty Bad Land,"* in African-American culture they can be badmen like Stagger Lee (also known as Stagolee, Stackerlee, and Stack O'Lee), Railroad Bill, and John Hardy. These were ruthless men who rebelled against society with violence, killing policemen and others who wronged them in addition to turning their violent fury on their own wives and girlfriends. Badmen evoked masculine anger, but they rarely succeeded in their rebellion—nearly all of the ballads end with their capture and punishment.

While badman ballads were most common in the nineteenth century, a later generation of "toasts," which emerged in the 1920s and '30s, also frequently employed the ballad's rhythm and rhyme scheme (Bryant 6). As oral street poems, toasts revised badman stories only slightly, maintaining the violence and demise of the main character but increasing emphasis on his exceptional sexuality. Like ballads, toasts celebrated the badman without offering moral commentary, and neither form typically portrayed his resistance as political. Instead, the badman resisted general social constraints rather than racism, and his victims were often black rather than white.

The ballad form was popular with black novelists and poets throughout the twentieth century. Bryant traces the softening of the badman figure in the Harlem Renaissance through the works of Arna Bontemps, Zora Neale Hurston, Rudolph Fisher, and Claude McKay, while he sees a more politicized, naturalist version of the badman in Richard Wright's *Native Son*. The badman character attracted novelists, and ballad form remained common in black poetry, especially in and around the Black Arts era. Gwendolyn Brooks's 1963 poem "The Last Quatrain of the Ballad of Emmett Till" memorialized the lynched boy and his mother while departing from the ballad form by remaining silent on the story of the lynching, and Dudley Randall's 1969 poem "The Ballad of Birmingham" eulogized the children who died in Birmingham's Sixteenth Street Baptist Church bombing. In 1975, Sterling Brown published a collection of nonstandard ballads that examine the ethics of the badman hero, *The Last Ride of Wild Bill* (Sanders). Altering and playing with the ballad form was common in black literature, including in the Black Arts era, and "Our Thing Is DRUM" participated in this tradition.

The LRBW ballad was lighthearted, like a playful toast, and it melded a narrative of oppression with the celebration of DRUM's resistant potential. While the toast and the badman ballad shock listeners with the hero's violence, the League evokes horror at the auto industry's violence—the workers are "dying in shit" and "strangled by a swine." The language is not especially graphic, but it describes both the auto industry and its workers in the language of the black worker. Although "Our Thing Is DRUM" was a printed text rather than an oral poem, it was anonymous, giving it the aura of the folk tradition, and its final line echoed worker chants of "long live DRUM!" at wildcat rallies. While the badman evoked vicarious pleasure in rebellion, schadenfreude in the badman's punishment, and amusement at the wild situation, "Our Thing Is DRUM" intended its readers to experience empowerment and anger.

It also encouraged them to see the political world through the lens of collective actors rather than individual ones. The badman ballad's melodrama focused on the rebellion of an individual, but the League's badman was a political organization poised for victory rather than defeat. Just as Haki Madhubuti derided the blues for its passivity in his 1969 poem "Don't Cry, Scream," the League rejected the badman ballad's acceptance of white law's inevitable victory over the black antihero. Madhubuti insisted that "we ain't blue, we are black. / we ain't blue, we are black. / (all the blues did was / make me cry) / soultrane gone on a trip / he left man images / he was a life-style of / man-makers & annihilator / of attaché case carriers. // Trane done went. / (got his hat & left me one) // naw brother, i didn't cry, / i just— / Scream-eeeeeeeeeee e-ed" (42). Jazz and its rebellious undertones, Madhubuti suggests, bring joy where the blues reveled in sorrow. This didn't mean that Madhubuti and his fellow Black Arts writers rejected the blues altogether (that repetition of "we ain't blue, we are black" recalls the doubled lines characteristic of the blues form, and Baraka celebrated the blues as a characteristic African-American form). It simply presented jazz as a new generation, an ancestor to the blues tradition with an insurgent edge. The League took the same step with its ballad, tweaking the folkloric ballad's lament to incorporate Black Power visions of revolt.

The League's poetry might not have attracted much notice from more famous Black Arts participants or literary critics, but it served a crucial function within the group. It told auto workers that they were not *simply* laborers. They had interests and aspirations beyond the plant, and they could participate in the Black Arts Movement as either writers or readers. Moreover, it asked readers to see abstract League metaphors through the lens of art. If metaphors need interpretation within a poem, and if a Black Arts poem is a political statement, then perhaps political statements, too, require interpretation.

"Jungle" Tactics: Spontaneity versus Organization

While the traditional ballad celebrated fallen heroes like John Henry or antiheroes like Stagger Lee, and the Black Panthers lionized Newton, Seale, and other imprisoned members, the League retained relative anonymity for its leaders. General Baker and Ken Cockrel did not take center stage in League publications or imagery. But the badman figure did—in poetry and in real life. The League's heroes were real-life badmen—workers who made the term *industrial jungle* come alive. According to this definition, the wildcat was the only acceptable form of strike, and even a wildcat strike was labeled a "pussycat strike" by *ELRUM* when union officials pressured workers to return to work. In ELRUM's estimation, the UAW had domesticated the "wildcat," transforming the virile panther into a submissive, feminized "pussycat." When they began describing even their own wildcats as "pussycats," it became clear that there was a growing disjuncture between the League's behavior and its rhetoric. The LRBW embraced aggressive, emotional language even when its organizational decisions were more staid.

This contradiction became especially clear after the 1970 James Johnson murders. Johnson was an employee at the Eldon Avenue plant who landed in the auto industry after a series of mental problems and physical fights had caused him to be ousted from jobs in the army and a restaurant (H. A. Thompson 16–18). As an auto worker, ELRUM and the UAW thought little of him before 1970: he didn't attend union meetings, participate in radical organizing, or even join coworkers at the bar after work. In May 1970, Johnson took a medical leave after a car accident and was denied coverage for his medical expenses. Soon afterward, he obtained permission to take several days off—only to learn upon his return that he had been fired for going "AWOL." Johnson filed grievances over both issues, and they eventually settled in his favor, but what he saw as insults from the management continued. On 15 July 1970, he expected to be promoted to job-setter after receiving a strong recommendation from a coworker. Instead, a foreman demoted him to the brake oven, an unpleasant task usually reserved for those with low seniority. Lacking the gloves needed to perform the job, he asked to see his union steward and was suspended for insubordination (124). Later that afternoon, he returned with a gun, killing the foreman who had relegated him to the oven, a second foreman, and a job-setter who tried to calm him down (125). After submitting to arrest, Johnson employed Ken Cockrel as his defense attorney, and he was eventually found not guilty by reason of insanity (137).

With its own Cockrel on the case, the League adopted Johnson as a hero, publishing stories about him and even altering newsletter mastheads to include drawings of his face, sometimes with the phrase "Hail James Johnson!" (H. A. Thompson 143). Johnson was not simply a badman figure—though he did share something with that tradition, and celebrations of Johnson resembled toasts. He was, in the League's assessment, a politicized badman who represented growing radical sentiment among the masses, and its interpretation of Johnson's behavior revealed the organization's delicate relationship to the industrial and the "primitive"—or to "civilization" and "barbarism."

Johnson's spontaneous attack exposed the racist "barbarity" beneath capitalist industry. His aggressive response also exemplified a style of combat suitable to the "industrial jungle." In LRBW stories about Johnson, references to the "industrial jungle" and "barbarism" abounded: an article in *Spear* described the "industrial jungle of Detroit" and Johnson's struggle with "industrialist barbarisms" in the auto plant ("Who Is James Johnson"; "Salute to a Black Patriot"). Such articles detailed the "barbarous" conditions that Johnson had endured both in life and at the plant, from witnessing a cousin's lynching to facing the disrespect of plant foremen. He responded, the League insisted, as any black radical would, by refusing to "buck [d]ance and grin" submissively for whites ("Who Is James Johnson"). Instead, he lashed out with violence, shooting those he felt had wronged him. In a poem titled "The Ballad of James Johnson: James Johnson Needed a Thompson," which appeared in many of the League's publications, the anonymous author writes that "nothing tames a man like James, / he does what he has to do." These representations suggest that an "untamed" response is inevitable in an "industrial jungle." Johnson's actions brought to fruition the League's aggressive rhetoric, and League newsletters dubbed him a "Black Patriot" (*ELRUM* 3.5; "Salute to a Black Patriot"; "Who Is James Johnson?"). Like a wildcat or the 1967 Rebellion, Johnson's rebellion was impromptu and unregulated.

This celebration of *dis*organization mimicked the way the League had merged auto workers and the black community to simultaneously privilege workers and suggest that all black Detroiters were workers. Here, the League smudged the boundaries between LRBW members and nonmembers—and between organization and spontaneity. When *DRUM* credited James Johnson's triple murder with "mov[ing] the Black Workers struggle at the point of production to a new and higher level" or identified him as "an armed guerrilla," it suggested that he was an honorary League member with valid political tactics ("Hail James Johnson" 4; *Spear* 26 March 1971: 2). Consequently the League appeared more unpredictable and threatening, whereas Johnson seemed more organized and ideological.

Such fascination with Johnson's spontaneity clashed markedly with the League's own political strategies. In fact, the LRBW aspired to an astounding level of structure and organization. With an executive board, a communication committee, and a central staff, the League guided potential members through a probationary period and asked them to submit letters of recommendation for admission. If admitted, they would participate in one of the League's "departments," such as social welfare, communications, or education, following strict procedures for reporting to leadership and handling money (*The Overall Program of the League*; "Confidential Communication for Internal Use"). While the League planned an orderly political organization, Johnson's disorderly behavior seemed romantic and exciting. Because Johnson was a political outsider, his impulsive mutiny allowed the League to revel in a moment of disorganized, dangerous dissent. Its newsletters thrived on the sense of disorganization and emotional behavior that characterized Johnson. Like an apparently spontaneous wildcat or the gossipy, fiery plant newsletters, the Johnson shootings replaced the UAW's sober negotiations with violent revolt.

This was not the only time that the League deliberately cultivated confusion between planning and impromptu revolt. Organizational lore held that the unplanned May 1968 wildcat sparked DRUM and, in turn, the LRBW. In fact, future LRBW members had long been waiting for such a "spontaneous" event to build their movement. As early as 1965, a group of future League leaders who also belonged to the Revolutionary Action Movement published a journal known as the *Black Vanguard* that declared itself the organ of the "League of Revolutionary Workers." An August 1965 issue included an array of texts that would later appear—in modified form—in *DRUM*, the *South End*, or *ICV*. A "Tom Chart" classified liberal civil rights leaders just as a later "Tom Chart" in the *South End* would publish names of community, union, and plant "Toms"; the *ICV*'s future John Henry image

appeared on the front cover; and General Baker's letter to the draft
board accompanied Robert F. Williams's "Negroes with Guns," both
of which later materialized in *ICV* (*Black Vanguard* 1.5; *South End* 23
January 1969). But the *Black Vanguard* didn't fit the LRBW's historical
narrative. The League was supposed to unite an already existing movement of radical workers, and in 1965, no such organization existed.
It wasn't until May 1968 that General Baker saw the discontent of his
fellow (white) workers and jumped into the fray. The resulting wildcat
was just the kind of impulsive event that the League's founders had
been waiting for. Now the League of Revolutionary Black Workers that
the *Black Vanguard* had envisioned could come to life.

Spontaneous revolt, whether in the form of the 1968 wildcat or
in James Johnson's attacks, elicited the feeling that anticapitalist revolution was really possible, and while the League knew it didn't have
the power to instigate it, members were looking for any sign that it
might be imminent. The LRBW critiqued the Panthers for taking up
arms too soon and too publicly, but Johnson's lack of affiliation with
any organization made his rebellion seem like a "natural" expression
of political radicalism. If radical violence emerged spontaneously, the
League would be ready with its Black Marxist ideology and organizational structure to harness discontent into socialist revolution. In the
prerevolutionary moment, moreover, an unplanned protest confirmed
the League's importance, suggesting that it expressed the real popular
opinion of workers. In reality, although Johnson became a countercultural hero among a segment of plant workers, the League's celebration
of Johnson did not indicate either the coming revolution or the hege-
mony of Black Marxism in the auto plants. Rather, it foreshadowed
the League's imminent demise.

In 1971, the group's executive board split into two factions. The
Cockrel, Watson, and Hamlin group left the LRBW for the Black
Workers' Congress, while the League reoriented itself to a strict
Marxist-Leninist (Maoist) cadre structure. It did not last long, how-
ever. In 1972, it dissolved into the Communist League (Georgakas and
Surkin 164). After fewer than five years, the LRBW was gone. Despite
its rhetorical and tactical flaws, the League used its brief time on the
political scene to successfully insert race into the center of the labor

movement. At a time when white workers, too, were questioning the value of bureaucratic unionism (as the next chapter will examine), the League presented black nationalism and wildcat strikes as alternatives to union-management cooperation.

Moreover, while the Black Panthers produced a widely circulated national newspaper and earned regular mass media coverage, the League largely addressed itself to its local black community. As a result, its metaphors were less concerned with rewriting racialized language and more centered on immediate tactical needs. It might not have had a national impact on public discourse as the Panthers did, but the League quietly reached out from Detroit's auto plants to the enormous, unwieldy Black Power movement. It asked Detroit's auto workers, stuck in the plant for upward of eight hours a day, to see themselves as key players in a national black liberation movement. The LRBW may have become distracted by James Johnson's badman revolt, but its toast/ballad "Our Thing Is DRUM" also allowed workers to view *themselves* as heroes. As members of a black community within and outside the plant, the League insisted, they could use small moments of worker-management combat to set the stage for larger political victories. Perhaps these victories never came, but the League brought poetic, unbridled, performative, frightening, aggressive, and often *fun* rebellion outside of college campuses and into the workplace. The factory, the LRBW insisted, could be a site of oppression or one of resistance—and in order for black workers to resist, they would have to bring their culture as well as their politics to the shop floor.

CHAPTER THREE

Becoming the Worker, Becoming the Slave

The Socialist Project of Industrializing and the Neoslave Narrative

In 1971, when Wendy Thompson submitted an application to the General Motors (GM) Chevy Gear and Axle Plant in Detroit, she replaced her four years of college education with four years of factory experience. As an employer reference, she listed "International Sonics" in New York City and gave the address of her socialist organization, International Socialists. She was cosmopolitan and well educated, having grown up in a liberal family that supported the Civil Rights Movement, attended college, and studied in France during 1968, where she witnessed the student and labor uprisings that seemed to verify the imminence of revolution. But this background didn't serve her well when she decided to join the labor movement as a member of the working class. Prospective employers saw her as management material, while she wanted to be part of the masses. Her trick worked—at least initially. She got a job, entering a factory where the LRBW's DRUM was still active and taking part in two wildcats before her International Sonics ruse was discovered and she was fired for falsifying her application. Undaunted, Thompson returned to auto work, and in 2005, she retired after thirty years in Detroit's factories.

Thompson represents a movement at the tail end of 1960s radicalism that is often overlooked. By the 1970s, radical groups that had thrived on college campuses began succumbing to internal strife and FBI infiltration. Activist youths were also transitioning into adulthood. While some abandoned radicalism for the "real life" of jobs and family and others continued to work as full-time activists, a different group, mostly comprised of those who belonged to socialist organizations, decided to combine the two by entering industrial jobs and organizing workers "from the inside." By participating in rank-and-file union work in the tradition of earlier generations of socialists, they hoped to build a base for revolution from the shop floor by challenging management exploitation and union bureaucracy. This work, known as "industrializing" or "colonizing workplaces," reflected a growing belief among New Left–era activists that working-class organization was more crucial than student activism.

Socialist organizations that encouraged members to "industrialize" created an aesthetic of collective change with the worker as the heroic central figure. By taking factory jobs, members of these organizations inhabited worker identities and established a first-person plural narrative for the story of revolution. This aesthetic appears in the newspapers they produced at the time and in the language that former members employ in retrospective personal interviews. In both cases, the first-person plural aesthetic was fraught. The working class was simultaneously familiar and foreign, self and other. Over time, as members became comfortable in their jobs, some socialists really did *become* working-class people, while their comrades in other professions began to see them as representatives of and windows into an authentic working-class experience.

This process of learning to absorb another identity is ethically and emotionally problematic, on the one hand, and entirely natural, on the other. There is nothing strange about taking a working-class job, and in America we take it for granted that class identity can change with time. It is the desire to move downward in economic or social status that seems suspicious in a capitalist culture of strivers. Socialists, of course, did not value the capitalist drive for wealth, and they believed that incorporating themselves into the working class was a strategic move to build a socialist labor movement and express solidarity with exploited workers. At the same time, they also viewed it as a way of gaining Marxist authenticity by becoming part of the only group that could really effect social change. As Marxists, they believed they were workers in spirit even if not in reality. They felt personal, emotional investment in the phrases "Workers of the world, unite!" or "Arise, ye wretched of the earth." Becoming a worker was like returning to an *originary* identity or fulfilling an ideological destiny.

The industrializing project was a strategic political decision with emotional implications. As we try to understand the complexities of the process, African-American authors Octavia Butler and Ishmael Reed offer insight into this particular brand of merging or adopting identities. Butler's *Kindred* and Reed's *Flight to Canada*, both neoslave narrative novels, demonstrate the ways that twentieth-century African Americans struggle with slave ancestry, which is an essential part of their identity but also is distant from their contemporary lives. These novels engage with the process of grappling with contradictory identities or perverse desires to inhabit the experiences of the oppressed. At the same time, both Butler and Reed see their work as part of the black liberation struggle. In other words, they mix pragmatic, antiracist politics with a recognition of their position as insider/outsiders in slave history.

For socialists, who tend to privilege practical political analyses over what they might dismiss as mere soul-searching, Butler and Reed offer a real theoretical perspective on the personal and affective issues that come from identifying with the oppressed. Their work illuminates both the aesthetic and tactical decisions made by the two Trotskyist groups that are at the center of my study: the International Socialists (IS) and the Socialist Workers Party (SWP).[1] These are by no means the only groups who industrialized, and I don't mean to suggest that their experiences offer a generic picture of all socialist industrializers. Rather, I think they offer a useful glimpse into a process that many socialists have employed. I focus on them because "industrialization" was a central aspect of each of their political programs, because the two organizations exhibit strikingly different rhetorical and tactical approaches to industrializing despite their similar political perspectives, and because the IS can help illustrate the successes that socialists had in establishing long-term democratic union movements in several American unions.

The Neoslave Narrative and the Process of Becoming

Before turning to the details of IS and SWP history and rhetoric, an analysis of Octavia Butler and Ishmael Reed will provide a theoretical groundwork for understanding how political tactics merged with desire in the industrializing project. Both socialists and African-American writers depended on a guiding narrative of liberation. In other words, socialists motivated themselves by believing in a founding story, and African-American writers did the same. Literary theorist Robert Stepto argues that black American literature reflects the "pregeneric myth" of literacy and freedom, and Elizabeth Beaulieu modifies the structure for female slave narratives and neoslave narratives to family-identity-freedom. In some instances, the triumph occurs within the text itself, but more often it hangs over the work as a promised future. Like Marxist mythology, which envisions a future rather than celebrating the present, the African-American liberation narrative remains unfulfilled.

These two utopian narratives don't simply parallel each other. They are also intertwined. As Cedric Robinson and James Smethurst outline, many black artists and theorists have belonged to American socialist organizations, and socialists, in turn, have seen the black freedom struggle as a key component of American politics. Moreover, both liberation stories center on a learning process undertaken by a heroic, sacrificing, and often frustrated figure. For Marxists, the hero is the industrial worker, and for African-American writers the hero is the black American who overcomes his or her condition—a condition that is rooted in the history of slavery.

Thus, the worker and the slave stand for historical group identity and the promise of future success. For socialists and African-American writers in the 1970s, however, these characters had special significance. The Civil Rights and Black Power movements had generated excitement among activists because revolution seemed imminent, whereas the 1970s and '80s marked a disappointing retreat. Both socialists and black writers responded by looking to the past for inspiration. Among writers, this appeared in the form of an imaginative return to slavery, while for socialists, it emerged in the resurrection of traditional socialist forms of organizing. Members of both groups sought to become or imagine the identities of oppressed people, and although the "identity politics" that began in the 1960s have been much maligned for ignoring complex human and political relationships in favor of simplistic definitions of identity, both socialists and novelists proposed a more complicated understanding of identity as a political tool.

Among black writers, this identification with slave history appeared in the neoslave narrative, which began with the 1966 publication of Margaret Walker's *Jubilee*. Walker's novel about the life of slave woman Vyry sparked literary interest in the slave experience, and the trend grew in the 1970s and '80s with Ishmael Reed's *Flight to Canada*, Alex Haley's *Roots*, Octavia Butler's *Kindred*, Toni Morrison's *Beloved*, and Charles Johnson's *Oxherding Tale*, among others. These texts imitate but also revise the original slave narratives, which were written or narrated by former slaves in antebellum America as abolitionist tracts. Original slave narratives were true stories of oppression, and as a rule they were highly mediated by editors, whereas neoslave narratives were fictional accounts of daily slave life imagined by people who lived more than a century later. Twentieth-century authors inserted resistant female heroines, posed ethical dilemmas about slave behavior, acknowledged the impossibility of truly accessing the slave experience, and provided fictional character studies of the slave experience. As Ashraf Rushdy notes, the authors of neoslave narratives responded to white novelists and historians who perpetuated racial stereotypes. William Styron's 1967 novel *The Confessions of Nat Turner* and Stanley Elkins's 1959 historical treatise *Slavery* were especially controversial targets. Styron was accused of presenting Nat Turner and his mother as oversexualized, and Elkins was criticized for arguing that the black Sambo personality was a real phenomenon resulting from the slave system (Rushdy 30). Neoslave narratives, Rushdy remarks, presented slaves as more complex and human than white-authored texts had. Moreover, as Timothy Spaulding remarks, neoslave narratives also broke down views about *how* history could be represented by rejecting realist techniques and embracing new forms, including postmodern fragmentation, fantasy, or science fiction. This expanded view of history, according to Angelyn Mitchell, demonstrates that it is not a transparent, self-evident object but a product of our contemporary ways of remembering. Finally, as Elizabeth Beaulieu and DoVeanna Fulton argue, the neoslave narrative often incorporated a feminist message, placing female slaves at the center of ethically difficult forms of rebellion.

These elements of neoslave narratives, and particularly of *Kindred* and *Flight to Canada*, create a theoretical perspective from which to view the socialist industrializing project. The representation of history as unknowable and contaminated by the present sheds light on the problems inherent in attempting to become or identify with others. But by creating new speakers for black history, neoslave narrative authors also suggested that, although we might not be able to fully *become* others, we might still be able to widen the story of oppression and liberation to include new actors, among them women and newcomers who might seem to be interlopers. Octavia Butler and Ishmael Reed suggest that political identification with others—in their case historical ancestors—is necessary. It maintains the impetus for change and builds feelings of solidarity across time and space. However, they also indicate that the process of identification leaves a gap between the subject and the object of identification. In neoslave narratives, the twentieth-century African American simultaneously inhabits slave history and remains estranged from it. The paradoxes of political identification in slave narratives provide a guide for analyzing the same kinds of problems in the socialist industrializing project.

Slave narratives were important to black novelists because they represented both personal and cultural history. To look forward as black Americans, they had to understand where they had come from as writers and as people. But nineteenth-century slave narratives offered limited perspectives. They portrayed the experiences only of slaves who had succeeded in attaining freedom, and women wrote only a few of them (such as the texts of Bethany Veney, Mary Prince, and Harriet Jacobs). Moreover, white abolitionists refereed the final texts. Twentieth-century novelists, on the other hand, wanted to imagine the lives of slaves that had not been recorded. They wanted to inhabit the lives of female slaves, rebellious slaves, slaves who had died in the act of rebellion, those who had failed to escape, or those who were not models of Christian virtue. In doing so, they built a new record of slave history, but they also constructed bridges of identification between contemporary black Americans and their slave ancestors.

Imaginatively becoming a slave was a kind of traumatic repetition for black writers—an involuntary recurring memory of a traumatic moment. The popularity of the neoslave narrative in the 1970s and '80s, however, suggests that there was also a *desire* among African-American writers to inhabit the slave's role. The slave was the foundational element of African-American history, and black writers felt intimately connected to the slaves they wrote about. Empathizing with slaves felt like an urgent means of understanding twentieth-century racism. At the same time, Butler and Reed lived more than a century after slavery ended, and their access to slave experience was limited. In their novels, they struggled to *become* slaves imaginatively while acknowledging the impossibility of this project.

Butler's *Kindred* relates the story of Dana Franklin, a black woman writer who is mysteriously whisked from 1976 California to 1815 Maryland. Dana's involuntary time travel becomes a pattern, and she soon realizes that it is linked to the survival of her white male ancestor Rufus Weylin, whose relationship with the black free-woman Alice Greenwood produced Hagar Weylin, the matriarch in Dana's family Bible. Whenever Rufus's life is in danger, Dana is pulled back in time to rescue him. She can return to 1976 only when she fears for her life, and although she often spends months in the nineteenth century, almost no time passes in twentieth-century California. Dana eventually facilitates Hagar's birth by acting as a bystander when Rufus sexually abuses Alice, and she attracts Rufus's lust after Alice's suicide. In the final moments of the novel, Dana murders Rufus as he attempts to rape her, and she loses her arm in the grip of the dying man while she travels back to the twentieth century.

Dana experiences the disjuncture between twentieth-century black life and slavery directly, able to literally live in both time periods through the magic of time travel. Throughout the course of the novel, she transforms from a twentieth-century black woman to a slave and back again. Dana is *both* a slave and a free woman, both a woman of the 1970s and a woman of the nineteenth century. Butler wants us to see that this paradox exists not just for the time-traveling Dana but for all black Americans affected by the history of slavery.

Like some of Butler's potential readers, Dana is a middle-class black woman of the 1970s who has benefited from new opportunities for education and advancement. She is a college-educated writer married to a white man, and she supports her writing through minimum-wage temp work. On the one hand, she is subject to economic and social discrimination as a black woman in America, and she sees her low-wage work as an example of both class and race oppression. She thinks of the temp agency as a "slave market" and insists that employers see temps as "nonpeople" (52–53). Here, Butler reminds readers that lack of economic opportunity grows out of the history of slavery. At the same time, she wants us to see that Dana's job is *not* slavery, and Dana herself remarks that the temp agency was *both* a "slave market" *and* "just the opposite of slavery," because workers were not held captive by bosses—in fact, the surplus of labor meant that bosses were particularly careless about maintaining worker loyalty (52–53). This new economic situation continues the tradition of worker exploitation and racism, but it also allows Dana to marry a white man by choice, go to college, and sell her labor "freely" in the marketplace.

This conflict of sameness and difference between the contemporary black experience and slavery builds when Dana travels back in time. As an ancestor of Rufus Weylin and the black woman Alice, Dana is not an outsider to the world that she enters. She is biologically related to both slaves and masters, and her existence depends on the slave master Rufus's survival. But her "sameness" with the slaves is compromised both by her relationship to the slave masters and by her twentieth-century culture. Although she wants to identify with her slave ancestors, she knows that she comes from both white and black lineages, and she finds herself liking Rufus despite his racist statements and violent behavior. Moreover, because she must protect Rufus so that he can rape Alice and produce Dana's family line, Dana is not only *different* from the slaves, she is their enemy. She finds herself in a bind, then, wanting to be an ally to the slaves even as she is aligned with the oppressors.

The slaves she meets in the nineteenth century initially concur with this assessment, and Dana is unprepared for their reaction. Upon entering the plantation's cookhouse, where the slaves prepare meals, Dana assumes that she has come to a safe place: "the cookhouse looked like the friendliest place I'd seen since I arrived" (72). But she quickly discovers otherwise: "The warmth I'd felt when I came into the room," she remarks, "was turning out to be nothing more than the heat of the fire" (74). The slaves are suspicious: they ask why she "talk[s] like white folks," question her practice of wearing pants like a man, and worry that her relationships with Rufus and her white husband make her untrustworthy (74).

In other words, Dana's political allegiance to the slaves cannot overcome her cultural difference from them. "We were actors," she remarks of herself and her husband. "While we waited to go home, we humored the people around us by pretending to be like them. But we were poor actors. We never really got into our role. We never forgot that we were acting" (98). Her fellow slaves feel distant from her, and as she enters their lives repeatedly over several decades, they begin to see her as a kind of magician. She appears and disappears suddenly, and she brings medical knowledge and literacy. Dana embraces the power that they award her, and she takes on the role of teacher: she tries to change Rufus's racist speech; she uses her limited twentieth-century medical knowledge to save lives; and she covertly teaches slave children how to read. When she returns to 1976, she researches slave history to prepare for future trips, and she prefers the slaves who are willing to accept her challenge to rebellion, scorning the Weylins' cook Sarah for playing the subservient "Mammy" role. Dana's education and teaching benefit the slaves, but they also confirm the gap between herself and them. She wants to identify not just with any slaves but with successfully rebellious slaves, and she is disappointed when her escape plans and those of her fellow slaves result in capture. Unable to assimilate as a fellow slave, she seeks the role of slave leader.

But this status as slave leader is not successful either, and after witnessing Alice's severe beating following an escape attempt and later experiencing the same abuse herself, Dana transitions from an actor to a slave. Education has not improved her skills at rebellion, and her belief in slave resistance has not made her capable of withstanding the physical and mental torture that it demands:

> We'd [Alice and Dana] both run and been brought back, she in days, I in only hours. I probably knew more than she did about the general layout of the Eastern Shore. She knew only the area she'd been born and raised in, and she couldn't read a map. I knew about towns and rivers miles away—and it hadn't done me a damned bit of good! [. . .] *See how easily slaves are made?* (177)

Dana can "read a map," analyzing her geographical location and her social or political situation; she has a sense of herself within the larger narrative of American history. Her fears, however, leave her without a metaphorical map for escape, and without a map or script, Dana loses her actor status. The differences between her and the other slaves fall away, but in exchange she loses her power as a leader. And even at this point, the other slaves do not feel that she is one of them. Alice accuses her of taking on the passive role that she once scorned: "That's what you for—to help white folks keep niggers down. [. . .] They be calling you mammy in a few years" (167).

In Butler's text, the twentieth-century newcomers who want to identify with and help slaves rebel are not simply the bearers of wisdom—they bring problems, misinterpretations, and inadequate analyses. Dana's most productive interactions with slaves occur when she accepts that, just as they can learn from her, she can also learn from them. In one of her first visits to the past, when she is especially frightened and confused by the experience, she sees Alice's mother as a source of wisdom about survival as a slave (38–39). Later, Sarah teaches her discretion around the slave masters and warns her that, despite her privileged status, her skin color will not protect her from the risks of slavery (150). The lessons that Sarah teaches, from momentary passivity to domestic skills, are hard to swallow for a woman who came of age during the Black Power era. They require less militant attitudes about resistance. But by changing her behavior to match her historical surroundings, Dana begins to acknowledge the ways that her ancestors are not simple extensions of her. Identifying with them means working on their terms rather than hers.

Ultimately, Dana finds herself forced to identify with her ancestor Alice more completely than she would have liked to. While Dana wants to fight against slavery, she does not want to experience slave traumas. But, as Rufus notes, Alice and Dana are "two halves of the same woman" (229). They look so much alike that they are frequently mistaken for sisters, and Dana elicits the same sexual attention from Rufus that Alice does. Their identification with one another initially causes strife. They fight frequently, and Alice taunts Dana for the same kind of passivity that Dana rejects in other slaves. Like Dana, Alice values overt defiance, and she risks her own freedom by marrying a slave and helping him run away. But both Alice and Dana fail in their rebellion, and they bond "like sisters" only after Alice becomes emotionally dead to her sexual abuse (249).

Dana is a mirror image of Alice, and she nearly suffers through the same sexual trauma, but she is also forced to identify with Rufus by the supernatural forces that help to assure her existence. She travels back in time to protect him, and as a result they develop a bond. She tutors him, mothers him, and acts as a friend even as she feels constantly angered and betrayed by him. She believes the time travel will end once her ancestor Hagar is born, but to her surprise, she finds herself transported once again when Rufus's life is in danger *after* Hagar's birth. Her identification with Rufus, then, is both biological and supernatural. She belongs to her violent white ancestor as much as she does to her oppressed black ancestor.

The deep connections between the trio of Rufus, Dana, and Alice come to a head when Alice commits suicide, and, in her absence, Rufus tries to make Dana his concubine. Acting through her identification with Alice rather than her supernatural bond with Rufus, Dana kills him as he attempts to rape her. She does this against her own inclinations—she is tempted to allow the rape, remarking that he smells good and that she feels sympathy for him. But she makes a political decision to kill him, aligning herself with her slave ancestor rather than her slaveholding one: "I could accept him as my ancestor, my younger brother, my friend," she thinks, "but not as my master, and not as my lover" (260). This statement reflects both her absorption of the slave role—she thinks of herself as a slave in this moment—and also her distance from it. Her twentieth-century body looks no different to him than the slave bodies that he owns, and it offers her no protection. On the other hand, Dana can kill Rufus in her strange role as an outsider-insider because she knows that she will return to the present, where the murder of a slave master will carry no consequences. The nineteenth-century slaves, by contrast, would face certain death for murdering Rufus.

Yet Dana does suffer one consequence from her rebellion: she loses her arm, which Rufus clings to when she transports back to the 1970s. Once again, her identification with slaves is both intense and incomplete. Her body is not entirely separate from slave bodies, and she carries a permanent mark of her encounter. The lost arm, moreover, is only the last in a series of physical scars. Each time she returns to California, she carries new bruises from her encounters with white slave masters in the nineteenth century. Because she must fear for her life to return to the twentieth century, physical injury and threat become fundamental to time travel. Butler's text indicates that the construction of African-American identity in the 1970s requires a physical, scarring confrontation with the ancestral traumas of slavery, including sexual abuse, failed resistance, or resistance left untried for fear of its consequences. Black identity and resistance did not emerge independently from this history, she suggests, and contemporary African Americans must understand it physically as well as intellectually. Even as they do so, however, they must realize that their identity *is* fundamentally different from the slave experience. Butler depicts Dana's return to the past as a form of problematic but highly necessary identification. Dana wants to and does fight with other slaves by joining their ranks, and she remains in limbo between her historical position and theirs.

Whereas Butler sees some promise in identifying with the oppressed, Ishmael Reed's *Flight to Canada* is more negative about the possibilities of accessing other people's experiences, either literally or imaginatively. Although Reed's postmodern text makes his purpose elusive, the one thing that does carry clear significance is the personal story: "A man's story is his gris-gris, you know. Taking his story is like taking his gris-gris. [. . .] When you take a man's story, a story that doesn't belong to you, that story will get you" (8–9). Many slave stories, Reed suggests, were corrupted by those who used them for personal benefit, and Harriet Beecher Stowe's transformation of Josiah Henson into Uncle Tom is his primary example. By attempting to imagine the experience of a slave, even for abolitionist purposes, Stowe exploited Henson and stole his story. Although Stowe's book was intended to be fiction, even ostensibly nonfiction slave narratives aimed to please white readers. In some cases, they included the testimonies of white "witnesses" willing to swear to the truthfulness and authenticity of the black writer's story, and in other cases editors or collaborators took liberties with the details of the story itself.[2] Nineteenth-century slave narratives, Reed reminds us, do not depict the slave experience transparently.

Reed demonstrates this inaccessibility through layered, anachronistic time in *Flight to Canada*. The novel is a satiric, postmodern telling of an escape made by former slaves Quickskill, Stray Leechfield, and 40s from the plantation of their master Arthur Swille. Although the action takes place during the Civil War, the characters use telephones, ride in airplanes, and watch Barbara Walters on TV. Swille is a Virginia planter whose anthropologist son was consumed by a crocodile in Africa and whose suffragette wife wastes away in bed on a hunger strike. The master's aristocratic plantation, Camelot, masks his sexual deviance. Not only does Swille collect whips and watch movies of slaves being beaten, but he has a necrophiliac relationship with his dead sister Vivian. Meanwhile, the apparently submissive slave Uncle Robin covertly rewrites his master's will so that he inherits everything. Swille dies, in homage to Edgar Allan Poe's "The Fall of the House of Usher," during a confrontation with what appears to be the ghost of Vivian (it may in fact be the slave Pompey imitating her). After Robin receives the inheritance, Quickskill returns to Camelot to write the former "house slave's" story.

Raven is the text's narrator and ostensible author. His poem "Flight to Canada" makes him famous upon his escape, giving him literary authority but also leading the slave catchers to his door. And although

Uncle Robin trusts that Raven will be able to protect his slave narrative in a way that white writers cannot, Raven struggles to hang onto even his own identity. In postmodern fashion, he finds it fragmented and multiple. Although he is an escaped slave, he also stands in for the Tlingit trickster figure Raven and for the slave narrative metaphor of escape as flight. Raven himself notes that "there was much avian imagery in the poetry of slaves," and just as he creates this imagery in his poem "Flight to Canada," his name Raven—and the names of Uncle Robin and his girlfriend Princess Tralaralara—indicates that he is not a singular person but a metaphor for the slave writer (89). The slave catchers who come to "repossess" him see him as an object, and readers of slave narratives are little better—for them, he is an abstraction. Even when the slave holds the pen, Reed suggests, he can't quite get a grip on his own name or his own story.

In Raven, Reed creates a cultural figure like the Native American trickster who is powerful but also frequently the butt of jokes—trickster is notoriously foolish and often humiliated in his attempts to dominate others. The trickster figure—not a person but a society's symbolic construction—must be constantly humbled to instruct the community in spiritual and social health. Raven, then, wants to lay claim to a personal identity, but as a trickster figure he becomes a vessel for African-American identification. The slave author's personal authority is subordinated to the needs of the black community. Reed highlights this by putting both the primary subject and the primary author of the novel in question. At first, the novel presents Raven as its protagonist and ostensible author. However, as the reader approaches the end of the book and learns that Robin wants Raven to write his story, it becomes unclear whether *Flight to Canada* is Raven's story or Robin's. The two are intertwined. As Ashraf Rushdy puts it, "Raven is able to embark on an autobiographical act not based solely on the representation of self but necessarily based on the imbrication of self and other" (129). This failure of singular identity, however, is not all bad, as it suggests the importance of collective identity. Raven cannot be himself without also being *all* slaves—or perhaps all African Americans. As the trickster figure, he is the bearer of community wisdom and the focus of group storytelling.

Reed highlights the positive elements of multiple identities more clearly with his other characters. Uncle Robin plays the role of a submissive Uncle Tom figure while actually betraying his master by leaving the estate to himself. His false identity as a submissive slave gives him the power to act. The young slave Pompey is even more successful at inhabiting multiple identities, as he appears to cause Swille's death by doing so. The narrator describes him as "so fast that some people are talking about seeing him in two places at the same time." He is also able to "appear from nowhere" and throw his voice, imitating all of the Swilles (175, 179). Reed seems to suggest that the walking "corpse" who chased Swille to his death in the household fire was actually Pompey. By creating this character, whose multiple identities signal a skill with hoodoo rituals and an ability to overpower his oppressors, Reed indicates that taking on the identity of the *master* reverses the exploitation of inhabiting the identity of the oppressed.

Reed has said that he views his writing as a form of "neo-hoodoo," so perhaps he sees himself in Pompey, taking on the roles of others for the purposes of liberation. As the writer of a neoslave narrative, however, Reed's version of neo-hoodoo doesn't seem to be as liberating as Pompey's was. Like Harriet Beecher Stowe, he is attempting to access the experiences of slaves, and he makes it clear to his readers that this process is full of land mines. The slave experience doesn't present itself transparently, and Reed's contemporary moment in the 1970s intrudes on the past. Anachronistic objects like airplanes, telephones, Coffee-mate, and television mediate our relationship with the slave characters. Twentieth-century readers, Reed suggests, can only understand Lincoln's assassination through the lens of Kennedy's televised assassination, and we can comprehend the abolitionist fight only through commodified metaphors of contemporary products and technologies. The past, in other words, no longer exists except as it is seen through contemporary media. No matter how hard we try, we will not be able to identify successfully with slave predecessors—they are fundamentally elusive. Reed is adamant about this point even as he produces a neoslave narrative that attempts to touch one small portion of the slave experience. He represents the past with anachronisms, clichés, and satire so that readers will see our relationship to others as a kind of vaudeville performance. Through Raven, Reed puts on the mask of his slave ancestor, and stuck in the role of a representative slave rather than an individual, he attempts to travel back in time. The result is both liberating—as it is for Pompey when he puts on the master's mask—and troubling. He can't quite capture the slave experience just as Raven can't quite command power over his own individual story.

Butler and Reed examine the political, emotional, and ethical complexities of identifying with an originary African-American slave identity. Although both see problems in such a process, they also offer positive moments of either merging or adding identities. Their texts help us understand the similar ethical, logistical, and emotional questions that socialists were dealing with. Reed's highly sexualized novel insists that appropriating others' stories or entering others' lives always has an element of desire, and socialists sometimes discounted this. Moreover, during this period, writers like Butler and Reed were looking back in time for sources of black inspiration and narratives of liberation. Stuck in a moment of activist retrenchment, they, like socialist industrializers, turned back to earlier liberation narratives. Although socialists were not *literally* identifying with people in a previous time period, they were constructing ideal working-class identities by looking to past moments of union power. Like Dana, they both succeeded and failed in becoming workers and joining the workers' revolution. They encountered the postmodern fractured identities that Reed highlights and the complication that real-life workers' struggles do not always fit neatly into the larger Marxist narrative—a problem that Dana ran into when she realized that her needs and slave needs were sometimes at odds.

Socialism and the New Left

By the 1960s, the United States was home to an array of socialist organizations. American socialists had organized in the nineteenth century, and the 1917 Russian Revolution inspired many of them to join forces in the new Communist Party USA (CPUSA), affiliated with the Soviet-inspired Communist Third International (Comintern). This sense of unity around the Comintern was short-lived, however.

Lenin's death and Stalin's rise to power sowed strife in global socialist circles. One of the earliest breakaway groups was the Trotskyists, who split with the Comintern in support of Leon Trotsky when he fell out of favor with Stalin's regime. In the United States, James P. Cannon and Max Shachtman were part of a small number of such dissenters who were expelled from the CPUSA in October 1928, and they became the founding fathers of the two major strains of American Trotskyism (Fields 131–33). At first, they remained united, founding the Communist League of America, Left Opposition of the Communist Party. In later years, they moved apart, with Cannon remaining the figurehead for the Socialist Workers Party and Shachtman acting as the inspiration for others. In 1967, some of Shachtman's followers (without Shachtman himself) formed the Independent Socialist Clubs of America, which would change its name in 1969 to the International Socialists. Meanwhile, the SWP remained organizationally intact from 1938 onward, and James P. Cannon continued to act as a leader and theoretical guide until his death in 1974 (Fields).[3]

By the 1960s, Trotskyists were marked by their critical attitude toward Communist regimes in the USSR and China, which differed from the more positive assessments of their cohorts in the Communist Party or the array of Marxist-Leninist (also known as "Maoist") groups. Despite their different ideological perspectives, both Trotskyists and Marxist-Leninists were interested in reviving the strategy of industrializing as the New Left period began to decline.

In doing so, they looked back to the 1920s through the 1950s, when many socialist organizations, including the CPUSA and the Socialist Party (SP), had entered the working class to reform unions. In 1934, the Communist League of America played a central role in the dramatic general strike led by Minneapolis Teamsters Local 544, while the SWP and the Workers Party had substantial success in trade union work of the 1930s and '40s (Dobbs, *Teamster Rebellion*; Dobbs, *Teamster Power*).[4] Although many participants in these struggles were already industrial workers when they became socialists, others left middle-class backgrounds or lucrative careers to take up union work. In 1952, for instance, Ben Stone of the SWP abandoned an entrepreneurial past as a toy manufacturer and a white-collar job as an office assistant to become a union painter (Stone 30–43).

The 1930s was an auspicious time for radical union organizing because many workers were disillusioned by the Depression. The subsequent economic boom of the war years, the anticommunist fears of the McCarthy era, and continuing factional fights among socialists left the radical labor movement depleted at the beginning of the 1960s. Moreover, young activists in this era were attracted to the civil rights struggles of the early 1960s and the anti–Vietnam War movement of the mid- to late 1960s. To many student radicals, the working class stood for racist, reactionary ideas, and socialism represented rigid hierarchy and following the party line rather than bottom-up democracy. Young activists proclaimed themselves a "New Left," and socialist groups suffered.

Nonetheless, socialists participated enthusiastically in New Left activities, sometimes entering and attempting to influence them (as Progressive Labor did in Students for a Democratic Society) and other times offering a visible alternative to the New Left in coalition work (as the SWP did in the antiwar movement). They also attracted young activists by molding their strategies to incorporate civil rights, black nationalist, antiwar, and student interests. The SWP, which had been focused primarily on labor issues since its inception in 1938, sacrificed some of its typical priorities for the interests of young activists. On this front, it formed a youth group known as the Young Socialist Alliance (YSA) in 1960 that was separate from the SWP and did not hold its members to the rules of party discipline. YSA members became key players in the antiwar movement, especially the Student Mobilization Committee, and both the YSA and the SWP adamantly supported civil rights and black nationalism (Fields 153–54).

The IS was a much newer organization with less investment in party discipline from the beginning. Although many members had come from earlier Shachtmanite incarnations such as the Workers Party or the Socialist Party, the International Socialist Clubs of America formed only in 1967, and it took the name International Socialists in 1969. Under its first name, the ISC participated in the antiwar movement, recruiting from the pool of student activists, especially those associated with Students for a Democratic Society; and while ISC members supported black nationalism, they were more critical than their cohorts in the SWP. They lamented, for example, the Black Panther Party's "strong-arm tactics" and the League of Revolutionary Black Workers' tendency to "assume[e] that whites are incapable of struggle" ("Hands Off the Panthers"; Pierce 5).

Their critiques led them back to the labor movement more quickly than the SWP. Both of these organizations were majority white groups, and the growth of black nationalism had left many white civil rights activists at a loss as they tried to participate in an antiracist movement that now favored all-black organizations. Moving into unions not only marked a return to a socialist tradition, but it also led socialists back into an integrated setting. For former ISer Wendy Thompson, who had spent her youth as a white civil rights activist, taking a factory job allowed her to join forces with the growing black and female population in the industrial workforce, supporting black radicalism through the labor movement (W. Thompson).

At the same time that the IS was moving into industry in 1969, a split in Students for a Democratic Society (SDS) brought a modest influx of former student activists into socialist organizations (Fields 152). Between 1969 and 1974, the SWP's membership jumped from 520 to 1,140 (Breitman, Le Blanc, and Wald 74). Marxist-Leninist groups and the SWP's fellow Trotskyist organizations experienced similar growth as loyal radicals turned to the "Old Left" structures they had once dismissed. Many, however, fled radicalism altogether. SDS had been an enormous organization, boasting between 60,000 and 100,000 members nationally in 1968 and 1969, according to Nigel Young's broad estimate (189). The SWP, at 1,140, was the largest of the non-Communist Party socialist sects, however, and the IS could claim only two hundred to three hundred members in the 1970s (Finkel; W. Price).[5]

While the IS moved immediately into factories in 1969, the SWP maintained its focus on campuses, the antiwar movement, and the feminist movement until a much later "turn to industry" that began in 1975 and deepened in 1979. In both cases, however, the focus on industry signaled a comforting return to Marxist principles. According to Marx, the proletariat, composed of wage laborers in industrial society, constitutes the primary revolutionary force when members reject competition among themselves (*The Communist Manifesto* 64).

In Engels's definition of scientific socialism, crises in the capitalist marketplace due to the need for constant expansion into new markets and the increased concentration of wealth in a few hands eventually lead the proletariat to unite and destroy the system (*Socialism: Utopian and Scientific* 60–79). Many interpreted Engels's definition of "scientific socialism" to mean that socialist revolution was inevitable. In the Marxist vision of revolt, workers would seize factories and restructure them around collective needs, first building a dictatorship over their former exploiters and later constructing a socialist society in which government falls away and the industrial system supports all fairly, "from each according to his ability, to each according to his needs" (Marx, "Critique" 531). Not all socialists in the 1970s believed that socialism was inevitable, but all were inspired by Marx and Engels's concept of revolution.

Socialist Time Travel

The IS and the SWP wanted to identify with workers, who they viewed through the lens of the nineteenth-century Marxist liberation narrative. The workers they wanted to become were both real and abstract, past and present, and their ability to transform from activists and "intellectuals" into workers was challenging. On the one hand, it was as easy as taking a factory job. On the other hand, it might mean changing cultural and social identities and hiding true political affiliations.

In 1969, the founding convention of the IS announced its intention to send cadres into factory jobs as rank-and-file agitators for union reform. Although there were only several hundred IS members in the country, they believed that concentrated effort on certain industries could have a national impact. As targets, the IS chose transport (represented by the International Brotherhood of Teamsters), steel (United Steelworkers of America), telephone (Communications Workers of America [CWA]), public employment (American Federation of State, County, and Municipal Employees), and teaching (American Federation of Teachers) (Tabor 15).

The IS attempted to send members into workplaces in small groups, which gave them "comrades" to rely on in local unions. In addition, IS members in each industry organized into "fractions" to guide the national strategy for union reform. The auto fraction, then, coordinated the IS's national goals for reforming the UAW. An even larger "labor fraction" united all industrialized members of the IS for larger political conversations. The fractions, in addition to regular IS branch meetings and union meetings, meant that workers were expected to devote an enormous amount of time to their political activism. They were full-time socialists, selling the IS's newspaper *Workers' Power* outside and inside workplaces (not always their own), talking politics with coworkers, publishing in-plant newsletters, and forming or joining caucuses that pressed for worker militancy and increased union democracy.

The SWP didn't begin its "turn to industry" until 1975, and it only demanded that most members take industrial jobs in 1979. Although the SWP's project resembled the IS's, its rules were more rigid. The IS's industrialization plan included teaching and public employment, where many of its members already worked, but the SWP limited itself to heavy industries like steel, mining, and auto. As Party leader Jack Barnes wrote, "secretaries, teachers, and social workers simply do not have the raw power that industrial workers have" ("A New Stage" 145). Moreover, whereas the IS used only moral pressure to induce its members to "industrialize," encouraging people like college professor Frank Thompson to take industrial jobs—as he did when he began driving a truck with the Teamsters—SWP leadership *ordered* members to move across the country to take particular jobs (F. Thompson). As a 1979 SWP document remarked, "there is no category of comrades with certain kinds of jobs or union situations who should be exempted from our turn to industry" (qtd. in Barnes and Clark 27). SWPers may have been less happy with their organization, but they had a broader program. While Elissa Karg worked with two other ISers in her auto plant, SWP members Paul Le Blanc and Dianne Feeley had approximately fifty comrades in their Metuchen, New Jersey plant.

Because industrialization was a revival of an old strategy, it encouraged members to adopt romantic notions of the past and deny the new economic narrative of "deindustrialization." By 1970, the proportion of white-collar and blue-collar workers in the United States had become approximately equal. The two major categories of industrial workers, craftsmen and operators, dropped from a peak of 34% of the total US workforce in 1950 to 26.8% in 1980 and 22.1% in 1990 (Sobek, "Occupations").[6] Some members were aware of this shift in the economy, while others were not. David Finkel recollects that the IS acknowledged the growth of the service and medical industries before it began industrializing. The group chose basic industry, he comments, because it was the country's most unionized workforce, and these unions still had economic and political clout (Finkel, Interview). Milton Fisk of the IS and Paul Le Blanc of the SWP, on the other hand, insist that members had little knowledge of deindustrialization. Le Blanc remembers speaking with a friend who cautioned him against the SWP's program: "these industrial jobs that they're getting into," she said, "they're going to be evaporating." Looking back, Le Blanc recalls that "I didn't know—is this propaganda from the bosses? How can it be that industry would be leaving?" Despite Le Blanc's surprise, deindustrialization was already in process—and his friend was not the only one to have noticed.

GREETINGS FROM MOTOR CITY

Figure 6. Trotsky, Lenin, Marx, and Rosa Luxemburg as auto workers by Lisa Lyons for the *IS Bulletin*. Courtesy of Lisa Lyons, artist

Because the IS and the SWP spent much of their time analyzing the economic situation, this denial of changing conditions suggested that the groups' utopian vision of the worker was rooted in the past. Both organizations used rhetoric and imagery that reinforced this fact. The SWP, for instance, used the term *worker-Bolshevik* to describe its ideal industrial member, using an image of a Russian revolutionary from the days before Stalinist corruption. The IS likewise depicted workers on its internal Discussion Bulletins as figures from an earlier era who were often dressed in striped overalls and soft caps. In one issue, cartoonist Lisa Lyons brought Marx, Lenin, Trotsky, and Polish-born German revolutionary Rosa Luxemburg into the present, portraying them as Detroit auto workers. The long-dead revolutionaries wave their "greetings from the Motor City" while holding wrenches and a shovel. Not only were the caps reminiscent of 1930s workers, but the tools they carried were timeless, bearing no trace of the mechanized assembly line.

In these cases, the imagined "worker" belonged to an era of simple industrial production. The technological realities that many SWPers and ISers faced as telephone operators, teachers, or truck drivers didn't evoke the requisite sense of Marxist industry that the wrench-wielding, cap-wearing worker did. Moreover, by depicting Marx, Trotsky, Lenin, and Luxembourg as workers or by referring to members as "worker-Bolsheviks," the IS and the SWP not only created a mélange of eras, but they also confused the definitions of workers and revolutionaries. The four socialists had been intellectuals who saw their role as leading workers, not becoming them. In IS imagery, identifying with Marxist predecessors became mixed up with working-class identification. To be like Trotsky, one had to become a worker rather than an intellectual. Or, to look at it another way, being a revolutionary intellectual made one into a worker. In either interpretation, the organizations relied on a romantic vision of the worker that bridged gaps in time and identity.

Because both the IS and the SWP made political decisions after detailed analysis, however, members had substantial self-awareness about these distortions. In publications and internal discussion bulletins, the romanticization of the worker elicited a great deal of debate. Although SWP leader Jack Barnes was adamant that the group's "obsession about getting large fractions of comrades into great concentrations of industrial workers" was not a "gimmick," others were more willing to explore their own shortcomings ("The Turn to Industry" 46). Lyons's cartoon depictions of Trotsky, Lenin, Luxembourg, and Marx may have contributed to the problem of romanticization, but they also forced members to confront it. Her lighthearted illustrations allowed ISers to simultaneously revel in their idealistic visions and laugh at how absurd they were.

Members of both groups expressed anxieties about their stereotypes by using the term *workerist*, which described an obsession with the working class. During the 1970s and '80s, the expression was often used as a weapon against comrades in factional fights, but in retrospective memoirs, former members sometimes employ it to explain their own behavior, as SWPer Tim Wohlforth demonstrates in his autobiography:

> We were very "workerist" in those days, devoting much energy to trying to build a base in the trade unions. For some reason we had a fixation on the docks. It could be that we were all impressed with Marlon Brando's performance in *On the Waterfront*. Every morning comrades would get up in the dark and make it to the piers as dawn was breaking. In San Francisco, this was a safe exercise, even sociable and jovial, as the union had a radical leadership and the dockers were happy to see anybody up at that hour. In Brooklyn it was a bit scary. Not many papers were sold when the proceedings were being watched from a Cadillac stretch limousine by large men in suits. (183)

Wohlforth suggests that the SWP's ideas about dockworkers clouded their understanding of the real political situation. Their image of a dock was based on a cinematic romanticism rather than 1970s experience. As the mafia looked on, subtly threatening retaliation, the socialists saw themselves as heroes in a script, able to break the mafia's hold on unions simply by selling radical newspapers.[7] Like Reed's Raven who wanted to be an individual but found himself trapped in the cliché of "avian imagery," socialists found themselves living through the *narrative* of working-class rebellion rather than what they saw around them. Their multiple identities made them into the foolish trickster figure unable to understand his surroundings. These visions of the Marxist liberation narrative intruded into their working lives, mediating the way they related to others. Although Reed sees the way that the present contaminates our understanding of the present, these socialists discovered that ingrained stories from the past could also contaminate analyses of the present.

Colonizing and Educating the Working Class

With these confused visions of the factory space as part of the Marxist liberation narrative, socialists entered industry much like Dana did: just as she thought she could be a more successfully rebellious slave because of her education, they saw themselves as teachers of working class militancy. SWP leader Jack Barnes insisted that the working class needed the SWP if it hoped to succeed. If socialists did not make the "turn to industry," he declared, "our program, which the world proletariat needs to chart a course to victory, will remain a lifeless document" (Barnes, "The Turn to Industry" 48).

The SWP expressed its pedagogical role metaphorically as well. Members spoke of "colonizing" workplaces with radicals, evoking the Western history of sending "civilized" people to live in "primitive" locations to build and enforce imperial rule. Like colonists migrating to another country, SWPers moved into industrial spaces, interacting with, leading, teaching, and becoming working-class people. Many former SWPers resist this reading of *colonization* through the lens of colonialism, and Paul Le Blanc equated it to a dead metaphor. But in 1970s America, *colonization* was *not* a dead metaphor. In fact, it was a key term in the leftist vocabulary. During the 1960s, the Black Panthers and the Chicano movement had identified black and Chicano communities as victims of "internal colonialism," and anticolonial movements around the world had revived socialist dreams of international revolution. If the term simply survived as a remnant of the CPUSA's

Depression-era language, when American radicals were less conscious of anticolonial movements as allies, then the SWP was not adept at analyzing and updating its rhetoric for the 1970s. The IS, by contrast, had made this leap by jettisoning *colonizing* for the term *industrializing*.

Colonialism is an economic and political system, of course, and not a metaphor, so the SWP use of *colonizing* did not mean that SWP members exploited fellow workers. And traditional colonizers do not aim to erase distinctions between themselves and the natives. In fact, SWP "colonizers" often made themselves even more vulnerable than their "native" counterparts because their radical politics made them management targets. The problem lay not so much in the decision to take factory jobs as in the choice of language to describe their experience. In some cases, this descriptor may have affected the attitudes that socialists brought to the job. *Colonization* evoked not only political and economic connotations but also associations with Christian missionaries. Stella Nowicki, a member of the CP's youth group, the Young Communist League, who worked in the 1930s in Chicago's stockyards, commented that "the colonizers were like red missionaries," and former SWPers Le Blanc and Dianne Feeley invoked the same simile to describe their discomfort with the tactics of some comrades who behaved like "Jehovah's witnesses" (Lynd and Lynd 72; Le Blanc, Interview; Feeley). These references to missionaries hinted that some "colonizers" felt a sense of superiority about their socialist knowledge—they saw their perspective as the ultimate truth, and their coworkers needed to be educated. They were missionaries bringing the word of socialism to the "industrial jungle."

The choice of the term *colonizing* was not only condescending, but it also paradoxically reinforced stereotypes against socialists. In the Cold War era, the US government presented communism as a virus that could brainwash innocents and communists as "infiltrators" or "outside agitators." As self-proclaimed "colonizers," SWP members allowed their own rhetoric to confirm the government's scare tactics by expanding the distance between activists and workers. Imperialism fostered distinctions between *civilization* and the *primitive*, and the notion of colonizing workplaces suggested that activists had come to urge workers out of "primitive" political stasis. It announced, moreover, the same kind of "inauthenticity" that Butler's Dana confronted in her interactions with other slaves. Because colonizers are travelers who immigrate into their new social situation, they do not necessarily adopt the identity of those around them. Like Dana, they might feel like "actors" whose job is to perform and teach rather than participate.

Socialist organizations played with the "colonizing" metaphor by defining their project as simultaneously educational and participatory. On the one hand, they believed the working class needed education about Marxism, current events, union-management relations, union bureaucracy, racism, and sexism. The SWP, like many socialist organizations, subscribed to the Leninist principle that one revolutionary party would act as the vanguard of the revolution, and it thought that the SWP would be that vanguard. On the other hand, the SWP and the IS (which did not consider itself the one vanguard party) entered unions because they believed the *workers* would lead the revolution, and they didn't want to miss the action.

Because the SWP saw itself as the vanguard of the revolution, it used its weekly newspaper the *Militant* to bring Party wisdom to the workers it hoped to recruit. In many articles, the *Militant* focused on basic socialist ideas and international politics, such as Trotsky's influence on the "founding of international left opposition" or "Why Cuba Has Jobs for All" (D. Williams; "Why Cuba"). But the *Militant* also allotted a great deal of space to advertising the SWP as an organization and validating its vanguard status. In 1973 the organization had sued the government over surveillance and blacklisting, and it published FBI records detailing its harassment in the *Militant* (Sheppard 329; Fields 171). It registered the same level of defensiveness with its own members. Then, in 1979 and '80, it publicized deportation charges against SWP members Hector Marroquín and Marian Bustin and denounced the workplace harassment of a member in an auto factory whose coworkers had doused him with gallons of oil and painted his workbench with a hammer and sickle (Cole 8; "Coal Miner Fights Deportation" 12; Jayko 8). Even the *Militant* was a major topic for the *Militant,* as the paper printed the results of subscription drives. In these instances, the SWP's newspaper depicts the Party as the central agent of change—the workplace simply provides the material needed to enact it.

Because the Party's goal was to educate the working class, the *Militant* also presented workers as material evidence of the SWP's success or failure. Articles frequently focused on the opinions of SWP members' coworkers. If the *Militant* could prove in 1980 that workers were opposed to war with Iran or to nuclear power, then the SWP was succeeding in spreading radicalism. Unlike the IS, which tended to present international and domestic politics as supplements to the detailed focus on labor struggles, the SWP saw national politics as a key factor in workplace recruitment. An interview with Marian Bustin, which ostensibly addressed threats to her American residency, actually served as a forum for discussions of Bustin's coworkers in a West Virginia mine. While the first four questions were devoted to Bustin's life (only the first addressed her immigration status), the last four concerned the opinions of her fellow miners on the upcoming contract fight, the women's movement, the draft, and nuclear power ("Coal Miner Fights Deportation" 12–13). Another article similarly interviewed industrialized YSA members about the opinions of their colleagues on Iran.[8] "Every black worker I've talked to says to send back the shah," one member proudly reported, while another commented that a tack welder at his shipyard had "[come] down a level of the ship to get me to come up there to talk to this shipfitter about what I know on Iran" (Singer 5). Industrialized members used their presence in the working class to act as gauges of class consciousness, and they publicized the positive responses they received as proof of emerging worker radicalism.

In this case, the SWP judged class consciousness by the tendency to agree with the Party on international politics. Such obsession with specific forms of worker education elicited mixed feelings among SWP members. Paul Le Blanc insisted that attempting to convert workers to socialism wasn't "elitist or vanguardist," noting that such fears justify the status quo by discouraging people from exploring dissent and analysis. Debby Pope, on the other hand, remembers working on the railroad in Chicago as a political disaster: "The idea that most of my coworkers were ready to hear about socialism or that I could reach out to them about something like the Cuban Revolution or Fidel Castro—it was preposterous! I could barely talk to these guys about how I'd been involved in the antiwar movement." Pope registers frustration both about the SWP's focus on education and about her fundamental ability to *become* a worker in her particular workplace. She felt culturally alienated from her coworkers, and they did not seem to represent the Marxist ideal of the working class.

While Pope saw this as a fundamental problem, Dianne Feeley remained optimistic about industrialization but critical of the SWP's approach to education. She felt that on-the-job activism was a two-way learning process. As a worker at Ford's Metuchen, New Jersey plant between 1979 and 1980, Feeley and her SWP coworkers, including Paul Le Blanc, talked politics with their coworkers regularly. They ran into trouble in 1980, however, when Ford announced the closing of a nearby plant in Mahwah and declared that high-seniority workers from Mahwah would move to Metuchen, displacing newly hired employees there. This posed a quandary. Socialists didn't oppose seniority, but at Metuchen as around the country, young auto workers included many women and people of color, while senior workers were mostly white males.

Faced with this situation, the SWP leadership was at a loss: it had nothing to teach. It could only offer stock answers, instructing cadres to sell the *Militant* and advocate thirty hours work for forty hours pay. Le Blanc and Feeley were furious: "how could we have a position on the Iranian revolution but not have a position on what should be happening in our own plant?" Feeley fumed. As Le Blanc recalls, the issue was urgent because for the first time workers were approaching SWP members for advice. Although Feeley felt that older workers should not be able to displace the younger ones, Le Blanc was not so certain. And the SWP leadership refused to take a position, leaving its members with no plan or political analysis. Feeley suggested turning to coworkers for advice by holding a discussion forum for affected workers. Although the SWP leadership initially rejected the idea, it quickly reversed itself, adopting the plan as though the leadership, not Feeley and Le Blanc, had introduced it. The proposed meeting, however, never happened. When SWPers introduced the idea at a local union meeting, the union's regional director prevented the membership from voting on it, and the workers from Mahwah displaced younger workers with no further debate (Feeley; Le Blanc, Interview).

While Feeley insists that "the SWP didn't really learn much from that experience," she and Le Blanc did. Like Butler's Dana, who found that her twentieth-century knowledge did not give her the skills to escape slavery, they discovered that their intellectual background and Marxist education did not make them experts at working-class politics. Just as Dana learned discretion and domestic skills to cope with the slave situation, Feeley and Le Blanc had to compromise their revolutionary priorities to deal with the quotidian problems of particular workers in specific plants. They were forced to focus on minimizing the damage of layoffs instead of striking for a reduced work week, and in the process they developed more complicated understandings of working-class people and their political challenges. The shift from imagining the working class to becoming the working class led many participants—if not the organizations themselves—to modify their mythologized understandings of revolutionary strategy and worker education. At the end of the experience, like Dana, they had successfully become the other with whom they identified, but they simultaneously remained distinct, shielded from the blows of layoffs by college educations and energized rather than frightened by conflicts with management.

Becoming the Working Class: The IS and *Workers' Power*

The IS faced a similar struggle to identify with the working class while also promoting socialism. Unlike the SWP, it did not consider itself a vanguard organization, and members tended to be somewhat more reserved in their socialist sloganeering, hoping to attract converts who were fed up with the more abrasive tactics of other socialist organizations. As a result, they used their biweekly newspaper, *Workers' Power*, to address workers in a way that they hoped would be accessible and nonthreatening. They did so by developing what they referred to as "class struggle unionism" language, which rejected the vocabulary of Marxist and American socialist traditions (Finkel). Phrases like "upsurge," "nature of the period," "revisionism," "opportunism," and "class collaborationism" became canonical within the radical tradition, and they signified a history of obscure factional disputes to readers who were in the know. Both the IS and the SWP avoided such expressions in their publications even as they used them freely in internal documents, but the IS specifically worked to create a public rhetoric that would be understandable to workers. *Workers' Power* staff writer David Finkel remembers that class struggle unionism was an attempt to discard internal discussions about such political issues as the "deterioration of the Russian revolution" in favor of everyday union politics (Finkel). As a result, *Workers' Power* focused on particular union struggles, downplaying the international coverage that was a staple of many socialist newspapers, including the *Militant* (Stacy). Instead, local union struggles, analyses of domestic political events, and cultural materials such as movie and book reviews comprised the primary content.

The newspaper's title, which first appeared in September 1970, reflected the intent of class struggle unionism language. It had previously appeared under the name *Independent Socialist: A Revolutionary Socialist Monthly*, which associated the publication more strongly with its organization. In May 1970, it even published a photo of Lenin on the cover for the centennial anniversary of his birth (*Independent Socialist*). Although the *IS* shared much with its later incarnation, the name shift to *Workers' Power* reflected the group's wholesale commitment, both in rhetoric and in action, to industrialization. It expressed a basic socialist concept without making wild declarations about revolution or employing overly intellectual terminology ("Fight for Workers' Power"). Moreover, both the title and the content deemphasized the IS as an organization. Each issue included contact information for IS branches and a "Workers' Power: We Stand for Socialism" section, but the majority of the paper focused on rank-and-file union issues.

The sources for such articles were often IS members who had industrialized. As a result, particular local unions became regular news items. In *Workers' Power*, readers could follow the struggles of CWA Local 1101, which represented New York telephone employees, through the reports of IS members Ken Morgan, Rose Veviaka, Brian Mackenzie, Bill Hastings, and Clinton McCain. Between 1970 and 1972, *Workers' Power* detailed Local 1101's fight to unite workers under CWA's banner by voting out an established company union known as the Telephone Traffic Union (TTU), leading two strikes, holding officer elections, and negotiating a contract ("Lessons of Our First Two and a Half Years in New York Telephone"). IS members in 1101 supported CWA's campaign against TTU while encouraging rank-and-file dissent against CWA bureaucracy. In the lead-up to the longer of the two strikes, ISers codified these demands by helping to found a group called United Action that challenged the union on its tactics in contract negotiations and the related strike.

The ongoing articles on CWA 1101 were directed in large part to non-IS workers in that local, exhorting them to take action or explaining complex political situations in their own workplaces. In the case of Local 1101, IS member and *Workers' Power* writer Rose Veviaka supplemented articles about the strike from her male comrades by explaining her situation among the women workers of the Bell System's telephone operators. These workers, who belonged to the company union TTU, were largely women of color, and they remained on the job while the mostly male craftsmen of CWA 1101 went on strike. Although Veviaka writes of her support for the strike, she also highlights the way women in the traffic and commercial departments had been ignored: "CWA never asked us to stay out and were not willing to formally support any of us who did honor the picket lines. [. . .] [T]hey did not even once attempt to explain the strike to us or to show how it was relevant to our struggles" (Veviaka, "Traffic Trouble" 16). Veviaka's articles often appeared on the same page as pieces written by male telephone workers, and the juxtaposition urged CWA members to confront gender and race issues while pressing TTU members to support the strike. When large numbers of operators finally did join craftsmen on the picket line six months later, Veviaka wrote a celebratory article encouraging operators to vote in CWA as a replacement for TTU (Veviaka, "New York Operators" 3).

For readers who were not IS members, the newspaper documented their own union struggles or made the union activities of other workers around the country into ongoing dramas, complete with personalities of union officials and their challengers. Worker-employer disputes are extraordinarily complex, involving workplace norms, disparate employee populations, specific contract provisions, and internal union disputes. Consequently, journalistic accounts of labor issues typically rely on broad analyses and reports from management and union spokespeople. The *New York Times*, for instance, which covered the long, seven-month telephone strike regularly, did not seek rank-and-file opinions or detail internal union conflicts. *Workers' Power* offered both rank-and-file perspectives on the strike and ongoing analyses of the conflict that created personalities for readers to hang onto. A March 1972 article, for instance, sported the title "N.Y. Phone Strike: Beirne Does It Again," suggesting that readers had some familiarity with CWA President Beirne as a "character" in this saga.

For those outside the IS and its targeted workplaces, such details may have been daunting. Within the IS, however, the ongoing articles about locals where ISers had industrialized generated a sense of collective accomplishment and identification. CWA 1101 was an *IS* local, while rank-and-file caucuses or organizations such as Teamsters for a Democratic Contract (later Teamsters for a Democratic Union), the United National Caucus of the UAW, or the New Caucus in the AFT were seen by IS members as *their* organizations. The elevation of local union politics to a national level allowed IS members to feel ownership over one another's work and to feel that it was influencing the entire working class. If industrializing as an individual was a way of taking on working-class identity, *Workers' Power* stories allowed IS members to feel that the IS was slowly becoming *the working class*. Together, their local union democracy movements took shape and meaning.

This process was reinforced by the fact that nearly all such articles reverted back to the first-person plural—even when they had begun in the third person. Although authors were usually identified as union members at the bottom of each article, many remained detached from the topic at first. Brian Mackenzie, for instance, began an article about the CWA 1101 strike in a journalistic style: "After two weeks, the strike of Local 1101, Communications Workers of America, against N.Y. Telephone was called off on Jan. 25 without even a partial victory." Although the term *victory* suggests his allegiance, not until paragraph five does he enter the first person: "The courts and the police were mustered by AT&T to destroy our union." Here, Mackenzie both addresses his coworkers and initiates other readers into the status of the worker.

The same collective initiation into worker identity occurred in John Weber's recurring column "Life on the Line," which described the physical and emotional impacts of his work in an auto plant. He opened the doors of the auto factory to readers, describing the daily life of a worker, publishing photos, and guiding new workers through the probationary process. Weber often addressed readers in the second person, telling them that "you don't need training or experience to get a job in an auto assembly plant" and "during the first 90 days of work, if you want to keep your job, you have to take any shit that's handed you." His use of the second person positioned the reader as a potential auto worker, and although he offered a daunting perspective on auto work, he also beckoned to the reader to share the experience by joining the industrialization project.

In Weber's column and in the serialized descriptions of local union movements, *Workers' Power* constructed itself as a text for its own membership. It built a sense of collective working-class identity and, by presenting all of the IS's union work in one publication, it imagined the connections between local struggles that would foster revolution. Although the collective first person and the second person ostensibly spoke to fellow workers and the public, they actually addressed IS members who took comfort in the sense of revolutionary progress.

Class struggle unionism language, then, largely generated the IS's own group identity, shifting it from intellectual to working class. As David Finkel reflects, class struggle unionism sometimes became "a highly rhetorical kind of pseudo-militant kind of discourse" (Interview). Although the title *Workers' Power*, for instance, aimed to express basic socialist ideas in a way that would appeal to workers, some members remarked that the name evoked too much militancy: "Hand the paper to a high school youth or anyone outside industry," member Scott Jacoby wrote, "and the obstacle is apparent. Hand it to a worker who is a solid militant and he or she will see us as trying to come on too big." Jacoby may have been right. SWPer Barry Sheppard recalls being told by a coworker at a nonindustrial job that he should avoid anything with "the word 'worker' in its title," because it would represent "communists in disguise" (16). Moreover, although the IS hoped to distinguish itself from other socialist organizations they saw as "crazy," its practice of selling papers outside the factory gates—like nearly all socialist groups—did not immediately mark it as "less crazy." Former auto worker and ISer Elissa Karg jokes that, on her way to sell papers outside the Jefferson auto plant on a cold winter morning in Detroit, "I hear this news story come on and it turns out to be one of my college roommates reporting on the death of Aristotle Onassis, and I thought: Oh my God, did I choose the wrong thing to do! You'd hardly ever sell a paper. You'd be out there for an hour and you might sell two papers!" (Karg).

While *Workers' Power* might not have attracted many workers as readers, the IS's smaller publications were more successful. Many industrial fractions established their own in-plant newsletters that addressed immediate union issues. Karg recalls her group's *Mack Safety Watchdog*, a newsletter produced for the Mack Stamping Plant, with much more positive feelings, recollecting that "everyone read it. [. . .] It wasn't like a propaganda thing—it was really about plant issues, and it was an issue people were very concerned about." Although the socialist dream of uniting all working-class people played out in *Workers' Power*, the specifics of plant publications had more impact on coworkers. They expressed collective identity between workers within one plant and demonstrated to industrialized ISers that they did not need to reinforce their working-class identities: they *were* workers, and they belonged.

Put Your Body on the (Assembly) Line

IS publications were extremely earnest in their attempt to build a collective working-class identity, and they didn't adequately acknowledge or cope with the way their desires for revolution and solidarity sometimes clouded their vision. Ishmael Reed and Octavia Butler gesture to the importance of confronting these emotional layers of political identification in an attempt to assuage its potentially exploitative elements. Both Reed and Butler see physical experience as a deciding factor in erring on the side of solidarity rather than appropriation, and the IS and the SWP certainly attempted to make this kind of commitment.

Reed demonstrates this position when he insists that Harriet Beecher Stowe's status as a free white woman makes her a poor candidate to write a slave's story, whereas Raven appears trustworthy with Robin's story because they experienced slavery together. Dana, likewise, gains an understanding of her slave ancestry only by traveling back in time to live through it, and she earns the trust of her fellow slaves slowly, by learning their skills and receiving their punishments. The neoslave narrative as a genre imitated Dana's experience of time travel, as twentieth-century authors imagined themselves undergoing the daily struggles and tackling the ethical problems of their slave ancestors. By examining people and situations that had been left out of original slave narratives, they approximated the experience of time travel to create a more nuanced sense of African-American history and collective identity. Instead of employing broad metaphors of a utopian Africa, as some of their predecessors in the Black Arts Movement and the Black Power movement had, they wanted to see black history as specifically as they could—or in Reed's case, to highlight how impossible it was to access such specificity.

Socialists, unlike black writers of the 1970s, had the physical opportunity to experience the lifestyle of those they identified with. Industrializing was *not* simply a theoretical political argument—it required members to change their daily lives. Many IS and SWP members had attended college, and although some came from working-class backgrounds, most had been encouraged by their families to pursue white-collar work. As a result, while industrialization was met with enthusiasm by IS members, its implementation was a source of strife. Discussion documents often exerted pressure on those who had not industrialized, acknowledging members' uneasiness but demanding that they overcome it. Member J.W.[9] insisted in 1971 that:

> Industrial work is no more unpalatable to the average ISer than it is to 99% of those engaged in doing it. Almost no one works on an assembly line by choice. If anything, a radical political-intellectual backround [*sic*] makes industrial work easier, not harder. ISers will find the work less alienating because they will have a reason for being on the

job above and beyond selling their alienated labor power in order to provide the necessities of life for themselves and their families.

Of course, the IS *was* asking members to volunteer for assembly line jobs, so J.W.'s argument assumed that IS members should be willing to sacrifice. ISers were told to "put your body on the line"—with any risks that might entail. The fact that so many comrades hesitated to make the leap, however, suggested that there remained a disjuncture between the narrative of working-class heroism and the reality of *being* a worker.

Anxiety sprung largely from the relationship between ideology and the body. Those who decided to enter industry were worried about how their bodies would be marked, strained, or injured by the transition. Dianne Feeley, who had just recovered from a severe illness, was afraid her body would be unable to handle the work, and Elissa Karg was terrified by a rumor that a man's head had been cut off in a press during her first week at a Detroit auto plant. The threats to the body deterred some from joining the industrial workforce altogether. David Finkel, for instance, who worked as an IS staff member, remarked that he chose not to enter industry because "it would not have been safe for me or for anyone around me" (Interview). No matter how politically sound the industrialization project was, its physical challenge was a deterrent for many.

For some members, on the other hand, becoming a worker meant proving one's mettle. While people who entered factory jobs from working-class backgrounds might not have seen the work as exhilarating, many socialists saw the physical challenge as an energizing confirmation of their political commitment. Men entering the working class from white-collar jobs wanted to confirm their physical abilities, as did women who were struggling to prove the feminist claim that women could do "men's" work. ISer turned truck driver Dan La Botz felt that "by learning to drive a truck I was proving that I too was a real man," and Dianne Feeley and Paul Le Blanc were proud when they became physically capable workers (La Botz 145; Feeley; Le Blanc, Interview). These feelings of accomplishment bolstered many members in their union work. Some left after a short time to pursue careers they felt more suited to, but others, including auto workers Wendy Thompson and Dianne Feeley, settled into their new roles, where both remained until retirement.

Those who came to terms with the physical challenge of industrial work began to see their bodies as part of a collective worker body. In fact, as Feeley remarks, fear became a tool for her to challenge safety standards in the plant. Macho disregard for personal safety among male workers had allowed corporate owners to ignore the egregious conditions in their auto plants, but newly hired women saw no reason to put up with these dangerous norms. Thus, while some male coworkers saw Feeley, an auto worker in a largely male plant, as a threat to their jobs and their masculinity, others viewed the entrance of women as an opportunity to question some of the plant's oppressive conditions. While speaking with coworkers, Feeley challenged the notion that coming to work should be risky. She introduced feminist notions by demonstrating that women could perform arduous physical labor and men could protect their health and safety without emasculating themselves.

Safety issues weren't the only impetus for socialists to view their bodies in tandem with those of their coworkers. In auto plants, the structure of the assembly line and the difficulty of the work fostered a sense of community. Le Blanc explains that, in his plant, "You and a worker coming the other way would say hi, and you didn't know that person, but it just felt good. It felt good to affirm your humanity" (Le Blanc, Interview). Dianne Feeley expands on this metaphor when she describes passing her probationary period at the same plant:

> That was a wonderful experience that I think anybody in industry feels, but especially a woman. That you can handle the work—that you find a way of being able to handle the work, of being able to handle the challenges of using your body, because you really are hands, and the line went 58 [cars] an hour, so you had to basically do your job in a minute and ten seconds.

Feeley's expression of satisfaction circles around the comment that "you really are hands." While it might disembody the individual, making her simply one node in the larger structure, Feeley's repetition of "handle the work" and "do my job" suggests a sense of agency even within the regimented and dehumanizing assembly line. Workers became limbs of the assembly line's body, literalizing the term *industrializing*, but they had control over those hands. Their labor initiated them into a collective working "body."

Disembodied hands have metaphorical currency for socialists. The raised fist as a symbol of radicalism had preceded the SWP and the IS, and it had been modified over the years by a plethora of organizations.

Solidarity, June 30, 1917.   The Hand That Will Rule the World—One Big Union.

Figure 7. Ralph Chaplin's *The Hand That Will Rule the World—One Big Union*, 1917.

Black Power displayed the black fist, the women's movement portrayed a fist rising out of the female symbol, and the IS produced a fist holding a wrench. The fist was a synecdoche for the strength of the group, and a 1917 drawing created by International Workers of the World (IWW) artist Ralph Chaplin illustrates this quite literally. In this image, which originally appeared in the IWW publication *Solidarity* and is reproduced in figure 7, a group of workers stands in a hole that they have either dug or been forced into, each one holding a shovel, pitchfork, or pick in one hand and raising the other to the sky. Together, the raised hands form one enormous fist that rises above the level of the land, dwarfing the buildings and smokestacks in the distance. The many hands appear in the wrist like veins in a united body, and the caption identifies the fist as "the hand that will rule the world—one big union." In Chaplin's image, the collective fist represents physical labor and political power. Even when confronted by the industrial infrastructure around it, the human element triumphs. In Feeley's case, her hand had this power because it ran the machine. If even one hand was missing, the assembly line failed to run—so one person taking a stand could make a serious political statement. As workers industrialized, then, they ripped apart the IS metaphor of industrialization: it was not they who became "industrial"—rather, the industrial system became human, run by a collection of human hands.

By confronting the physical aspects of working-class life, socialists forced themselves away from mythologized views of the working classes while also making new room for women to play heroic physical roles. Octavia Butler, Toni Morrison, and Sherley Anne Williams, as authors of neoslave narratives, rewrote stories of slave rebellion and escape to put women at the center, and socialists modified their liberation narrative in a similar way by putting women on the assembly line and finding that, as Feeley remarked, the strangeness of their presence actually facilitated discussions of change among her coworkers. In both cases, identifying with a mythic liberation narrative morphed into a process *changing* that narrative, allowing it to grow and accommodate the needs of a new generation of radicals.

Both socialists and neoslave narrative authors like Butler and Reed found that the collective identity needed for solidarity is impossible to achieve fully. It is, however, possible to *approximate*, but only through minute-by-minute physical or intensely imaginative identification. The liberation story, in other words, needs more complexity. It needs the experiences of women, the lunchtime discussions, the moments of betrayal, and not simply the major plot points that lead to victory. Hands and bodies were important metaphors for socialists because they represented this basic, quotidian kind of identification. Becoming a revolutionary worker was a physical, emotional, cultural, and social process. It meant taking and keeping a job that might be physically uncomfortable, working with new people from different backgrounds who have different interests, and attempting to influence those people to adopt your political perspective or at least to take action on local union issues. This was different from being a "salt"—the term unions use to describe people who enter workplaces to incite a union drive. Unlike "salting," industrializing was intended to be permanent (though in practice it often wasn't), and it frequently meant making an enemy of the union as well as the boss. Those who stayed in union jobs their entire working lives did become workers, just as Dana became a slave by experiencing beatings, rape, and lack of self-possession. But successfully transforming socialists into workers in the real world did not mean merging socialist and worker identities but adding to the political and cultural diversity of the working-class population. Like writers of neoslave narratives, however, the process of identifying—whether with workers or with slaves—had real political meaning. Identification was a way of living out the economic and social wrongs of slavery and capitalism in an attempt to change them.

As socialists realized in their union work, the simple Marxist narrative of liberation could not explain or manage the realities of daily oppression. Nonetheless, members of the IS and the SWP continued to see value in the old narrative structures even as they realized that it wasn't a one-size-fits-all narrative. Taking union jobs forced them to tear holes in the Marxist narrative even as they hung onto it as their ultimate goal. For them, becoming a worker meant valuing the political importance of identity without seeing it as rigid and unchangeable. And while they, like Butler's Dana, originally entered the working class as "actors," they didn't remain in that position for long. Wendy Thompson might have initially had to falsify her résumé when she applied for a job at a Detroit auto plant, portraying herself as a working-class woman rather than the college graduate that she was. But decades later, as a retired auto worker with thirty years in the plant, it would be impossible to call Thompson an actor. She was a genuine auto worker, union member, and working-class person. Her experience demonstrates the paradoxical role of identity in politics: it is both real and unreal. Working-class identity was real for IS and SWP members because it gave them clout in unions and among fellow workers. As "real" workers, they could speak and lead in ways that "outsiders" couldn't. At the same time, their identity as workers developed and changed over time. Posers, with enough patience, can become the real thing.

In this process of identity transformation through industrialization, socialists of the 1970s and '80s didn't relight the spark of mass radicalism. They did construct small but influential and long-lasting movements for union democracy in some of the nation's most powerful unions. Most notably, Teamsters for a Democratic Union, a union reform movement within the Teamsters that some IS members helped to form, has offered an alternative to the bureaucratic power structure of the Teamsters union since 1976, and the United Action Caucus has performed a similar role in the American Federation of Teachers since 1971. These organizations continue to survive, offering a rank-and-file perspective on union organizing among twenty-first-century workers and sometimes supporting leftist political issues within the union. Other efforts were more short-lived, though still significant. The UAW's United National Caucus led an antiracist campaign, supported the right to strike, and opposed wasteful UAW spending measures between 1967 and 1972; and the SWP was inspired by and also supported the 1977 reform movement in the United Steelworkers of America led by Ed Sadlowski, which lost, but not without gaining substantial support from the membership ("United National Caucus Meets in Detroit"; H. A. Thompson 108; Wohlforth 270).[10]

Even failures leave an impression on the union landscape, and these movements sent a message to unions and bosses alike that there was a more democratic model of worker solidarity than the bureaucratic international union. The beauty of these union movements, moreover, is that they were not created by socialist "infiltrators," and they don't belong to either the IS or the SWP. They were created by both socialist workers and nonsocialist workers, including those who developed radical politics in the workplace and those who entered the workplace because of their radical politics. Instead of "uplifting" the downtrodden, socialists became workers who needed to organize if they hoped to save their own bodies from dangerous machines and unhealthy chemicals or to prevent their own jobs from leaving town. They felt the consequences of loss much more often than they felt the exhilaration of victory. They participated in wildcat strikes, attended union meetings, wrote newsletters, and experienced the economic devastation of layoffs. Although their decision to enter unions might have been based on romantic notions of industrial workers, those who did stay in working-class jobs became workers in the same sense that Butler's Dana became a slave. They were unusual workers with different life histories than their colleagues, perhaps, but workers nonetheless.

CHAPTER FOUR

Urban Hunter-Gatherers

Anarchism and the New Primitive

Revolutionary leftist organizations have declined in the United States since the 1970s. Socialists who saw the labor movement as the site of revolutionary change have witnessed a seismic economic shift. While approximately 24% of wage and salary workers were union members in 1973, that figure declined to 12.1% by 2007 (Hirsch and Macpherson 352; United States Department of Labor). In part because of this, the metaphors of the industrial and the primitive no longer seem as current as they did in the 1960s and '70s. With the end of the Cold War and the rise of globalized capital, networks, both virtual and real, have replaced the poles of the previous era. Few would use the term *primitive* unthinkingly to describe people of color, and the American working class, gutted by neoliberalism, two-tier wage structures, and the bankruptcies of American auto manufacturers, has become an increasingly unlikely sector for mass revolt.

Nonetheless, radical sentiment has not disappeared. Today, an eclectic movement of anarchists is the dominant strain in America's radical left, and though it might seem out of touch with the twenty-first century, many of these young anarchists recuperate primitive and industrial metaphors. Many also view themselves as admirers and ancestors of the Black Power tradition, and several former Black Panthers, including Lorenzo Komboa Ervin, JoNina Abron, Ashanti

Alston, and Kuwasi Balagoon, have become prominent anarchist voices, critiquing the mostly white movement for its inadequacies in race politics while insisting that anarchist anti-authoritarianism offers a necessary corrective to the Panthers' corrupt centralized leadership. As these crossover voices demonstrate, anarchism is by no means a dramatic departure from the socialist-inspired organizations of previous chapters. Anarchists are today's most vocal left-wing radicals, and their interest in economic, racial, and also environmental justice makes them clear companions of the socialist tradition. Their use of industrial and primitive imagery, moreover, demonstrates an aesthetic continuity with previous radical generations. The Panthers, LRBW, IS, and SWP interacted with and benefited from the commentary of African-American writers, and the same is true for today's anarchists. Young anarchists are well read and eager to incorporate literature and culture into their political repertoires. Unlike the Black Panthers, they do not see culture as a threat to authentic action.

Today's anarchists employ the stock metaphors of the primitive and the industrial in a variety of new ways. While socialists in the 1970s identified with and hoped to become industrial workers, many anarchists today celebrate the train-hopping hobo of the early twentieth century instead. The hobo had been a hero to the most famous American anarcho-syndicalist organization, the Industrial Workers of the World, which attempted to form "one big union" in the early twentieth century while also lauding the hobo as a revolutionary figure. The industrial worker may seem problematic to this new radical generation because factories contribute to environmental contamination, whereas the hobo evokes working-class solidarity in the form of a man who moves in and out of industrial and rural spaces without destroying the environment around him. The industrial world, this generation of radicals claims, is not a neutral territory for economic battles between capitalists and the proletariat. It is a landscape that represents human abuse of the environment.

The hobo figure does not belong to industrial capitalism or to a high-tech global community. He is a nomad with basic survival skills to cope in any environment. Many anarchists take the hobo figure even further, imagining an ideal nomad as a new hunter-gatherer, trained in the "primitive" skills of tracking, plant identification, basic shelter construction, and nontechnological medicine. Their vision of resistance combines "primitive" skills with the remnants of an urban environment.

One segment of the anarchist community, known as anarcho-primitivism or green anarchism, depicts this future of neoprimitive survivalism in apocalyptic terms. These anarchists, I believe, could enhance their theoretical perspectives and propaganda strategies by paying attention to the relatively recent work in speculative fiction by African-American writers Octavia Butler and Nalo Hopkinson. These authors address the pressing late twentieth and early twenty-first-century fears of environmental and political collapse that motivate many anarchists. Their books set up the perfect scenarios for capitalist collapse and an ensuing anarchist utopia. But unlike anarchist bloggers and writers of do-it-yourself "zines" who revel in the idea of industrial society's demise, Hopkinson and Butler force readers to confront hard questions about ethics and race relations in moments of revolutionary crisis. They offer friendly lessons that are surprisingly compatible with anarchist beliefs even as they question some of the assumptions that anarcho-primitivists rely on.

Anarchists Come Into Style

Broadly defined, anarchism is a rejection of the state, and anarchists believe that humans can thrive in its absence by instituting other forms of collective organization. They differ in their understanding of these alternate forms. Nearly all anarchists reject hierarchy and favor economic and social justice, and many, especially those in the anarcho-syndicalist tradition, identify as libertarian socialists. Most anarchists depart from socialist tenets, however, when they declare their opposition even to a temporary state during the period of revolutionary transition. Instead, small communes and collectives will organize themselves, either remaining autonomous or forming federations (Guérin). Despite the lack of a state, anarchism is not simply another word for chaos. Anarchist theorist Michael Albert, for instance, creates a model for a highly organized anarchist society in his socioeconomic tract *Parecon*. Albert's model stresses egalitarianism and social justice, and other anarchists exhibit varying degrees of commitment to social or individualist values.[1] While Albert envisions a large-scale anarchist society that functions through mass participation in an array of inter-locking democratic committees, other anarchists believe that a world without a state can only survive if humans remain limited to small, autonomous democratic communities.

Anarchism is an old radical tradition, with strong roots in the nineteenth and early twentieth centuries, and it has experienced a global resurgence in the late twentieth and early twenty-first centuries. Even in the 1960s and '70s, the New Left had employed anarchist strategies as it shifted away from the hierarchical structures of traditional social-ist organizations. Movements like the American Yippies or the French situationists offered explicit outlets for anarchist ideology.[2] The collision between anarchism, punk music, and do-it-yourself (diy) ethics in the 1970s gave anarchism a new style and subculture for the late twentieth century that appealed to disaffected youth. Punks became known for their simple music, homemade clothing, and personal adornments such as safety pins and spiked collars.[3] The diy attitude made punk style ostensibly accessible to anyone, as it denounced corporate products in favor of personally constructed items. This radical subculture served an important social function in the 1980s, when the Reagan and Thatcher administrations in the United States and the UK popularized conservative ideas even among working-class people. Punk allowed young dissenters to express their frustration with mainstream politics and culture. Although punk anarchism did not become dominant in the social movement scene until the 1990s, the punk subculture had been growing since the late 1970s.

When punk anarchism did take a key position in 1990s activism, it came in the wake of a long period of activist retrenchment. During the 1980s, specific issues such as apartheid, Central American solidarity, and environmentalism attracted many leftists, but it wasn't until well into the 1990s that young radicals began once again adopting broad anticapitalist analyses en masse. Entrepreneurs were looting the spoils of fallen Communist nations, and the neoliberal policies of the World Trade Organization (WTO), the World Bank, and the International

Monetary Fund (IMF) earned the ire of radicals who saw their policies as expressions of Western economic power.[4] In protest against the
neoliberal globalization that these institutions represented, a movement,
sometimes known as the "antiglobalization movement," arose in the
late 1990s. Although leftists of all stripes participate in it, anarchists
are key players, and the famous 1999 ministerial meeting of the WTO
in Seattle showcased this fact. Organized labor, socialists, and liberals took part in the Seattle marches, but the direct actions planned
by anarchist affinity groups succeeded in shutting down the meetings
entirely. Many participated in civil disobedience, locking arms across
street corners as they were attacked by police. Others, including members of the infamous Black Bloc, masked themselves and participated
in property destruction, targeting the windows of corporate giants such
as Starbucks, Nike, and the Gap (*The Black Bloc Papers* 47–48).[5] Since
then, anarchists have remained visible in a variety of venues, from the
antiwar movement to radical environmentalism.

Today's anarchists are extraordinarily diverse, and although
socialists exhibit a similar degree of ideological heterogeneity, they
tend to express their conflicts by joining different socialist organizations. Anarchists are much harder to pin down by group affiliation
because many have no affiliation at all. It is perfectly acceptable to
label oneself an "anarchist" while working in nonanarchist organizations, such as environmental justice, human rights, animal rights, or
labor rights groups. Those who do choose to affiliate only with other
anarchists frequently work in small, self-selected, and ever-shifting
"affinity groups"[6] established for planning an action or undertaking a
specific campaign. Others take on the name of a publicly recognized
entity such as Earth First!, the Black Bloc, or CrimethInc. None of these
organizations actually admit members in a formal sense, so affiliations
are loose and adopted simply by individual choice, and the ideologies of
the organizations are likewise fluid. While Earth First! is not officially
an anarchist organization, it has a large concentration of anarchists,
and it organizes participants around core beliefs in direct action and
"biocentrism," the perspective that the earth and nonhuman creatures
have the same rights to existence that humans do. The Black Bloc, on
the other hand, is adamantly anarchist and focuses solely on the issue

of direct action. It is known for its tactics of property destruction, and its adherents typically gather in black clothing and bandannas at major antiglobalization rallies. Historically, they have broken windows in corporate storefronts, challenged police barricades and defied police rules about protest locations, or simply offered a visual image of militancy for mass protests. Black Bloc cells are organized for mass actions and do not typically function in quotidian settings. CrimethInc., on the other hand, does exist outside of mass protests, but it, too, denounces formal membership, organization, or even a firm ideological perspective. It does produce a national website and a host of publications, however, that spread its particular brand of anarchist politics, which includes a denunciation of capitalism, a critique of work, and a celebration of a contemporary "hobo" culture that includes surviving by squatting, dumpster diving, stealing from major corporations, and generally living off the abundant refuse of consumer culture. Anyone may take action or form a local group in the name of CrimethInc., and the national "organization," embodied in anonymously produced literature and a website, has no authority to declare such actions invalid.

The instability of anarchist groupings means that individuals often pick and choose among ideological perspectives. A teenager who encounters CrimethInc. ideas online may emotionally and intellectually affiliate with that group, participating in national "convergences" and living the lifestyle that CrimethInc. espouses. Meanwhile, the same activist might participate in Earth First! actions as well as other, nonanarchist activism, and if he or she chooses to drop the self-identification of CrimethInc. at any point, the lack of formal membership would make the transition easy. As a result of this fluid ideological and organizational culture, it is difficult to generalize about anarchists—no comment will describe all anarchists or even all anarchists within one ideological group.

Nonetheless, I think it is important to analyze, with admitted imprecision, two overlapping trends in anarchist culture that have recently gained in popularity. One is antiwork anarchism, which arose in response to Bob Black's 1985 manifesto "The Abolition of Work." Black declares that anarchism and socialism have been plagued by a valuation of working-class labor, and he calls for a revolutionary new culture of play. Black sees this as a break with modern civilization in favor of premodern social forms. Hunter-gatherer societies, he maintains, do not discriminate between work and play as industrial cultures do but instead see the two as continuous and interchangeable. For them, "work" at hunting, gathering, cooking, or building is not alienating because it allows time for rest and play. Black's antiwork ideology has led to a rise in squatting, train hopping, dumpster diving, stealing corporate merchandise, and "primitive" living. These strategies allow participants to avoid traditional "work" in favor of full-time activism and "play." In fact, activities like dumpster diving have become so common in activist communities that they are no longer identified simply with antiwork anarchists—young anarchists of all ideologies tend to see dumpster diving as a community norm.

Among antiwork anarchists, anarcho-primitivists, also known as anticivilization or green anarchists, are the most extreme in their rejection of mainstream life. They believe that, as a result of excessive population growth and environmental destruction, civilization will and should fall in the near future. In its place, they hope to see humanity transformed into small bands of hunter-gatherers. The hunter-gatherer social system, they claim, is healthier for humans and more sustainable for the planet. In order to "return" to such societies, the human population must fall below the global "carrying capacity." This point has been the subject of much debate, and anarcho-primitivists have often been accused of racism and misanthropy for dismissing the significance of mass death. In response, anticivilization writer and activist Derrick Jensen insists that this decrease in population need not result in an *increase* of violence or deprivation. Our contemporary world already generates mass poverty and frequent warfare, so the anticivilization vision of population reduction may actually reduce current levels of violence, in Jensen's analysis (129). The collapse of civilization will, Jensen concedes, be a major calamity, but he believes that it will eventually lead to a more sustainable and just world.

Anticivilization anarchists like Jensen consider environmental concerns equal to or more pressing than human needs. Consequently, many participate in radical environmentalist and animal rights organizations. They also tend to identify their belief in "primitive" living as a move that will align humans more closely with animals, and some therefore refer to such lifestyles as "rewilding" or "going feral." As "feral" humans, they will experience life in its natural state.

Primitivists are often derided by fellow anarchists for their anti-technology perspective. A cartoon from Chaz Bufe's *Listen Anarchist!* for instance, depicts a man and woman dressed in leopard skins and sitting around a fire. The man holds a pair of broken eyeglasses, declaring "Well, at least that severs our last contact with technology." The cartoon suggests that anticivilization activists are shortsighted and foolish, giving up even the most useful of tools in a misguided attempt to return to the Stone Age. Anarcho-syndicalist writer Michael Albert produces a similar analysis when he complains that green anarchism attracts too much media attention, overshadowing more sophisticated anarchist work:

> Primitivism, usually in the persona of John Zerzan, is given attention by the mainstream as compared to other strands of anarchism whose better substance is literally ignored, precisely in the same way Stalinism's vile aspects were given attention as compared to other strands of anti-capitalist organization in the past whose better substance was ignored. ("Albert Replies to Critics")

Nonetheless, as Albert elsewhere acknowledges, primitivists excite young activists by presenting a concrete vision of a fascinating, exciting, and liberating future ("Anarchism?!"). The increasing popularity of Derrick Jensen's ideas throughout the radical left suggests that we cannot simply ignore anarcho-primitivist thought. Instead, it is worth examining what makes their rhetoric and ideology so appealing to young radicals.

A New Primitive

Anarcho-primitivist rhetoric arises out of the diy tradition, espousing the belief that anyone can be a hunter-gatherer, and anyone can be a political theorist. Thus, both practical knowledge and political ideology travel through diy channels, especially zines and internet sources (blogs, forums, and websites). Zines are homemade magazines common to fan cultures and activist communities. Produced with varying degrees of sophistication, they may be periodicals or stand-alone publications, small sheets of white paper stapled together featuring handwritten text or colorful, carefully illustrated pages with hand-sewn bindings. Zines usually have a small distribution through alternative bookstores and direct barter with the author. Although they first became popular before the Internet or sophisticated word processing programs, they have retained a central stature among activists in part for their diy "authenticity." Sites like Zinelibrary.net have mixed the zine tradition with the convenience of online distribution by collecting PDF versions of print zines and offering them for free online. The zines themselves, however, continue to highlight their homemade status, usually employing handwritten text even though typed text would be more time effective. And Zine Library reinforces the importance of the physical zine rather than the virtual one by displaying page proofs that could be printed and stapled into a book. Online, the pages appear out of order.

Anarchist zines offer intimate communication from others committed to a diy lifestyle. They often include autobiographical accounts, political analysis, or cartoon illustrations. Anarcho-primitivists are especially interested in teaching survival skills, along with narratives about the author's experiences implementing them. The anonymous author of *The Ghetto Garden*,[7] for instance, includes directions on how to build a composting toilet, and the author of *Feral Forager*[8] instructs readers on mushroom hunting and hide tanning while providing insight on the risks and rewards of eating roadkill.

Most anarcho-primitivist texts are adamantly inclusive, blurring the boundaries between the reader and the author by encouraging reader commentary and addressing the reader as a friend, but some of them adopt the diy ethic in a completely different way. While zines tend to look intentionally homemade and raw, some anarcho-primitivists have gone to the other extreme in blogs and videos by producing professional, corporate-style imagery. In some ways, this strategy mimics the media-friendly behavior of the Black Panthers, who mixed newspaper stories, stylized dress, violent rhetoric, and provocative images to attract public attention. Anarchists likewise use YouTube videos, blogs, and glossy photographs to widen the net of possible readers and to produce a tongue-in-cheek approach to primitivist symbols.

The blogs of "Urban Scout" and Emily Porter, "Tracker of Plants," use these methods to popularize anarcho-primitivist ideas on the web, though both express some reservations about the ideological label. These twenty-something primitivists share their political ideas and personal lives with readers, revealing pictures and videos of themselves under the guise of dramatic primitivist pseudonyms. Urban and Porter, formerly known as Penny Scout, are a former couple who both reside in Oregon, and they express their ideology by playfully imitating the style of com-modified radicalism. Although Urban Scout refuses to label himself an "anarchist," his avowedly primitivist ideology aligns him practically with those who do proclaim themselves "anarcho-primitivists."

Figure 8. Penny Scout in homemade "primitive" gear. Courtesy of Emily Porter

Figure 9. Urban Scout with teepee and MacBook. Courtesy of Peter Bauer

Figure 10. Urban Scout and Emily Porter/Penny Scout. Courtesy of Peter Bauer

If Urban Outfitters appropriates leftist politics by selling Che Guevara T-shirts, these bloggers reverse the process by presenting do-it-yourself primitivist projects *as though* they were corporate products. They blunt the power of corporate commodification by taking it into their own hands, producing mock-corporate style images so that when their work is appropriated, their original humorous attitude remains. Porter and Urban Scout use fashion and entertainment news as their aesthetic model. A report by Porter about a survivalist camp, for example, includes photos of her in a model's stance, wearing short shorts, fur wrist bands, a hip belt for a knife, and mock Ugg boots that she sewed out of felt, as seen in figure 8. Urban Scout generates similar photos, which are often stylized in the manner of corporate promo shots, that depict him (and Porter, in figure 10) in humorous poses as hunter-gatherers. One, figure 9, portrays him sitting in front of a teepee, wearing a T-shirt that reads "Portland." A MacBook, a homemade bow and arrow, a backpack, a "Rewild" hat advertising his online anarcho-primitivist forum, and a collection of cardboard signs reading "Apocalypse Now" and "The End Is Near" surround him on the grass. He holds two rocks in his hand, striking one against the other, and in the background a fence is visible, suggesting that he may be "camping" in a backyard.

In these photos, "rewilding" retains the marks of civilization. It takes the guise of a fashion shoot and includes backyards, Portland T-shirts, and computers. Even the cardboard signs are designed to resemble homeless pleas for help rather than activist picket signs, allowing Urban Scout to jokingly portray his version of the "primitive" as simply a glorified version of urban homelessness. In all of these images, Porter and Urban Scout brand themselves before they can be branded by corporate America. He, especially, welcomes media attention to fund his projects and promote his cause.

Urban Scout's video footage is even more explicit in using corporate strategies for activist "propaganda." He advertises his annual "Nuclear Winter Formal" dance, for example, by posting YouTube videos of "red carpet" interviews. Primitivist Molly Strand carries what appears to be a lead pipe as a microphone and mimics E! Entertainment Network interviews with celebrities on the red carpet, asking each of the partygoers about their views on fashion and the apocalypse. Strand and the Nuclear Formal guests are intimately familiar with the details of the "red carpet" interview, and they perform the expected banter on cue. "Who are you wearing tonight?" she asks one guest. "Squirrel," the beaming woman replies, twisting the stock red-carpet question about fashion designers to incorporate anarchist ideology ("The Radioactive Runway with Molly Strand"). In these mock-mainstream encounters, anticivilization activists revel in the contradiction between mass media spectacle and primitivist sentiment. By using blogs, YouTube, and red carpet events, they acknowledge the success of corporate strategies of "selling" ideologies, and they insist that their antitechnological perspective can best be spread through the very media that they hope to destroy.

The corporate and mainstream art worlds have taken the bait. In fall 2007, the website for *GQ* and *Details* magazine published a photo of Porter in a "Trend Report" piece titled "Apocalypse Soon." Wearing a shift dress and her homemade knife belt, she appears as a capable postapocalyptic woman walking amid abandoned industrial infrastructure as she wanders down railroad tracks—and even in this scenario she maintains her fashion sense. The caption, meanwhile, advertises her then-boyfriend's $25 rewilding workshops ("Apocalypse Soon"). Urban Scout, meanwhile, has attracted the notice of his local press, including the *Portland Tribune,* the *Oregonian,* and the *Willamette Week.* An LA firm even considered him as a subject for a new reality show. Although he didn't land this potentially lucrative gig, he did produce an art installation in December 2007 for a Washington, DC event titled "New Future," where he displayed his handmade stone tools in museum cases, set up his teepee with a TV inside, and demonstrated survival skills for visitors while wearing his Rewild cap, a T-shirt, and homemade buckskin shorts. In this humorous performance reminiscent of artist Coco Fusco and Guillermo Gómez-Peña's early 1990s installations of themselves as undiscovered "primitives," Urban Scout advertises himself while deconstructing museum displays of "primitive" artifacts. Museum artifacts, he suggests, can be TVs or hats with corporate logos as easily as "primitive tools," and in Urban Scout's installation they appear with their creator, in their "urban primitive" context rather than in isolation.

While Fusco wanted to highlight the way Westerners stereotype and exploit indigenous peoples, Urban Scout puts his white male body on display, insisting that the tools and skills associated with "primitive" people are not simply located in certain bodies, locations, or time periods. He questions the museum's sterile and often decontextualized depictions of indigenous tools and art, and displaying his own imperfect knowledge of survivalist skills, he brings them back to life as changing, developing ways of life. At the same time, as he shows off his legs in short shorts, he mocks the seriousness of the entire endeavor—both the museum as a transmitter of knowledge and history and himself as a model of the future.

Urban Scout's imitation museum display inserts an actual human into the museum setting, generating space for a personal narrative as well as an abstract historical one. By relying on personal blogs as companion pieces to their corporate-style imagery, Urban Scout and Porter do the same thing. They combine performative strategies with mundane stories of life and activism. Their focus on slow personal narratives and their attempt to live out primitivist lifestyles have something in common with the 1970s and '80s work of labor activists who became workers, while their use of spectacular media-friendly imagery borrows from Black Panther techniques. Porter and Urban Scout acknowledge that their political perspective appears absurd to many, and they take their contradictions to extremes. Knowing that they will be accused of hypocrisy for living in Portland and using computers while espousing primitivist values, they accept these contradictions, mocking them and using them as core identifying features. In a 2010 video of Emily Porter performing "primitivist standup," she announces to her audience that "like all good anarcho-primitivists, I have a blog" (Porter 28 January 2010). Urban Scout is equally proud, naming himself according to this contradiction and using the photo of himself with the teepee and laptop as his signature photo on his "About" page. He insists that his goal is not to isolate himself in the wilderness but to use his Portland community, with all of its technological trappings, as the starting point for a new lifestyle. Moreover, by recounting personal struggles with depression and tales of failed attempts at hide tanning or shelter building on their blogs, Porter and Urban Scout also portray themselves as appealing and human.

Ultimately, the two make themselves vulnerable and visible because they believe that political change must be on a grand scale. Their vision of radical political change is certainly different from that presented by labor activists. It does not center on the workplace or value taking over the means of production. However, it similarly relies on recovering a more genuine human experience from the alienation and oppression of industrial culture. They see smaller social structures and more simple technologies as the key to human liberation. But, like socialists, they too must attract broad-based interest to spark change, and they are willing to take the risks of corporate corruption and derisive laughter for the possible rewards of finding a mass audience. That said, because Urban Scout vocally distances himself from the anarcho-primitivist movement rather than accepting the critiques and laudatory attention that self-professed anarcho-primitivists offer, he may isolate himself even more in his own ideological perspective.

Anthropological and Cultural "Primitives"

Urban Scout's recycling of Fusco and Gómez-Peña's installation indicates some sophistication about the ways the "primitive" has been used in American culture as a symbol of racial difference and inferiority. But although he has moments of skilled analysis, he and those who do claim the label anarcho-primitivist often fall into the trap of romanticizing a generic idea of the "primitive" that is rooted in old stereotypes about racial and cultural differences. Moreover, their celebration of rewilding from within corrupt American culture fails to confront the hard ethical questions about what it would mean to build a neoprimitive world *after* civilization's crutch has collapsed. The chaos in the wake of natural disasters such as the 2010 earthquake in Haiti, Hurricane Katrina in New Orleans, or the 2004 tsunami in Southeast Asia reveals the more tragic potential of infrastructural collapse—even if a more sustainable world might later emerge.

This is not to say that anarcho-primitivists don't attempt to address some of these problems. Urban Scout, for instance, avows his intent to respect tribal cultures and to avoid abusive cultural appropriation. Other anarcho-primitivists attempt to tackle the racial history of the term *primitive* by using it in an anthropological way, which would supposedly take their analyses out of the realm of stereotype. Unfortunately, however, they rely on dated studies, refusing to account for more recent debates within the discipline about hunter-gatherer lifestyles, the use of the term *primitive*, and the methods of anthropological study. Although they cite a wide array of scholars, they do so to make general claims that idealize hunter-gatherers as remnants of precivilized life, a perspective held by few contemporary anthropologists. Anarcho-primitivists depend especially on founding texts of hunter-gatherer studies from the late 1960s and early 1970s, including Robert Lee and Irven Devore's collection *Man the Hunter* and Marshall Sahlins's essay "The Original Affluent Society." These pieces retain respect as seminal disciplinary works, but their conclusions have been updated by later generations of scholars.

In the New Left era, Devore, Sahlins, and Lee, among others, became fascinated with hunter-gatherers as representatives of an ancient, more egalitarian era—exactly the perspective that anarcho-primitivists embrace. This trend arose in part because of the growth of radicalism and anticolonialism in the world at large. In a contributing essay to the 1968 anthology *Man the Hunter*, Claude Lévi-Strauss argues that the collection represents a shift in the discipline from a politics of assimilation to a celebration of cultural difference (349). Years later, anthropologists Barbara Bender and Brian Morris remarked that indigenous resistance in the Vietnam War led their colleagues to interpret hunter-gatherer lifestyles as "an alternative, highly adaptive and ecologically sensitive system" (5). Radical politics, in other words, encouraged anthropologists to see utopian promise in hunter-gatherer societies.

Today's anthropologists, of course, are likewise affected by their social and cultural moment, but that cultural moment has changed, and newer anthropological studies have altered basic conceptions about hunter-gatherer societies. As early as the 1980s, anthropologists such as Thomas Headland and Lawrence Reid suggested that ancient hunter-gatherers did not survive *solely* on the fruits of their hunting and gathering. Instead, they traded with and depended on relationships with peoples from agricultural societies (Headland and Reid). Today, scholars usually depict hunter-gatherers as fully modern people whose lifestyle has evolved in response to relationships with agriculturalists, colonizers, and postcolonial capitalists. Whether their societies were egalitarian is a source of much debate (Winterhalder; Barnard).

Instead of taking on such questions, anarcho-primitivists often employ sound bites from older texts. Mark Nathan Cohen's *Health and the Rise of Civilization* (1989) is one favorite. John Zerzan and others cite Cohen to argue that hunter-gatherers have better health and life spans comparable to contemporary Westerners (Zerzan, "Elements of Refusal" 68). They are correct that Cohen's survey of medical and anthropological material suggests that hunter-gatherers avoid a wide array of "First World" diseases, including heart disease, high blood pressure, diabetes, and high cholesterol. Cohen does note, however, that they experience a variety of infectious diseases, depending on their environment, and that they exhibit high infant mortality rates and low life-expectancies (48). Their life spans and infant mortality rates, Cohen argues, are better than those of contemporary Third World peoples but not comparable to First World peoples.

John Zerzan's pro–hunter-gatherer research also incorporates clearly disputed or discredited evidence. Zerzan's most widely known essay, "Future Primitive," cites studies of the Philippine Tasaday, a supposed group of Stone Age hunter-gatherers "discovered" in 1971. Although it was deemed a hoax in 1986 and controversy over the truth or falsity of the group's lifestyle still continues, Zerzan continues to reference the Tasaday as late as 1994 without any mention of the controversy (Headland; Hemley). Similarly, Zerzan cites the dubious evidence of Arnold DeVries's 1952 *Primitive Man and His Food* to bolster his position that primitive people have near painless childbirth. DeVries's only evidence for this claim was based on the testimony of eighteenth- and nineteenth-century white observers of Native American life: Lewis and Clark and Washington Irving, among others, observe that "squaws" seem to give birth with greater ease than white women (12).

By circulating outdated or discredited information among themselves rather than participating in a vibrant debate in anthropology about hunter-gatherer lifestyles, anarcho-primitivists focus on an idealized myth of tribal life instead of earnestly attempting to analyze its benefits and flaws. Some of the academic debates in hunter-gatherer studies might be especially useful for anarcho-primitivists because they stress that hunter-gatherer behavior exists not in a vacuum but in a social context, and this might be a more productive model for understanding how to incorporate some hunter-gatherer behaviors into an industrial or postindustrial society.

When they refuse to take contemporary anthropological debates seriously, however, anarcho-primitivists suggest that they are primarily interested in the imagery and rhetoric about hunter-gatherers, which is rooted in primitivism, including modernist aesthetic primitivism and racist primitivism. In these understandings, hunter-gatherers are mirror opposites of Westerners—sometimes more vicious and lawless and sometimes more egalitarian and happy. As examples like Josephine Baker demonstrate, these assumptions slip from their targets—tribal hunter-gatherers—and attach themselves to Africans, Polynesians, and African Americans as racial groups. This tired problem of idealizing the "primitive" reflects a breakdown in the transmission of radical rhetoric across generations. Even though the Black Panther Party and its former members exert influence on anarchists, anarcho-primitivists adopt the term *primitive* without sufficient critique. Because they speak only of hunter-gatherers when they reference the "primitive," they do not acknowledge how the concept has demeaned people of color as a whole. They fail to recognize that aesthetic and anthropological definitions of the primitive are culturally intertwined.

Anarcho-primitivists have taken their metaphors and beliefs about the "primitive" from anthropology, radical history, and the history of racialized tropes. By claiming solely an anthropological history, however, they obscure the way primitive tropes have shaped American racism. Thus, although they speak out against racism that affects Native Americans, they do so because Native Americans were persecuted for their tribal structures and because Native American communities continue to value tribal lifestyles. They do not recognize the ways that the "primitive" label or the celebratory depictions of people of color wielding spears can be seen as racist rather than simply resistant. They also struggle to understand the *variety* of political needs that contemporary indigenous people have, including economic justice and, in some cases, greater access to the tools of civilization.

Moreover, the anarcho-primitivist interest in biocentrism creates tension with the history of racism and animal representations. While primitivist racism presents the racial "other" as animal-like, anarcho-primitivists break down the distinctions between human and animal. Biocentrism puts life rather than *human* life at the center of ethics, claiming that animal and plant life have an equal right to exist and consume resources as humans do (*Barbaric Thoughts* 6). In this system, the environment and its creatures have intrinsic value, not simply as resources for human use. As a result, anticivilization rhetoric declares that humans are animals. When participants "drop out" of civilization to live as squatters, foragers, and hunters, they refer to the process as "rewilding" or "going feral." Both of these terms define postcivilization life not by a lack of technology or a tribal community but by an association with wild animals. The terms *wild* and *feral* suggest ferocious, uncontrollable, and independent animals, evoking the chaotic reputation of anarchism, not egalitarian structures. While the Black Panthers struggled to reclaim the humanity that Western culture had denied, anarcho-primitivists embrace an animal identity. In doing so, they usefully insert new environmentalist perspectives into activist metaphors, but they also sacrifice the modifications that the Black Panthers and the LRBW had made to the "primitive."

And a New Slavery

Green anarchists are not the only ones who believe society is on the verge of collapse due to industrial and environmental abuses—or, perhaps, due to religious prophesy. Doomsday saturates twenty-first-century culture, appearing in such venues as Cormac McCarthy's post-apocalyptic novel *The Road*, the zombie epidemic film *28 Days Later*, the film *2012*, based on the end of a Mayan calendar cycle, or the Christian best-selling book series *Left Behind*, which prepares viewers for the Christian rapture that will remove all but a few Christians from the Earth. As literary critic Tom Moylan notes, this resurrection of dystopian fiction dates back to the 1980s, with the work of writers like Margaret Atwood, William Gibson, and Octavia Butler. I would add that, while some of Moylan's examples of early 1980s dystopian fiction fall into category of Cold War–era apocalypse—when nuclear catastrophe and totalitarian regimes were present fears—post–Cold War apocalyptic novels and films reflect the new fears of our globalized world, including terrorism, epidemic, environmental catastrophe, and divine retribution. Twenty-first-century apocalypse is more self-inflicted than it was during the Cold War, when an enemy stood watch over the nuclear button.

Anticivilization anarchists are in conversation with a key strain of contemporary culture because of their interest in apocalypse. This synchronicity makes anarchism compelling for many young people, and it offers opportunities for theoretical and political development. On the one hand, anarchists can take advantage of apocalypse's popularity to attract followers. On the other hand, writers who are interested in apocalypse can offer theoretical critiques of the anarcho-primitivist project, and the work of black speculative fiction (sf) writers Octavia Butler and Nalo Hopkinson does just that.[9] Moylan sees the recent generation of dystopian writers as political critics who use dystopia to introduce underlying utopian possibilities in the culture (3). In other words, they perform the same function as green anarchist theorists, predicting the demise of civilization while presenting openings for a more sustainable future.

Butler's and Hopkinson's dystopian worlds could come directly out of anarcho-primitivist zines. Butler's *Parable of the Sower* (1993) and *Parable of the Talents* (1998) depict the fall of civilization into brutal chaos, and Hopkinson's *Brown Girl in the Ring* (1998) imagines Toronto decimated by economic catastrophe and white flight. Both writers portray impending apocalypse and a return to "primitive" culture that anarcho-primitivists envision. By focusing on the crisis rather than the contemporary moment or the future utopia, however, they offer some essential critiques for green anarchists. They laud "primitive" survival skills, but they also suggest a host of other considerations for the transition into a postapocalyptic world, including labor rights, racial equality, and crime management that have concerned both socialists and mainstream politicians for years.

Octavia Butler's series seconds anarcho-primitivist commentary on civilization's excesses, but it also targets the common flaws in utopian alternatives. Her novels tell the story of Lauren Oya Olamina, an African-American girl growing up in a social crisis. Affected by a drug her mother took while she was in the womb, Lauren is a "sharer," meaning that she feels the physical pain and pleasure of others as though it were her own. During her youth, Lauren watches American civilization destroy itself slowly. In 2024, when *Sower* begins, global warming runs rampant as a hurricane decimates the Gulf Coast, California struggles with drought, and seaside towns disappear due to erosion and rising sea levels. Economically, the gap between rich and poor becomes so severe that middle-class people can no longer afford televisions, cars, vaccines, or even shoes. As a result, epidemics of curable diseases like measles spread across the country, and towns sell themselves to corporations for environmental help and physical protection. Privatization, the loss of labor rights, and environmental abuse sow chaos.

The country begins to resemble a postcivilization world. A huge array of stars is visible in the night sky because cities no longer generate as much light, and Lauren's family replaces expensive white and wheat flours with homemade acorn flour from the community's oak trees. Because social crisis has led to a *loss* of technology for the masses rather than new, oppressive technologies that appear in famous dystopias such as Huxley's *Brave New World* or Orwell's *Nineteen Eighty-Four*, Lauren adopts the survival strategies of many anarcho-primitivists. She trains with rifles, learns to process animal skins, and reads books on wilderness survival, natural medicine, and the historical plant cultivation of California's Native Americans. Her goal is to "get ready for what is going to happen, get ready to survive it, get ready to make a life afterward," a statement that could easily have come out of the mouth of an anticivilization activist (*Sower* 48).

When Lauren is eighteen, the drug addicts and rabid scavengers who have become common invade her family's walled middle-class neighborhood, killing those inside and looting their homes. This signals the further collapse of civilization and the beginning of anarchy. Lauren leads a small group of survivors North in search of safety, gathering new travelers as she walks down California highways that rarely see automobile traffic. In the process, Lauren becomes the prophet for her own religion. Known as Earthseed, it posits that God is change and that humans can only survive by seeking "heaven" in space colonization. At the conclusion of *Sower*, Lauren establishes an egalitarian community based on Earthseed in Northern California. In *Parable of the Talents*, however, her utopian community breaks down when government forces invade and enslave its members. Although Lauren and some of her followers eventually escape, they remain separated from their children, who were placed in adoptive homes during their imprisonment. Resigned to the loss of her daughter, Lauren pursues space exploration and Earthseed, becoming detached from family as her fame increases.

Although Lauren and anarcho-primitivists share an interest in survival skills, their differences in rhetoric demonstrate that the "neoprimitive" can incorporate both ecological and antiracist elements. On the one hand, Butler's novel makes an environmentalist statement. Lauren's utopian solution includes "sustainable living," and her collection of followers builds a cooperative community based on low-technology skills in Humboldt County, a region famous for attracting hippie "back-to-the-land" communes (in addition to marijuana growers) beginning in the 1960s. The group does not live a nomadic hunter-gatherer lifestyle, but it combines small-scale farming and stationary living with basic nontechnological living—Butler's corrective to the environmental destruction that created pandemics and natural disasters. On the other hand, Butler also emphasizes her characters' relationship to the history of Afrocentric black nationalism. Although she had viewed her 1979 novel *Kindred* as a critique of black nationalists who were "angry with their parents for not having improved things faster," Butler is more positive about them in the *Parable* series (Kenan 496). Both Lauren Oya Olamina and her new husband Taylor Franklin Bankole bear names that grew out of this period. Their grandparents and parents, respectively, chose Yoruba names in the 1960s in solidarity with black nationalism. In turn, Lauren and Bankole name their child Larkin Beryl Ife Olamina Bankole, maintaining the two Yoruba names and adding a new one (*Talents* 157). With these details, Butler insists that black nationalism remains not only an important legacy but also a continued component of twenty-first-century activism.

Black nationalism remains significant, Butler indicates, because the United States of the future still struggles with racism. In other words, she still thinks that black nationalism is important in a post-civilization world, indicating that she believes race—and perhaps even separatist views of race—are crucial to building a new social structure. Black nationalism is also significant to the anarchist tradition. Many anarchists admire the Black Panthers for their direct action tactics and uncompromising rhetoric. Moreover, environmentalist and animal rights anarchists who feel targeted by the new label of "eco-terrorist" see the Panthers' struggles with the FBI's COINTELPRO as akin to their own. They, too, risk prison sentences for their activist tactics as many black nationalists did.

But this respect for black nationalism has been somewhat less prominent in the anarcho-primitivist community. Despite its prevalence in Earth First!, the home of many green anarchists, it is more common among anarcho-syndicalists, those with stronger ties to the labor movement. Moreover, the former Black Panthers who have entered the anarchist movement have avoided green anarchism, seeing more commonalities between their "revolutionary nationalist" roots and the work of anarcho-syndicalists. We can see why they might have made this choice when we look at the gaps in green anarchism's politics on the issue of race. Some anarcho-primitivists believe that civilization's fall will ultimately eliminate problems of racism, sexism, and oppression. This perspective, which dropped out of most socialist ideologies many years ago, still maintains some currency among green anarchists. Those who do recognize the problems of racism and oppression before, during, and after the crash sometimes minimize them. Earth First!, for instance, focuses so much on the environment that it sometimes scorns the needs of humans, and this can mean subordinating the immediate needs of people of color or workers to saving the environment. I do not mean to suggest that Earth First! or the majority of anarcho-primitivists trivialize racial and economic justice. As part of the broad radical left wing, they tend to see the importance of racism as self-explanatory, and Earth First! builds anti-oppression policies into its journal and its national convergences. However, the rhetoric and political tactics that dominate in green anarchist communities rarely identify racial and economic justice as *primary* components of social change, and this is the perspective that Butler critiques.

Anarcho-primitivist Ran Prieur, for instance, describes a "Sci-Fi Utopia" that includes war that turns the world against the United States, an economic crash, race riots, class riots, martial law, and mass deaths in its early stages. Prieur's utopia concludes with the emergence of autonomous tribes who produce windmills and bicycles, interacting with the land as well as one another. Imperialism doesn't die, he notes, but empires come and go rapidly and are more susceptible to dissent. Although Prieur acknowledges the likelihood of race and class riots even in his utopian imagination, he relegates them to one sentence. His notion of a postcollapse world does not address how these new communities can overcome problems of race, class, and empire.

CrimethInc., likewise, trumpets the importance of racial justice while employing language and imagery that offer a kind of inept, self-centered solidarity. One example is the use of the label "wage slavery" in its 2001 book *Days of War, Nights of Love*. This phrase was popular among Marxists in the nineteenth century for the same reason that it has attracted anarchists today—it drew a comparison between the evident exploitation of slavery and the capitalist exploitation of wage labor. The equation itself is problematic, as it relies on the racialized form of slavery that existed when Marx adopted the term. Slaves were marked by their race as a different caste of people, and Marx wanted his readers to see workers the same way. Instead of correcting Marx's nineteenth-century racial insensitivity that equated exploitation with slavery, CrimethInc. heightens it by comparing the mundane humiliations of "putting a price on your time or wearing a uniform or having a boss" to lynching (245). In a section that elaborates on its antiwork philosophy, the group presents a drawing of a person hanging by a noose that is captioned by the word "work," as seen in figure 11. The androgynous individual appears in silhouette, and the strands of hair and the light-colored hand in the foreground suggest that he or she is white. The surrounding discussion of "wage slavery" makes no reference to lynching, race politics, or American slavery. When CrimethInc. presents the lynched figure, then, it does not comment on race politics. Rather, it uses an iconic image of black oppression to define generic suffering without analyzing real relationships between class, labor, and racism in American society.

The group employs the lynching spectacle to describe capitalism's quotidian impositions on the body, and in CrimethInc. those bodies

Figure 11. CrimethInc.'s definition of "wage slavery."

are primarily white. Lacking a membership list, CrimethInc. cannot be definitively identified as a "majority white" group, but nearly all CrimethInc. photos and illustrations depict whites, and the group recruits from the largely white punk music scene. Its anarchist manifestos, moreover, include no analysis of race. CrimethInc.'s lynched figure instead invokes members' sense of work as a form of embodied victimization. The work-as-lynching image relies on the experience of racial oppression to define suffering, and it employs the black body solely as a signifier of pain, not as an agent of resistance.

Octavia Butler offers a corrective to this language. She, too, plays on the term *wage slavery* by depicting labor rights as an issue that affects Americans of all races, but she makes a distinction between fair and unfair labor conditions while insisting that the lynched body and the slave are not simply metaphors for oppression. As events in African-American history, they should appear in political discourse with adequate context, especially because they evoke such intense public emotions. In an increasingly corrupt society, Butler observes, it is the middle classes who have the leisure to develop neoprimitive survival skills as Lauren does. The poor, on the other hand, are stuck in the corrupt labor pool, turning first into indentured servants who are forced to live on their worksites and use company scrip while their employers overcharge them for the basics of life. When workers inevitably fall into debt, employers hold them and their children as slaves until the debts are paid. Later, in *Parable of the Talents*, the system morphs into outright slavery in which slaves are sold by traders and controlled by electric slave collars. Butler suggests that the chance for utopia emerges in such a collapsing economy, but so does the possibility of a new form of slavery.

Butler's twenty-first-century slaves are not defined by race but by class, and as a result they share something with the Marxist/anarchist notion of the "wage slave." In other words, Butler does not deny the equation between slavery and economic exploitation. But it is no coincidence that the former slaves in Lauren's original community are people of color. The first former slaves the group encounters are Grayson Mora, a black Latino male, and Emery Solis, a woman of Japanese and African-American parentage (258, 261). Later, in *Parable of the Talents*, white slaves appear when the Noyer children arrive in Lauren's Acorn community. This new multiracial slavery indicates the intersection of race and class oppressions. Capitalist civilization, at its breaking point, forces working-class people of all races into poverty, debt, and eventually slavery. Then as now, people of color disproportionately fall into this category.

By toying with the boundaries between labor rights abuses and slavery, Butler ties the labor movement's concept of "wage slavery" to the African-American experience with bond slavery. In doing so, she revises anarchist uses of the phrase. The "antiwork" strain of anarchism views *all* capitalist employment as "wage slavery," no matter what labor conditions the worker toils under. Butler tempers this comparison by reminding her viewers of the real abuses of bond slavery and the intimate connection between slavery, economic exploitation, and race.

Anarchist Microcommunities

The racial insensitivities that some anarcho-primitivists display should not condemn all anarchists. Those who are most successful in addressing race and class politics are able to move beyond personal lifestyle transformations and interact successfully with larger communities of people who might not share their politics. Because anarchists squat or rent cheaply in urban settings, they frequently find themselves in the midst of racial political struggles over gentrification, homelessness, or police brutality. The realities of local politics and grassroots activism force them to question their physical status in minority neighborhoods in addition to their methods of interacting with community members.

We can see the challenge of the microcommunity in an example of an anarchist squat in the Berkeley area detailed in a zine by a woman who identifies herself as "Hannah Potassium." After moving into an abandoned boat motor and turbine sales office that had been known as "The Power Machine," Potassium originally lives without electricity, water, or other amenities. As she invites friends to join her and acquires other unwanted squatters, however, Potassium and the others slowly accumulate the amenities of "civilized" life, including water, electricity, a hot plate, and a radio. Potassium identifies it as a

> small-scale industrial revolution. [. . .] I was addicted to progress. It bemused me to picture a time when we huddled around a candle on the floor. Primitive times. Uncivilized times. A time we should never hope for again. (4–5)

Although Potassium had begun squatting to avoid the corruption of civilization, she finds herself quickly lured by technological "advancement." Living in an abandoned building named "The Power Machine," she is at an industrial center, and her "primitive" experience must be a relationship with civilization rather than nature. She can "dumpster" at Trader Joe's across the street, but she cannot subsist from "nature."

As the group's technology grows, its physical and social situation deteriorates. The trash they have been piling in the corner begins to stink, and "wars" erupt about who has the right to use the squat. Angry about sexual intimidation from a male squatter, Potassium and her friend finally booby-trap the building's entryways to prevent him from entering and establish a "safe space" for women in the squat. The zine, in other words, becomes an allegory for the growth of civilization, even as it reflects the real experiences of urban squatters. And because the squat represents the whole of "civilization" and the "neoprimitive" response, the activist work they do—in this case the feminist work of establishing a "safe space"—takes place within the squat rather than outside its walls. It affects only their microcommunity.

By developing what anarchist theorist Hakim Bey refers to as a "temporary autonomous zone," the members of the squat feel that they have some control over an otherwise oppressive environment (Bey).[10] Potassium and her companions recycle and conquer a space that had previously represented capitalist neglect. Potassium admits, however, that their ability to develop a "temporary autonomous zone" is limited by their status as young, white, formerly middle-class kids. She tells us that, although she had occupied the building without permission, the landlord tacitly agreed to their squatting and told them to "keep the riff-raff out" (21). Potassium concedes that "most recreational squatters (i.e. not squatting out of necessity [. . .]) can have pretty good luck doing it. Meanwhile, 50-year-old black men will automatically have trouble" (9). White privilege frames her squatting experience, and by keeping the "riff-raff" out, she and other anarchist squatters sometimes become the first white faces in gentrifying neighborhoods.

Most contemporary anarchists, like Potassium, are aware of these contradictions, and they usually seek to remedy them. A central debate rages, for instance, about the role of "lifestyle anarchism" in political movements. Anarcho-primitivists and squatters often earn the dismissive title "lifestyle anarchists" from their cohorts who value organized political work in the community over personal decisions about diet, employment, and housing. In many ways, this debate mimics the antagonism between "cultural nationalists" and "revolutionary nationalists" during the Black Power era. Just as the Black Power factional fight hid the similarities that bound cultural activists and political activists together, it can likewise be difficult to separate "lifestyle anarchism" from action-oriented anarchism. Anarcho-primitivists may be involved in larger-scale environmentalist activism, and anarcho-syndicalists often work on animal rights, environmentalist, or antiglobalization projects, usually under the purview of issue-based organizations or affinity groups.

Skill Shares and Nalo Hopkinson's *Brown Girl in the Ring*

Although environmental analysis might be anarchists' biggest ideological contribution to the larger activist world, diy skills are their most pragmatic gift, and they are also the keys to branching out from microcommunities to more broad-based activism. Nalo Hopkinson's science fiction/horror novel *Brown Girl in the Ring* identifies the potential that anarchists have to combine diy skills with urban politics to make real progress on issues of racial and economic justice. Today, some anarchists practice diy because they want to protest corporate culture, while others laud it as a way of favoring simple technologies over more complex ones. Hopkinson demonstrates that, whether linked to notions of the "primitive" or not, diy traditions have the potential to launch participants into positive interactions with larger communities. Her depiction of an urban Toronto collapsing into a "neoprimitive" city stresses that any "primitive" lifestyles must be filtered through the lens of industry, modernity, and postmodernity. Moreover, she provides correctives to romantic understandings of "traditional" practices, industrial collapse, and community cooperation.

As a writer who has lived in Jamaica, Trinidad, Guyana, and Canada, Hopkinson incorporates Caribbean Obeah traditions into her novel (Hopkinson and Nelson 97). Hopkinson's protagonist Ti-Jeanne lives in a postcivilization Toronto, which fell into economic crisis after the Temagami Indians filed suit against the Ontario government over indigenous land rights. The government and its wealthy, mostly white citizens abandon the city, leaving the impoverished barricaded inside Toronto without electricity, plumbing, or public transportation. Although the rest of the world presumably retains capitalist civilization, Toronto's urban center becomes the hole of an economic "doughnut." Residents turn to subsistence farming and hunting squirrels, pigeons, dogs, and cats. Ti-Jeanne's grandmother Gros Jeanne is the local healer, practicing with a nursing degree and an understanding of Caribbean folk medicine. Meanwhile, a posse of drug dealers headed by Gros Jeanne's ex-husband Rudy rules over the newly "primitive" society.

Hopkinson's crash begins with an act of resistance when indigenous people assert their land rights. It is not the white community that suffers, however. Instead, the Temagami victory creates a crisis for other communities of color. Hopkinson never mentions the status of the Temagami again, and the reader doesn't know whether they have achieved anything in return for Toronto's collapse. Instead, we simply see how ethnic communities become isolated from one another as the dominant system employs the "divide and conquer" method. A victory for the indigenous rights movement does not result in a positive domino effect for others. The "fall," then, appears in Hopkinson's text as an undesirable event that targets people of color, leaving them with no choice but to turn to "primitive" means of survival. Just as socialist countries took up their new experiment while surrounded by hostile capitalist neighbors, this new postcivilization Toronto is one pocket of destruction within the larger world. The people who live there are those who have neither the means nor the power to escape, and Hopkinson's characters are more interested in escaping Toronto than in forging a neoprimitivist utopia.

While Hopkinson highlights the way that poor people and people of color are oppressed by civilization's fall, however, the crisis appears to slightly increase community cooperation. Gang violence and political corruption run rampant, but at the same time, Caribbean Canadians find some new forms of cultural freedom: "Among Caribbean people," Ti-Jeanne thinks, "bush medicine used to be something private, but living in the Burn changed all the rules" (14). Now, folk medicine and Western medicine come together because of a lack of Western pharmaceuticals, an example of privation that opens the culture to Caribbean traditions. In addition to cultural changes, the entire community begins to adopt habits that anarchists would celebrate as egalitarian and diy: the major Toronto newspapers are replaced by a hand-made zine; a street vendor sells reconditioned bicycles to replace cars; and a woman at the market repairs shoes with discarded rubber. The local market involves bartering as well as sale, encouraging many people to develop skills that are useful to the community. With these details, Hopkinson portrays a neoprimitivist lifestyle as ambiguously positive. However, because the residents of Toronto, unlike anarchists, did not seek out this economic shift, many want to escape to the suburbs where they could return to industrial capitalist civilization.

The corrupt rule of Ti-Jeanne's mob boss grandfather in this postcivilization society calls anarchist attention to the dangers as well as the opportunities of social crisis. Without strong organization for egalitarian values, a corrupt leader quickly fills the power vacuum. With this warning, Hopkinson stresses the dangerous elements of crisis while also offering some hope for productive change. Preindustrial tradition, however, does not simply lead to increased human cooperation. In post-civilization Toronto, voodoo practices and traditional forms of medicine fill in the gaps as Western norms collapse, but voodoo supports both the drug lord Rudy and the heroes Ti-Jeanne and her grandmother.

There are opportunities for a better world in the crisis, Hopkinson suggests, but they require community members to build survival skills in tandem with family and religious bonds. With these efforts, the new society Hopkinson envisions is not a utopia or a return to tribal lifestyles, but a cooperative social structure that is more than simply a collection of surviving individuals. Hopkinson's depictions of community building do not differ dramatically from what many anarchists would advocate. In that sense, she is not presenting a deep critique. Her novel, however, outlines both the benefit of diy skills and the fact that these skills will only spark widespread change if their proponents move outside their own microcommunities and interact with the larger culture. She highlights the significance of developing diy skills as a process that initiates personal and social change. At the same time, she doesn't want her readers to fetishize diy skills or traditional beliefs as the *keys* to social change. And she reminds anarchists that even a postcivilization world will require activists to live with and within the remnants of industrial civilization.

Hopkinson's protagonist gains optimism about postcivilization Toronto by learning skills that will be useful for both her family and her community. Initially, Ti-Jeanne is a reluctant teenage mother who refers to her little boy as "Bolom," meaning fetus, and shakes him or tells him to "shut up" when he cries. She is also unwilling to help others in the community—when a group of street children arrive at her grandmother's home to beg help for one of their crew with a broken leg, Ti-Jeanne flinches at the children's filthiness. Her grandmother, on the other hand, appears gruff on the outside, but she welcomes the children and fixes the leg. With Gros Jeanne's guidance, Ti-Jeanne transforms from a pouty teenager into a capable seer woman when she learns traditional Obeah practices and defeats posse leader and fellow Obeah practitioner Rudy. As both the protagonist and antagonist practice Obeah, Hopkinson's novel values tradition not for itself but for its potential community and family benefits. Rudy uses Obeah to break his family relationships, transforming his daughter Mi-Jeanne into a spiritual slave or duppy[11] and demanding that his minions kill his wife and granddaughter to satisfy the demands of the Canadian prime minister for a human heart. When Ti-Jeanne matches her Obeah against Rudy's, she succeeds because she has built connections with others in the community. The children find her an escape path, and she mitigates the effects of Rudy's duppy bowl by appealing to Mi-Jeanne's motherly love. Although the duppy Mi-Jeanne *must* obey Rudy's order to kill Ti-Jeanne, Mi-Jeanne postpones carrying out the order to give her daughter time to save herself.

Hopkinson argues that breaking down the binaries of Caribbean versus Canadian or traditional versus technological does not necessarily produce positive results. Rudy, after all, uses Obeah to support the drug trade and his plush Western lifestyle in the midst of Toronto's destruction. Instead, Hopkinson suggests that diy skills and the mixture of modern and traditional Caribbean lessons occur most productively in concert with community organizing. Stepping outside of one's individual interests and accepting social and family ties helps transform diy skills into a more egalitarian community. The "Burn" is at its best when residents pool their "neoprimitive" skills at the market or when Ti-Jeanne seeks help from her family members or the wandering children. Diy skills are not the key to a better society, but Hopkinson argues that they help when those who practice them are willing to learn, teach, and interact with others. When Ti-Jeanne finally becomes a healer and a seer woman like her grandmother, she has reason to connect with others, offering her skills and building relationships that lead her to feel that burned-out Toronto is a genuine home.

Hopkinson's perspective about blending skill development with community organizing may seem obvious, but it can be a useful reminder for anarchists struggling to integrate community activism and personal lifestyle changes. One project that attracts many anarchists is the squatting movement—and, in part, the attraction grows out of the fact that many anarchists are squatters who want to avoid rent and wage labor. Aware that their status as squatters can sometimes trigger gentrification in poor neighborhoods, many anarchists participate in antigentrification projects or homeless advocacy groups. In New York City, for example, a long history of squatting and "homesteading" has linked anarchists to community members and the homeless.[12] In 1987, a local activist started the Inner City Press, a group that organizes and defends squats for willing participants. Since then, it has occupied many buildings, establishing and attempting to renovate housing for both anarchist activists and local working-class citizens (Bearak). After numerous showdowns with police over eviction orders, Inner City Press and several other groups of New York City squatters earned the right to stay in 2002, on the condition that they bring the buildings up to code (Ferguson). Squatting projects like this in New York and elsewhere force anarchist squatters to immerse themselves in local politics of race, poverty, and housing while also developing their diy skills. Residents in the squats learn to pirate electricity, replace plumbing, and set up alternative heating systems, and they frequently set up community gardens for vegetables and fruits, developing skills to benefit poor urban communities (Ferguson).

In these squatting scenarios, which have only become more popular in the wake of the recent foreclosure crisis, anarchist diy abilities are essential both for survival and for gaining community support. Homesteading has long had substantial public support in New York City because of its association with hard work and personal improvement, whereas the notion of living "rent free" has not. City Councilmember Margarita Lopez made this distinction to the *Village Voice* in 2002, when the squatters' settlements were approved as homesteads:

> Before, the majority of the people were single white individuals who came from outside the neighborhood. It was easy to identify them; they had Mohawks or whatever you call those things. They were in total rebellion with everybody and everything. They were a movement against the rental buildings, because the people believed everything should be free and that nobody should ever pay. (Ferguson)

Village Voice reporter Ferguson goes on to remark that "In fact, quite a few of the folks living in these buildings were once young punks and wild-eyed idealists. But for every radical in the streets, there were always many more who shunned the spotlight, quietly working to carve out homes inside their rubble-strewn buildings." Ferguson and Lopez contrast punk anarchists with the "hard-working" squatters who are worthy of homestead rights, though Ferguson notes that many of the hard workers were *once* "young punks and wild-eyed idealists." She indicates that the willingness to work rather than simply defy property rights transforms activists from outsiders into part of the community. Anarchist squatter Rick Van Savage confirms this phenomenon: "If you have been there for a number of years, and you are really trying to incorporate people from the neighborhood into your squat, and you are not just a bunch of white suburban kids coming in for the summer, they will be much more sympathetic" (Van Savage). In New York's squats, the nonanarchist community includes many Latino/a and African-American residents. Consequently, developing skills that foster relationships between anarchists and fellow squatters means confronting the reasons that anarchism is a majority-white movement and attempting to assuage these problems.

This has become even more significant in the 2009 recession and foreclosure crisis. In Miami, a black radical organization known as Take Back the Land, led by Max Rameau, has begun claiming foreclosed houses and installing original residents or homeless families into them. Take Back the Land has received national media coverage, and although it is an all-black group, members have been willing to cooperate with white radicals from the anarchist tradition, including the local Lake Worth Global Justice group (Rameau 51). Movements like this offer an opening for anarchists to use their diy skills and their knowledge as squatters to build alliances with the black left.[13] In such cases, diy skills can be translated into "survival skills" that are applicable in twenty-first-century urban life. Instead of glorifying urban "hunting and gathering," anarchists become involved in issues of economic and racial justice. They suggest that any alternative lifestyle will be filtered through the infrastructure of industry and technology. There is no way to return to the past but only to "repurpose" civilization's tools. Remnants of civilization become "artifacts" (members of Urban Scout's *Rewild.info* forum use this term to refer to civilization's items), and in this new world, artifacts of the past will be used rather than simply displayed or studied. Nalo Hopkinson also emphasizes this point when she houses her protagonists in a nineteenth-century farmhouse that, in "civilized" Toronto, used to be a museum. There, children and families could watch actors take on the roles of farmers, milking cows and collecting eggs from the henhouse (34). In industrialized Toronto, the nineteenth-century farm was a source of entertainment. In "the Burn," however, the farmhouse takes on its formerly fictional roles. Ti-Jeanne and Gros Jeanne inhabit the rooms, cook on a wood stove, and dig their own outhouse to replace the public bathrooms. In one sense, this use of the farmhouse indicates a shift to an earlier era when nineteenth-century technologies were necessary. In another sense, the display house is just one more remnant of civilization that can be "repurposed" for postapocalyptic use. Like Urban Scout, they bring the museum to life by making it simply another place for human habitation, not a place to judge relative levels of progress or social development.

Taking Out the Dams

This ability to incorporate *both* industrial and "primitive" landscapes allows anarchists and writers like Nalo Hopkinson and Octavia Butler to combine dystopia with the promise of a just future. Novelist Cormac McCarthy demonstrates the consequences of refusing this combination in his 2006 novel *The Road*, which portrays a world left in ashes by an undefined cataclysm that kills nearly all animal and plant life. Physical structures and a small human population remain. In a conversation between the two main characters, a child asks his father about the relationship between industrial infrastructure and life:

> Will the dam be there for a long time?
>
> I think so. It's made of concrete. It will probably be here for hundreds of years. Thousands, even.
>
> Do you think there are fish in the lake?
>
> No there's nothing in the lake. (17)

Anarchists maintain a different perspective, and for them, the dam is a poignant symbol. Dams are environmentalist shorthand for harmful industrial structures, as they flood animal and human habitats and destroy rivers that fish like salmon need to spawn. Edward Abbey's famous 1975 novel *The Monkey Wrench Gang* revolves around a desire to bomb the Glen Canyon dam, and anticivilization activist Derrick Jensen employs the dam as the symbol of civilization, using the phrase "taking out dams" as a metaphor for resistance (306). By referencing a dam as an example of the surviving infrastructure, McCarthy offers an extremely pessimistic view of the environment's future. Anarchists, by contrast, do not see the dam as a permanent structure that will outlive the fish. Abbey's monkey wrenchers and Jensen's saboteurs are lurking in the background, ready to destroy the dams and renew the environmental equilibrium. Both fish and humans will survive, living in, on, and around the ruins of industry. This anarchist reading of the dam transforms the metaphors of the industrial and the primitive, making them into a new tool for the future.

This, of course, is the most optimistic anarchist vision of a postcivilization world. Hopkinson and Butler are more negative than anarcho-primitivists about the experience of civilization's collapse, and they stress that the process of destroying civilization will be a costly one, especially for people of color. Anarchists who reject work *choose* to be homeless, unemployed scavengers, and they have the ability to move in and out of such a status, whereas the characters in Butler's and Hopkinson's stories are relegated to scarcity by social and economic status.

As the ranks of people of color in the anarchist community increase, they have begun to challenge their comrades on some of these problems. The first Anarchist People of Color Conference, held in 2003, took some steps in this direction, and participants followed up by publishing a two-volume collection titled *Our Culture, Our Resistance* and establishing a website known as *Illegal Voices* (Aguilar). The essays in these forums, in addition to a growing number of other zines and websites, address the race politics of contemporary anarchists. Many of the writers came to anarchism because of its antihierarchical structures. Former Black Panther Ashanti Alston, for instance, sees anarchism as both a corrective to the BPP's hierarchical structure and a fulfillment of its core values. He feels that the Panthers gave too much power to their leadership and that only anarchism offers *all* power to the people, as a famous Panther chant had promised. Other young radicals of color are attracted to anarchist militancy, including a willingness to take physical risks that recalls the daring behavior of Panther predecessors. As African-American anarchist Greg Lewis puts it in *Our Culture, Our Resistance*, "The anarchists did things. They took over buildings and lived in them, they chased the Nazis off the streets, [and] they would go to community meetings and blast the so-called 'experts' on homelessness or youth issues" (77).

Anarchists of color criticize their peers, however, when they fail to understand race as a problem worthy of direct action tactics. Victoria Law, a Chinese-American activist, recalls being accused of instilling notions of authority and hierarchy in her daughter by sending her to preschool. Law, however, saw preschool as a space for her daughter to meet other Chinese children, learn Cantonese, and feel comfortable with her ethnicity. Fellow activists saw *refusing* school as a radical act, but they did not view immersion in a culturally diverse setting as a similar statement.

The Planting Seeds Community Awareness Project combats similar misunderstandings in a zine titled *Answers for White People on Appropriation, Hair and Anti-Racist Struggle*. Citing mohawks as imitations of traditional Native American hairstyles and dreadlocks as part of the African diaspora's Rastafarian tradition, authors Colin Donovan and Qwo-Li Driskill request that white activists refrain from wearing them: "A true appreciation of other cultures," they write, "means fighting against the forces trying to destroy them, not taking them on as your own" (3). Donovan and Driskill insist that metaphorical and cultural histories of race matter. They ask anarchists to see cultural choices within American histories of race even as they recognize the resistant possibilities of anarchism. Critiques like these from anarchist people of color supplement the commentary of fiction writers like Butler and Hopkinson. Together, writers and fellow anarchists urge their activist peers to analyze the histories, contexts, and implications of their metaphors because these metaphors are essential building blocks of direct action.

Conclusion

I have argued for the value of political language, but I want to end by returning to the question of propaganda. Political speech is ultimately about persuasion, and it forces us to consider the ethics of persuading others. The television show *Mad Men*, which traces the professional and personal lives of 1960s-era advertising executives, offers one perspective on the ethics of persuasion by portraying advertising as an art form. Although the show's creators acknowledge the corrupt motives of some of their characters, they offer little ethical analysis of the commercial messages. The young creative talent Peggy Olson struggles to answer the political critiques of radicals in the emerging counterculture around her, but the firm's creative "genius" Don Draper reassures her that advertising deserves respect as both commerce and culture. Perhaps it is a problem to see too much aesthetic value in persuasive speech—it allows us to minimize the real motivations of its creators. Ethical, transparent communication should be a goal for political speech. Today, however, in a media-rich world where our attention is under siege by ads, political messages, tweets, and Facebook entries, political movements must work even harder to compete for public attention. And those who succeed may feel that they have to do so by corrupt methods. After all, George W. Bush successfully built a false link between Iraq and September 11 simply by repeatedly associating the two. Even when he disclaimed the connection, it remained ingrained in the public consciousness. This was a savvy rhetorical tactic that offers plenty of fodder for academic critical analysis, but it is not an ethical use of political language.

Great literature can capture the reality of political or existential conflicts so beautifully because it does not have to guide pragmatic decisions. Toni Morrison's 1987 novel *Beloved* shows us the tragedy of broken family bonds in slavery and asks us to question the social and psychological triggers that might lead a mother to kill her children. And although Morrison might have an opinion on how the justice system or our culture should have responded to the crime of Margaret Garner, her historical inspiration, the author does not have to put her protagonist Sethe on trial in the real world. Readers end with philosophical questions but not necessarily a firm view of whether and how a woman who kills her children in such circumstances should be punished.

Political language lacks the luxury of ambiguity because it asks for action. Although the same questions and uncertainties exist, political speakers can represent them only as a prelude to a decision. And listeners are often uncomfortable making decisions based on complex, conflicting, or fraught evidence. We are more likely to support action if the decision seems clear and simple. When ambivalent themes appear in the imagery of political organizations like the Black Panthers, it often reflects ideological splits and anxiety about how to make the right political decisions. Such uncertainties are ethically acceptable, but they can often make it difficult for an organization to achieve—or even fully define—its political goals. It is no wonder, then, that some of the most successful examples of political speech are spectacular in both language and imagery but morally questionable. Leni Riefenstahl captured Hitler's persuasive, mobilizing, and often visually compelling spectacle in *Triumph of the Will*—and the right-wing activist "Tea Partiers" of 2009 gain supporters by making wild but emotionally loaded associations between Barack Obama and Hitler.

Obama himself, on the other hand, attempts to appeal to populist enthusiasm while delivering complex messages about the decisions he makes. The success of this model of political rhetoric and action remains to be seen, especially in an age that privileges sound bites over extended arguments. His strategies, even if they are successful in regaining momentum on the liberal left, will not translate easily to political actors who do not have the benefit of the presidency, a remarkably beautiful and photogenic family, and the public enthusiasm generated by the end of the Bush era. Moreover, activists for radical change may not wish to imitate Obama's actions and rhetoric, which stress moderation, pragmatism, and compromise, not radicalism.

The interaction between Obama and his critics, however, represents the way that the American language of radical political change continues to be bound up in race. In his case it appears in a different form than it did for the Black Panthers or anarcho-primitivists. Obama came of age listening to the language of radicalism, and his connection to liberation theologian Jeremiah Wright betrays the aesthetic and emotional appeal that radicalism had for him. At the edges, where Wright's speech loses touch with intellectual complexity, however, it became an embarrassment to Obama. When Wright spoke of the "United States of KKK-A" or when he shouted "God damn America"—phrases that belonged to the Black Power era of indignation and that would have flowed easily from the lips of Panthers or LRBW members—he privileged the aesthetics of anger and insurgency over those of electoral politics (R. Goldman). Wright's ability to motivate and inspire the black community through language became a literary example for Obama. After all, Obama's second book, *The Audacity of Hope*, takes its title from a moving speech Wright delivered in 1988 ("Wright's 'Audacity to Hope' Sermon"). He captured Wright's potent turns of phrase while tempering the fiery rhythms and vocalizations of the black church for his own more staid persona.

Obama's moderate Democratic politics and his rhetoric rooted in black radicalism were persuasive enough to elicit enthusiasm among those on the far left who were willing to support the Democratic Party—or at least to vote for it. Former SDS leader Tom Hayden and well-known progressives Bill Fletcher, Jr., Barbara Ehrenreich, and Danny Glover published an editorial in the *Nation* and a variety of other left-leaning publications in early 2008 that declared Obama's candidacy a sign that "the future has arrived." "There is no doubt," they added, "that the campaign is a social movement, one greater than the candidate himself ever imagined." The piece was supplemented by a blog and website under the name *Progressives for Obama*, which attracted an array of publicly left-wing supporters, including former

1960s-era activists and academics who publish on labor rights and antiracist organizing. Radical academic writers Ariel Dorfman, Robin D. G. Kelley, and Cornel West made the list, as did former SDS members Robert Pardun and Todd Gitlin, along with one-time Weatherman Mark Rudd. At Obama's inauguration, a performance by folk singer Pete Seeger confirmed that avowed left-wing radicals were celebrating the election of the first African-American president as earnestly as liberal Democrats and America's black population at large.

This does not mean, however, that the radical left in the United States saw Obama as a radical candidate. Indeed, though some may have voted for him, many contemporary activists could not summon the kind of enthusiasm that Hayden, Fletcher, Glover, and Ehrenreich did. Anarcho-syndicalist academic and political scholar Noam Chomsky urged listeners to "vot[e] for Obama without illusions," while Pete Seeger admitted prior to the election that he "would've liked Kucinich" in addition to a modification in the electoral system to allow for instant recount voting (Chomsky; A. Green). Socialist groups around the country reminded members that Obama was fundamentally a Democrat, and as such, no harbinger of revolution: the socialist organization Solidarity urged members to support third-party reforms to the electoral system by voting for Green Party candidate Cynthia McKinney, while Freedom Road Socialist Organization advocated a "vote against McCain" without explicitly encouraging a vote for Obama, "the candidate of the Democratic Party, the other party of big business" ("The 2008 Elections"; Freedom Road Socialist Organization). Likewise, in the International Socialist Organization's newspaper *Socialist Worker*, Todd Chretien argued that "voting and giving political support to Barack Obama and the Democratic Party will weaken the fight for a fundamentally different kind of world, a socialist world" (Chretien). Anarchists largely took a similar approach, though they were less likely to consider third-party candidates and more likely to renounce the elections altogether. Those at CrimethInc. led a "counterelection" campaign, and a diverse set of anarchists and radical leftists turned out at both the Republican National Convention and the Democratic National Convention to express their discontent with the limited options of the American electoral system. Even among those on the radical left who were positive about Obama, Hayden and company's attitude was much less common than the "positive opposition" advocated by Malik Miah, a member of Solidarity who writes for its journal *Against the Current.* As Miah noted in the run-up to the election, Obama's victory would be "relative progress but not a solution to underlying class and social issues." He encouraged socialists to vote for a third-party candidate without actively disparaging or opposing Obama supporters, allowing that their enthusiasm for a black president was warranted even if Obama's politics were fundamentally flawed.

Whereas leftists themselves were often reluctant to claim Obama, many conservatives locked onto him as the incarnation of leftist radicalism. In part, this had to do with his link to Wright and his much more tenuous link to former Weatherman Bill Ayers, both of which received exhaustive press during the elections. On another level, however, Obama's campaign message of "change" and his status as the first African-American president called up the longtime associations Americans have between race and radical change. American leftists have long associated change with the "primitive/industrial" binary—and although they haven't always seen it as a dialogue about race, discussions of radicalism and uses of this binary in particular regularly return to race. American right-wingers in the years following Obama's election, on the other hand, see a black President as a symbol of radical change. He is not simply a political opponent but a sign of coming socialism or even, paradoxically, fascism. Radical change and race, they suggest, go hand in hand. Moderate, compromising rhetoric and continuations of the wars in Iraq and Afghanistan notwithstanding, Obama's face evokes the visceral fear of socialism.

It does so because our nation's fundamental changes have always been steeped in discussions of race relations. The American Revolution brought with it questions of slavery and citizenship, the expansion of the nation elicited questions about how to deal with Native American difference within the nation, the Civil War centered on the question of slavery, and the cultural changes of the 1960s came through and alongside the Civil Rights Movement. Change and race have literally gone hand in hand throughout American history, and they have accompanied one another metaphorically as well. The primitive/industrial binary that attracts those who want social change cannot be separated from metaphors and stereotypes of race.

The language of the right radicalism against Obama, then, confirms the link between American change and race on several fronts. Right-wing radicals see racial conflict as a primary impetus for radical change, and they want to invoke metaphors of racial oppression for their own benefit while marking Obama's race as a symbol of looming socialism. The twenty-first-century "Tea Party Patriots," as they identify themselves, resist Obama's national government in favor of states' rights. Like radical leftists, they envision an ideal past, though theirs is not a utopian tribal lifestyle but a return to the American origins of the Revolution. The Tea Partiers fancy themselves antitaxation advocates struggling, by turns, against an imperialist monarchy, a fascist government, or a socialist "welfare state." They identify with a time of rebellion against colonial rule, when there was no democratic representation for colonists in the British colonial structure. The Tea Partiers, then, see Obama not as a corrupt elected official but as a symbol of colonial oppression. And although they don't make this connection explicit, the era that they long for was also a period when black Americans were slaves rather than political leaders. They don't envision conservative change through the lens of the industrial and the primitive, but their vision of nostalgic change also has racial implications.

In a 2010 *New Yorker* piece about the Tea Party, Sean Wilentz comes to the opposite conclusion—that Tea Party radicalism is an inheritor of John Birch Society conspiracy theories concerning the Federal Reserve and the IRS. Wilentz reminds us that many radical conservatives, like their John Birch Society predecessors, identify Woodrow Wilson and Teddy Roosevelt as the beginning point of this American slide into "socialism." While he concedes that racial fears have arisen in some of Tea Party discourse, Wilentz insists that "'socialist' is not a racial slur" (37). On the one hand, the statement is self-evident. The term "socialism" has been used as an all-purpose slur against liberals as well as radicals in the United States, and the Cold War relationship with the Soviet Union prompted the American public to associate socialism with its Russian enemies. However, on another level, fears of socialism in America are frequently wrapped up in anxiety about racial equality. The height of the Cold War and the rise of the John Birch Society coincided with the beginnings of the Civil Rights Movement. Racial equality and class solidarity across race were key beliefs for socialists in this time period, and the John Birch Society, in turn, opposed the Civil Rights Movement on the ground that it was organized by Communists. Likewise, in 2009, the emergence of Birch-like conservative radicalism coincided with the election of a black president and the accompanying accusation that he is not a United States citizen. Fears of socialism and fears of black power frequently emerge together. Wilentz is right that race is not the only factor in the Tea Party's sudden emergence, but we shouldn't downplay its role. Socialism can, in certain cases, be a racial slur. To many radical conservatives, frightening social change comes in the guise of the Native American or the African American—through the voice of the oppressed victim. Those who are racially oppressed demand equality and government protection—civil rights—that strike fear in the hearts of those who fundamentally reject government programs, government protection, "special treatment," or collectivist ideas. As a result, Obama's very status as the first black President seems to make him a symbol for socialism. Racial conflict has brought radical change in the past, and Tea Partiers see Obama's black identity as a portent of more radical change.

By identifying with the Boston Tea Party, however, these conservative radicals also position themselves as the *colonized*—a term we now associate with racial minorities. The historical "Tea Partiers," who were colonists but not racial minorities, also made the association between colonization and racial oppression in their attempt to establish a new American cultural identity separate from their British rulers. As Philip Deloria notes in his study *Playing Indian*, at least one of the original Boston Tea Party participants famously dressed as a Native American—in part as a statement of American *difference* from Britain. Americans identified with natives in their rebellion, not with the British, and the tea they dumped into the ocean revealed disdain for their own links to British culture. Even as the Native American costume recalled British traditions of carnivalesque misrule and spoke to the importance of tea in both American and British culture, the Boston

Tea Party advocated a cultural as well as a political break with England (Deloria 25). By taking on the role of the colonized racial "other," Tea Partiers of 1773 and 2010 portray radical political change through the medium of racial and cultural conflict. Twenty-first-century Tea Party Patriots may not dress like Native Americans or African Americans, but they do don the mantle of white victimhood by citing Affirmative Action and Mexican immigration as signs of "favoritism" toward racial minorities or a threat to the culture at large. They view themselves as victims while also rejecting Obama as a symbol of black victim-hood, illustrating their understanding that American change can't be decoupled from racial metaphors, even if it is the Tea Party's brand of individualist, conservative change.

The "otherness" that Tea Partiers claim for themselves, of course, is simply white identity cast in the light of victimhood, and the change that this kind of victimhood brings is portrayed as comforting in its return to American foundations—not to a "primitive" past but to a past of secure boundaries between whites and blacks and opportunities for geographical and economic expansion. Obama's African-American identity, on the other hand, poses the threat of "primitive" chaos. At rallies, posters carried by some Tea Partiers even reference racist visions of the primitive by creating images of Obama in which the pixels are monkeys or by depicting him as a half-clothed witch doctor. In these cases, the Tea Partiers, like their Revolutionary ancestors, are separating themselves both culturally and politically from their political leader, but they are identifying with the tradition of white power rather than the supposed freedom, lawlessness, and political oppression of the Native American. They associate Obama's brand of change with racial fears in addition to radical socialism.

Obama himself works hard to separate his vision of change from socialism and primitivism. In part, he does so to distance himself from the more radical tenets of black nationalism, but he is also making a point about political rhetoric. He hints that romanticizing primitive or industrial utopias is problematic, and his own brand of pragmatism includes an imperfect world constantly in the process of modification through community organizing, band-aid solutions, and political com-promises. There is much to admire in this attitude, and Obama's skills as a public speaker certainly continue to offer a "dream" of a better future—even as this dream refuses to submit to a simple romanticism often associated with such dreams. Moreover, his rhetoric is intentionally inclusive. His well-received speech "A More Perfect Union," delivered during the 2008 campaign election about the state of racial relations in the United States, asked white listeners to appreciate black anger and radical rhetoric even as it requested that black listeners comprehend the anger and lingering racism of whites who feel disenfranchised. As a politician, of course, Obama did not dismantle the primitivist attitudes of the US state, which express themselves in occupation, invasion, and economic pressure on nations that America deems "backward" or in need of guidance. His failure to translate rhetoric into genuine victories against climate change, corporate exploitation of workers, and military spending increased levels of skepticism among even his most fervent supporters from 2008. Nonetheless, Obama's face and voice remind Americans that we envision radical leftist change through the lens of race relations. Those who oppose such change see socialism in Obama's face, while those who support leftist perspectives *want* to see hope for such change in him, even as they realistically understand that, as the current bearer of American international power, he will not and cannot support such change. Obama's position forces us at least to see and acknowledge this knot of meaning in American culture. Does it matter that we associate race and leftist radicalism? There is a distinguished history of leftist African Americans and a genuine relationship between radical politics and abolitionist, antiracist causes. But nostalgic, romantic images of the industrial and the primitive, with all of their generalizations and imperialist histories, have also hampered our ability to see race in our discussions of change, and they have often simplified what should be complex and more pragmatic discussions of political realities. Obama teaches us the value of political language that is direct and straightforward about its pragmatic implications and contradictions. These lessons need not come with Obama's own moderate political perspective. Although the Black Panthers, the LRBW, the IS, the SWP, and many neoprimitive anarchists employ intricate, compelling, and often beautiful rhetoric, the complexity requires historical and literary interpretation. This is satisfying, perhaps, for academic critics, but is it the most productive political strategy? Would such rhetorical tactics be better if they were paired with Obama's discussions of implications and political difficulties? Would it have been better, for instance, for the Black Panthers to discuss candidly their anxiety about the ethical and legal implications of the phrase "kill the cops," or would that have killed the movement's fire? Can a movement build a more sustainable, long-term base with a mixture of engaging rhetoric and philosophical discussions?

Regardless of his specific political perspective, Obama has brought these questions to the surface. The primitive and industrial metaphors, in his rhetoric, reveal their romantic flaws. In their place, however, Obama has sometimes presented technology as a romantic solution to global warming and compromise as an idealistic way of overcoming conflicts. In a speech before the United Nations in September 2009, he spoke of "unleash[ing] the creative power of our best scientists, engineers, and entrepreneurs to build a better world," promising his listeners that technology would step forward as an environmental savior even while acknowledging the difficulties of this process ("Obama's Speech on Climate Change"). The rhetoric of technology is the new romantic industrial language. Although technology can certainly be different from industry, and the information age has made dramatic changes in the way consumers *relate* to technology, the term *technology* as a descriptor in the information age allows twenty-first-century political thinkers to use romantic visions of technology without evoking the Marxist history of *industrial* utopia. Many leftist radicals still cling to their industrial and primitive visions—though in constantly modified forms—and Obama's technologically based solution to global warming also has romantic overtones.

Moreover, there may be value in rhetoric that requires interpretation—as long as political speakers offer viewers the tools they need to make those interpretations. One twenty-first-century political movement makes the case that interpretation might be a necessary and desirable part of engaging with politics. The Beehive Collective, centered in Maine and broadly based in the anarchist tradition, produces radical artwork, especially large posters, which it distributes for free in the communities affected by the issue in the illustration. These posters are often commissioned by local activists, and the Collective bases its intricate images on extensive discussions with community members. All of their illustrations use animals as subjects (bees and ants are the most common), and they do so to depict the confluence of environmentalism with labor rights, human rights, feminism, and antiracism. Using a Latin American saying, "Revolution is the work of ants" as its inspiration, the Beehive depicts tiny ants working together as they tunnel under systems of oppression, carry heavy weights, and take on enormous political tasks (The Beehive Design Collective, *Free Trade Area of the Americas*).

The Beehive's drawings provide a big-picture view of resistance and oppression while demonstrating how that view is composed of millions of tiny, complicated, almost invisible interactions. Their posters are so good at depicting a swarm of political insects that they are almost impossible to comprehend at first glance. And although members insist that alternate interpretations are welcome, the Beehive also narrates its art through explanatory pamphlets and speaking tours that display the posters. The networks they depict, including the insidious Free Trade Area of the Americas spider web and the promising network of underground ant burrows, are literally enormous: the posters can stretch up to six feet. Each ant, however, works from its own position as just one player in the international activist network; and although it knows that the network exists, it might not be able to see the full scope of it. Likewise, even the human viewers who can see the whole network on the poster may not be able to comprehend it as a coherent narrative without breaking it into component parts.

The artists are self-conscious about the history of animal metaphors, consulting with local activists about the connotations of using certain animals to represent groups of people. As a result, the Beehive establishes a new set of images that are adamantly environmentalist without being racialized. In their illustrations, the actions of ants and bees are not determined by their species. Either creature can be a worker, an activist, or an oppressor, depending on the context or the individual. And the value the Beehive artists place on biodiversity translates into a celebration of political diversity as well.

By creating such opaque, complicated illustrations, the Beehive announces to viewers that they *must* critically analyze the political texts in front of them. It isn't possible to interpret their statements at face value. This is the flip side of Obama's strategy of incorporating his philosophical conflicts into public speeches. There is nothing wrong, the Beehive Collective insists, with political rhetoric and imagery that requires interpretation—as long as the public actually *does* interpret it. Black Panther calls to "off the pigs" and neoprimitivist diatribes about the end of civilization, by contrast, can be understood simply without interpretation, and although critical analysis can illuminate the complexities of their political perspectives, many listeners absorb them as mere propaganda. Romantic language and overblown rhetoric have a place in mobilization, but the public needs to see them in tandem with lucid analyses or at least imperatives to analyze.

Literature is powerful because it naturally achieves the same thing as the Beehive Collective. Literature announces its representational status, and viewers must parse out the meaning of fictional events and figurative language. Although literary criticism's "hermeneutics of suspicion" has been lambasted recently as an overly politicized and cynical way to demean great artists by interpreting their work with a skeptical eye, a "hermeneutics of suspicion" might be valuable for political language. Suspicion is a useful analytical strategy when it comes to radical change. Mere celebration of abstract values like solidarity, justice, or equality will leave us unequipped to deal with the real problems that accompany any kind of political project. By combining literary and political language in clear ways, political activists can encourage the kind of deep analysis that allows for complexity rather than propaganda. It isn't new for radicals to consider these kinds of questions. Activists have always discussed the philosophical and ethical implications of their decisions, but they typically do so within their organizational structures. Their public rhetoric rarely exposes the striations that run through group ideology. A pragmatic radical rhetoric can and should make these ethical questions public, admitting ideological weaknesses and acknowledging the opposition's valid critiques with a sense of confidence that they can be managed. The line between propaganda and literary-caliber political rhetoric does not separate reason from emotion but delineates between absolute certainty and the courage to admit doubt, anxiety, and conflict in the process of organizing radical change.

Notes

Introduction

1. I will use quotes to mark the "primitive" unless referring specifically to primitive metaphors because I do not mean to use this often derogatory term literally. Instead, I am invoking a history of representations associated with the word. I will not use quotes to set off the industrial, however, simply because it does not evoke negative connotations. This should not suggest that I believe the industrial is a simple term that describes certain objects or environments unequivocally.

2. See JanMohamed's "The Economy of Manichean Allegory" for more on how binary categories define the colonizer and colonized in metaphysical rather than social, cultural, or historical ways.

3. See McClintock's *Imperial Leather* and Robert J. C. Young's *Colonial Desire* for theories of racial difference in the nineteenth century.

4. See Barnard's *Hunter-Gatherers in History, Archaeology and Anthropology* and Panter-Brick, Layton, and Rowley-Conwy's *Hunter-Gatherers: An Interdisciplinary Perspective* for a history of hunter-gatherer studies.

5. The interview originally appeared in André Malraux's 1974 *La Tête d'obsidienne*.

6. The popularity of black American dancer Josephine Baker suggests that African-American culture also contributed to European understandings of the "primitive." Although the paintings have been lost, it is believed that Baker posed for Picasso, making explicit the connection between French pop culture's fascination with an African-American "primitive" and the Cubist interest in "primitive" aesthetics (Wood 138–39; Mao and Walkowitz 172). See Tyler Stovall's *Paris Noir* for more links between European modernism and African-American culture.

7. Primitivist metaphors had currency in interracial and majority white organizations as well. The countercultures of the 1960s embraced primitivist tropes as alternate social ideals, channeling the "primitive" through communes or the adoption of Eastern and tribal religious practices. In doing so, they replicated both primitivist and Orientalist assumptions about the "Other" even as they distanced themselves from the oppression of Western culture.

Chapter 1

1. The ten demands are as follows:

1. We want freedom. We want power to determine the destiny of our Black Community. . . . 2. We want full employment for our people. . . . 3. We want an end to the robbery by the white man of our Black Community. . . . 4. We want decent housing, fit for shelter of human beings. . . . 5. We want education for our people that exposes the true nature of this decadent American society. We want education that teaches us our true history and our role in the present-day society. . . . 6. We want all black men to be exempt from military service. . . . 7. We want an immediate end to POLICE BRUTALITY and MURDER of black people. . . . 8. We want freedom for all black men held in federal, state, county and city prisons and jails. . . . 9. We want all black people when brought to trial to be tried in court by a jury of their peer group or people from their black communities, as defined by the Constitution of the United States. . . . 10. We want land, bread, housing, education, clothing, justice and peace. And as our major political objective, a United Nations supervised plebiscite to be held throughout the black colony in which only black colonial subjects will be allowed to participate for the purpose of determining the will of black people as to their national destiny. . . . (Foner, *The Black Panthers Speak* 2–6)

2. The North American panther does not appear in an all-black, or melanistic, form. As a result, the "black panther" is an exotic and even mythic figure in the United States, and it has been the subject of many local legends and rumored sightings.

3. Baker's animal was a spotted feline referred to alternately in the press as a leopard, panther, or cheetah. Ean Wood argues that the animal was in fact a cheetah (165).

4. Many of these groups were short-lived, and they did not all share the same ideological perspectives. After joining the fray, the BPP forced the Oakland Black Panther Party to change its name to the Black Panther Political Party and subsequently overpowered it entirely (Smethurst, *The Black Arts Movement* 302).

5. Some police officers did try to rescue the "pig." Geronimo Pratt recalls that a fellow Panther saw a scoreboard in an LA station reading "Pigs 11, Panthers 0," and Erika Doss notes that some officers created "P.I.G." buttons for pride, integrity, and guts (Olsen 231; Doss 186).

6. A buba is a loose-fitting Nigerian Yoruba shirt worn by either men or women.

7. Churchill and Vander Wall reproduce FBI documents illustrating the government's escalation of the conflict between Us and the BPP, including threatening cartoons sent to both organizations by the FBI on behalf of the other organization. M. Wesley Swearingen, a former FBI agent, claims that the Us members involved in the shootout were infiltrators working for the FBI.

8. Stanford's Huey P. Newton Foundation Records contain evidence of FBI surveillance. For more on Hampton, see Wilkins and Clark.

9. Jimmy Garrett's *We Own the Night* portrays a dying revolutionary who shoots his mother for threatening to betray the cause, and Ed Bullins's *Death List* depicts a political movement with an ever-growing list of enemies that includes mainstream civil rights figures like Martin Luther King, Sr.

10. Today, many activists reject the term *Third World* in favor of the *global South*. I employ *Third World* because it was the accepted terminology during the New Left period. At the time, activists viewed "Third World" solidarity as positive and nonderogatory.

11. His codefendants were white antiwar activists Abbie Hoffman, Jerry Rubin, Dave Dellinger, Rennie Davis, Tom Hayden, Lee Weiner, and John Froines.

12. Copyright restrictions prevent me from duplicating the image of Seale bound and gagged, but it is visible on the cover of the *Seize the Time* video at <http://www.bobbyseale.com/html/books.htm>

13. See Self for a description of these processes in Oakland.

14. Foner's *Organized Labor* traces the history of race and organized labor.

15. See Pritchett's *Brownsville, Brooklyn*; Gordon's *Why They Couldn't Wait*; Ritterband's "Ethnic Power and the Public Schools"; and Podair's *The*

Strike that Changed New York for more on Brownsville. In 1970, when the *Black Panther* article appeared, Brownsville had just emerged from a racially divisive struggle between Jewish, Puerto Rican, and African-American communities over control of the school system (Gordon 4).

16. As the Vietnam War escalated during 1965 and 1966, approximately 21% of US casualties were African Americans, though the percentage of blacks in the total population was only 11% (Binkin, et al. 76). Anger over this racial disparity led the military to restructure combat assignments, and casualties for blacks reverted to 11.5% of the total by 1969 (Segal and Segal 21–22; Binkin, et al.76). Today, however, the problem persists. In 2002, African Americans accounted for 22% of enlisted men and women, compared to 13% of the overall American population (Segal and Segal 21–22).

17. Working for the Panthers could also be alienating. See Austin 273–84 for elaboration on Panthers' daily activities.

18. Air Force Ones are a popular basketball shoe.

Chapter 2

1. A "wildcat" is a strike that has not been sanctioned by the union. Corporations and unions often agree to "no-strike clauses" that permit legal strikes only during the contract negotiation period. Wildcats are unapproved worker protests.

2. Historically, Hamtramck and its assembly plant were populated largely by Polish workers, and by the late 1960s young African Americans were entering the plant in large numbers.

3. Black presence in auto factories had been increasing for decades, but Detroit's July 1967 Great Rebellion sparked a larger influx of young African Americans. In the three months before November 1967, General Motors (GM) hired 12,200 new workers, 5,300 of whom were black (Widick 193; "G.M. Joins Campaign"). Chrysler and Ford admitted 4,000 and 5,000 black workers, respectively (Widick 193). Moreover, the UAW estimates that approximately 36% of Chrysler's workers in 1969 were less than 30. At GM and Ford the numbers were 33% and 30% (Foner, *Organized Labor* 411; "How Membership Has Changed").

4. *The Inner-City Voice* appeared under a variety of names. From its inception in October 1967 until summer 1968, it was the *Inner City Voice*. Between September 1968 and May 1969, the paper was replaced by Wayne

State's student paper the *South End*. When *ICV* returned in September 1969, it changed its name to *Sauti*, the word for "voice" in Swahili. Beginning in October 1969, it took the name *Sauti: The Inner-City Voice*, and by February 1970, the title had become the *Inner-City Voice*.

5. General Baker speaks only of men wearing the necklaces, though photographs of Black Panthers in the Bay Area around the same time period depict women wearing similar jewelry (Shames).

6. RAM was a revolutionary organization that advocated self-defense and was a major influence on the Black Arts Movement. Its largely clandestine actions make it difficult to trace, but several prominent League members, including General Baker and Glanton Dowdell, were active in RAM, and the group clearly had an influence on the League. The extent to which the two organizations were intertwined is uncertain.

The history of the Detroit Black Panther Party is similarly hazy. James Geschwender and Georgakas and Surkin suggest that the League assigned John Williams and Luke Tripp to establish a BPP chapter aligned with Newton and Seale's party as a way of influencing Panther recruits to support the League. Geschwender argues that this new Detroit BPP emerged in the spring of 1969, but according to testimony of a former Detroit Panther member during US Congressional Hearings on Internal Security, the Detroit chapter had been functioning since approximately 1966, suggesting that there may have been some overlap between the RAM Black Panther Party and the later Oakland affiliate (Geschwender, *Class, Race* 121; United States, *Black Panther Party, Part Three* 4,430–431).

7. It is unclear whether this meeting actually took place. The planning for it is recorded in the FBI's phone tap logs on the Black Panther's national office in Oakland.

8. According to John Taylor, a white radical in the plant who sympathized with ELRUM, such comments hurt ELRUM's reputation among many workers, both black and white ("ELRUM is Asking All Concerned"; Taylor).

9. Cooperation with whites was controversial. At a March 1971 meeting, for instance, Mike Hamlin complained that some members claimed to be unable to work with whites or behaved rudely to them (Bracey and Harley, Reel 9).

10.

We've spent century after century
us black children
trying to find and give our
love

but all we have found is injustice
in the eyes of the peace loving dove

century after century after torture
pain and strife
like days of old we're still being
sold black brothers, daughter and wife

but still we're not to be angry
or show signs of militancy

but just cast loving eyes to heaven
head bowed on our bloody
prayer worn knee

no Muslim movement says our black king
let them bomb our churches kill our
children democracy liberty will
ring

while black martyr's [*sic*] walk down hot
southern roads a greasy white finger
twitches and the barrel of a shotgun
roars

while the pope in his perfumed palace
welcomes bigots by the scores and
black steely eyed leadership sell
their bodies like common whores

no black power now young fellas that's
no way to get yourselves free, don't
burn down those filthy black
ghettoes never, don't speak of unity

cause this is the promised land

Oh say saint Malcolm can't you see
by the dawns [*sic*] stench and light

X slavemaster bringing fear to the east
cutting out hearts and kissing
sex symbols at night

but I am not to fight standing here
in the Mekong Delta with a punji stick
in my groin

eyes bloodshot bulging with terror
as I watch them X slave master my enemy
dragging bloody bodies across
the living color horizon
instilling fear into young black minds
and courage to exploit bloody atrocities into sad youthful white
     souls
to the tune of white soap operas
while long haired rape artists sing
while bigot strangle the sound of the bell
me black me standing here bleeding and going
to hell to the sound of the music I know so well
let freedom ring

let freedom ring while black martyrs walk down hot southern
     roads a greasy white finger twitches and the shotgun roars
KA PING KA PING KA PING

don't duck black brother don't cry and frown black sister damn
     fool don't you know that freedom rings
          let freedom ring
          let freedom ring
          let freedom ring to the rhythm of blond quivering hips
               while death sees angry loving black lips let freedom ring

11. "Our Thing Is DRUM" was published anonymously, and it
appeared regularly in League publications. The full text is below:

     Deep in the gloom
     of the firefilled pit
     Where the Dodge rolls down the line,

We challenge the doom
of dying in shit
While strangled by a swine . . .
. . . For hours and years
we've sweated tears
Trying to break our chain—But we broke our backs
and died in packs
To find our manhood slain. . . .
But now we stand—For DRUM's at hand
To lead our Freedom fight,
And from now til then
we'll unite like men—For now we know our might—
and damn the plantation
and the whole Dodge nation
For DRUM has dried our tears. [*sic*]
and now as we die
we've a different cry—For now we hold our spears!
U.A.W. is scum——[*sic*]
OUR THING IS DRUM!!!!!"

Chapter 3

1. The IS had a companion organization in Britain with the same name. Though the two groups were not formally linked, they maintained good relations. In 1977, the British IS transformed itself into the British Socialist Workers Party, which is unrelated to the American Socialist Workers Party. In this text, IS and SWP refer to the American organizations with those names.

2. See Marion Wilson Starling or Charles J. Heglar for more on the publication of pre–Civil War slave narratives.

3. The history of socialist organizations in the United States is dauntingly complex. To understand the backgrounds of different sects, several texts are helpful. Robin Kelley's *Hammer and Hoe* investigates the relationship between the Communist Party and black Americans in the 1930s; Breitman, Le Blanc, and Wald's *Trotskyism in the United States* and Robert J. Alexander's *International Trotskyism* provide a history of Trotskyist challengers to the Communist Party; and Max Elbaum's *Revolution in the Air* offers a discussion of Maoist sects in the 1980s.

For the purposes of this chapter, the organizational histories of American Trotskyists are most relevant, as both the IS and the SWP fall into this category. In 1934, the Communist League of America, Left Opposition of the Communist Party merged with the American Workers Party and took the name Workers Party, and in 1936 the Workers Party in turn dissolved itself into the larger Socialist Party. The one-time Workers Party members of the SP, however, were eventually forced out over political differences, and in 1938 this group formed the Socialist Workers Party. In 1940, a minority group of the SWP led by Max Shachtman left to form another incarnation of the Workers Party. From this point onward, "Shachtmanites" distinguished themselves from the SWP's "Cannonites." Shachtman's Workers Party eventually became the Independent Socialist League and later merged with the Socialist Party yet again. In 1967, a small group of SP members split to form the Independent Socialist Club, which would later become the IS (Fields).

The major political factor in the Shachtmanite split with the SWP was the characterization of the USSR. Shachtman saw the Soviet Union as a "bureaucratic collectivist" state whose new bureaucratic class had destroyed the "workers' state." As a result, Shachtman and his followers believed, the Soviet Union no longer warranted socialist allegiance. The SWP, on the other hand, continued to support the USSR, conditionally, as a "degenerated workers' state" (Alexander 795–96). Similar differences reemerged in the 1960s and '70s, when the SWP supported the Cuban Revolution, which the IS viewed more critically.

During the 1970s, both groups were at their height, having garnered membership from the dissolving New Left student movements. Today, the SWP remains a relatively small organization that still operates the Pathfinder Press. The IS had a more tortuous history. A "Left Faction" formed in the late 1970s, which argued against the IS's policy of pressuring students and academics to become workers and disputed the IS's position on radical developments in Portugal (Finkel, E-mail). In 1977, this group was expelled and went on to form the International Socialist Organization (ISO), which continues today and maintains a democratic centralist, Leninist tradition (Fisk, *Socialism from Below*; Finkel, E-mail). In 1979, another faction split from the IS over concerns that the group was abandoning its rank-and-file program and capitulating to union bureaucracy. These former members began a rival organization known as Workers Power. The remaining IS had suffered a serious loss of membership, and in 1986 it resolved this problem by "regrouping" with other socialists to form a new organization known as Solidarity. Solidarity united Workers Power, the IS, and a group of former

SWP members known as Socialist Unity, and it survives today with several hundred members (Finkel, E-mail).

Each of these organizational splits and recombinations reflects political and personal conflicts that are too extensive to detail here. See Fields's *Trotskyism and Maoism* and the array of autobiographies by participants, as well as the texts listed above, for descriptions of such debates.

4. Farrell Dobbs, SWP member and local Teamster leader, wrote a four-part account of his trade union work: *Teamster Rebellion, Teamster Power, Teamster Politics,* and *Teamster Bureaucracy.*

5. The IS also grew at the end of the 1960s. According to former member Milton Fisk, it emerged from the 1969 SDS split with only 180 members and grew to about 350 in 1970 (Fisk 50).

6. Kim Moody argues that "deindustrialization" does not adequately describe the move to "lean production" and a global division of labor. His critique may be right, but it did not change the facts on the ground for socialists in industry: jobs were leaving the United States, and American unions had less clout.

7. Historian Max Elbaum notes that the same desire to put on an imagined working-class identity appeared in Marxist-Leninist groups at the time. The Revolutionary Union, he says, adopted working-class dress and language reminiscent of the 1930s, rejected unmarried living arrangements as affronts to working-class morals, and sometimes even developed drinking habits in order to "fit in" with the working classes (170–71).

8. At the time, support for the Iranian revolution was a major focus of the SWP's international politics.

9. Socialists in the IS and the SWP often masked their identities to avoid government or employer surveillance. I have replicated pseudonyms or abbreviated names as they appeared in organizational documents.

10. See Kenneth Crowe on TDU's development.

Chapter 4

1. In the most extreme cases this can lead to anarcho-capitalism, a libertarian approach to the market and society. This rejection of leftist attitudes is rare, however, and many leftist anarchists deride "anarcho-capitalism" as a contradiction.

2. Today's anarchists often cite these movements as inspiration.

3. For discussions of punk culture and its relationship to anarchism, see Dick Hebdige's *Subculture*, Ian Glasper's *The Day the Country Died: A History of Anarcho Punk 1980 to 1984*, Craig O'Hara's *Philosophy of Punk*, Ross Haenfler's *Straight Edge*, and Jeff Ferrell's *Tearing Down the Streets*.

4. The World Bank and the IMF offer loans to poor nations but encourage repayment through government "austerity" plans that slash social services and privatize government-owned resources. The World Trade Organization complements this work by policing trade agreements between nations. It has been criticized for ensuring the free flow of capital with little regard for labor or the environment. For more on neoliberalism, see Price's *Before the Bulldozer*, Stiglitz's *Globalization and Its Discontents*, and Yates's *Naming the System*.

5. See Purkis and Brown's *Changing Anarchism*; Cockburn, St. Clair, and Sekula's *Five Days that Shook the World*; and Martinez's "Where was the Color in Seattle?" for more on the antiglobalization movement and the Seattle 1999 protests. *The Black Bloc Papers* offers insight on the history of the Black Bloc.

6. An "affinity group" is a nonhierarchical group of people who come together for a specific purpose, which is usually concrete, such as planning an action, but may be broad, such as promoting anarchist politics. Affinity groups are usually small (under twenty members) and composed of people who know each other well. Their intimacy and impermanence (they usually disband after completing the task) are intended to prevent police infiltration or a concentration of power within the group.

7. The zine was uploaded to *Zine Library* in November 2005, and references place its composition between 2001 and 2005.

8. This was uploaded to *Zine Library* in 2005, and context indicates that it was written between 2002 and 2005.

9. "Sf" can denote "speculative fiction" or "science fiction." In this chapter, I will use it in reference to the broader term, speculative fiction, which includes science fiction and fantasy.

10. Hakim Bey is the pen name of Peter Lamborn Wilson. His phrase "temporary autonomous zone" describes spaces of resistance within capitalism that privilege fleeting pleasure and insurrection over the long, contaminated process of revolution.

11. A *duppy* is a spirit, often malevolent, that remains on earth to haunt the living. In *Brown Girl in the Ring*, Rudy transforms humans into duppies by trapping their souls in his "duppy bowl." While the bowl survives, the duppy must do his bidding. If the bowl breaks, the soul can return to its body or, if the body is dead, it can escape the human world.

12. Homesteading is a process of earning the legal right to keep an abandoned property by improving it. At various times, New York City has permitted homesteading to revive declining neighborhoods and housing prices. In 1986, the city pulled back support for homesteading as property prices skyrocketed. Since then, it has not outlawed homesteading, but it has not approved new properties, effectively eliminating support.

13. The same opportunity arose in 2005 after Hurricane Katrina. The medical and rebuilding skills that anarchists brought to New Orleans, most famously through the group Common Ground, allowed them to establish relationships with the black community and its activists. Former Black Panther Malik Rahim was a major factor in constructing this alliance.

Bibliography

Abatino, Pepito. *Pepito Abatino présente Josephine Baker Vue par la Presse Française*. Paris: Les Editions Isis, 1931. Print.

Abbey, Edward. *The Monkey Wrench Gang*. New York: Avon, 1975. Print.

Abron, JoNina. "'Serving the People': The Survival Programs of the Black Panther Party." *The Black Panther Party Reconsidered*. Ed. Charles E. Jones. Baltimore: Black Classic, 1998. 177–92. Print.

Acoli, Sundiata. "A Brief History of the Black Panther Party and Its Place in the Black Liberation Movement." *The Talking Drum*. The Talking Drum Collective, 2003. Web. 2 Jan. 2007.

Aguilar, Ernesto, ed. *Our Culture, Our Resistance: People of Color Speak Out on Anarchism, Race, Class and Gender*. N.p.: Creative Commons, 2004. *Zine Library*. Web. 21 Feb. 2007.

———. *Our Culture, Our Resistance. Further Conversations with People of Color on Anarchism, Race, Class and Gender*. N.p.: Creative Commons, 2004. *Zine Library*. Web. 22 Feb. 2007.

Ahmad, Akbar Muhammad. *The League of Revolutionary Black Workers (A Historical Study)*. N.p.: n.p., n.d. Print.

———. "RAM: The Revolutionary Action Movement." *Black Power: In the Belly of the Beast*. Ed. Judson L. Jeffries. Urbana: U of Illinois P, 2006. 252–80. Print.

Albert, Michael. "Albert Replies to Critics of His Anarchism Essay." *ZNet*. Z Communications, n.d. Web. 27 Feb. 2008.

———. "Anarchism?!" *ZNet*. Z Communications, n.d. Web. 27 Feb. 2008.

———. *Parecon: Life after Capitalism*. London: Verso, 2003. Print.

Alexander, Robert J. *International Trotskyism, 1929–1985: A Documented Analysis of the Movement*. Durham: Duke UP, 1991. Print.

Allen, Ernest Mkalimoto. "*Detroit: I Do Mind Dying*: A Review." *Radical America* 11.1 (Jan.–Feb. 1977): 69–73. Print.

————. "Dying from the Inside: The Decline of the League of Revolution-ary Black Workers." *They Should Have Served that Cup of Coffee: Seven Radicals Remember the '60s*. Ed. Dick Cluster. Boston: South End, 1979. 71–109. Print.

Alston, Ashanti. "Anarcho-Pantherista." *Anarchist Panther*. Mayfirst/Panther, 1995. Web. 12 May 2008.

"Apocalypse Soon: Fall 2007 Trend Reports." *GQ*. Condé Nast, 2007. Web. 11 May 2008.

Asante, Molefi K. *The Afrocentric Idea*. Philadelphia: Temple UP, 1998. Print.

"Attention Black Workers!" Handbill. N.p.: n.p., [1969–1970?]. Box 3, folder 3–12. Dan Georgakas Collection. Walter P. Reuther Library of Labor and Urban Affairs, Wayne State U, Detroit. Print.

Auerbach, Jeffrey A. and Peter H. Hoffenberg, eds. *Britain, the Empire, and the World at the Great Exhibition of 1851*. Hampshire, England: Ashgate, 2008. Print.

"Augusta, Jackson and the Movement." *Independent Socialist* 20 (June 1970): 2. Print.

Austin, Curtis J. *Up Against the Wall: Violence in the Making and Unmaking of the Black Panther Party*. Fayetteville: U of Arkansas P, 2006. Print.

"The Auto Industry: It Could Keep Customers Happy." *UAW Solidarity* 12.3 (Mar. 1969): 8. Print.

Ayers, Bill. *Fugitive Days: A Memoir*. Boston: Beacon, 2001. Print.

Baker, General. Personal interview. 15 Mar. 2007. Print.

Balakrishnan, Gopal, ed. *Debating Empire*. London: Verso, 2003. Print.

"The Ballad of James Johnson: James Johnson Needed a Thompson." *Inner-City Voice* 3.2 (Apr. 1971): 11. Print.

Baraka, Amiri. *The Autobiography of Leroi Jones*. Chicago: Lawrence Hill, 1997. Print.

————. *Dutchman and The Slave; Two Plays*. New York: Morrow, 1964. Print.

————. *The LeRoi Jones/Amiri Baraka Reader*. Ed. William J. Harris and Amiri Baraka. New York: Thunder's Mouth, 1991. Print.

Baraka, Imamu Amiri, and Fundi. *In our Terribleness (Some Elements and Meaning in Black Style)*. Indianapolis: Bobbs, 1970. Print.

Barbaric Thoughts: On a Revolutionary Critique of Civilization. Portland: Venomous Butterfly, 2004. Print.

Barkan, Elazar, and Ronald Bush, eds. *Prehistories of the Future: The Primitivist Culture of Modernism*. Stanford: Stanford UP, 1995. Print.

Barnard, Alan, ed. *Hunter-Gatherers in History, Archaeology and Anthropology.* Oxford: Berg, 2004. Print.

Barnes, Jack. "A New Stage of Revolutionary Working-Class Politics." *The Changing Face of U.S. Politics: Building a Party of Socialist Workers (Reports and Resolutions of the Socialist Workers Party).* New York: Pathfinder, 1981. 90–160. Print.

———. "The Turn to Industry and the Tasks of the Fourth International." *The Changing Face of U.S. Politics: Building a Party of Socialist Workers (Reports and Resolutions of the Socialist Workers Party).* Ed. Jack Barnes and Steve Clark. New York: Pathfinder, 1981. 34–51. Print.

Barnes, Jack, and Steve Clark, eds. *The Changing Face of U.S. Politics: Building a Party of Socialist Workers (Reports and Resolutions of the Socialist Workers Party).* New York: Pathfinder, 1981. Print.

Bartholomew, Gloria. "A Black Woman's Thoughts." *Black Panther* 2.7 (28 Sept. 1968): 11. Print.

Bay Area Black Panther Party Collection, 1963–2000. Dept. of Special Collections, California Ethnic and Multicultural Archives. Davidson Library, U of California, Santa Barbara. Print.

Bearak, Berry. "Turf Wars." *Shelterforce* 75 (May/June 1994). National Housing Institute. Web. 22 Mar. 2008.

Beard, Miriam. "Wild Urban Jungle Has No Terrors for Man." *New York Times* 14 Mar. 1926: SM2. Print.

Beaulieu, Elizabeth Ann. *Black Women Writers and the American Neo-Slave Narrative: Femininity Unfettered.* London: Greenwood Press, 1999. Print.

The Beehive Design Collective. *Free Trade Area of the Americas and the Global Resistance to Corporate Colonialism.* Machias, Maine: The Beehive Design Collective, n.d. Web. 31 May 2011. <http://www.beehivecollective.org/PDF/narratives/FTAA_narrative-english.pdf>. Print.

The Beehive Design Collective Home Page. Beehive Collective, 2009. Web. 9 June 2009.

Bell, Daniel. *The Coming of Post-Industrial Society: A Venture in Social Forecasting.* New York: Basic Books, 1973. Print.

Bender, Barbara, and Brian Morris. "Twenty Years of History, Evolution and Social Change in Gatherer-Hunter Studies." *Hunters and Gatherers, Volume 1: Evolution and Social Change.* Ed. Tim Ingold, David Riches, and James Woodburn. Oxford: Berg, 1988. 4–14. Print.

Benjamin, Tritobia Hayes, and Loïs Mailou Jones. *The Life and Art of Loïs Mailou Jones.* Rohmert Park, California: Pomegranate, 1994. Print.

Benston, Kimberly W. *Baraka: The Renegade and the Mask.* New Haven: Yale UP, 1976. Print.

———. *Performing Blackness: Enactments of African-American Modernism.* New York: Routledge, 2000. Print.

Berger, Dan. *Outlaws of America: The Weather Underground and the Politics of Solidarity.* Oakland: AK, 2006. Print.

Bey, Hakim [Peter Lamborn Wilson]. *T.A.Z.: The Temporary Autonomous Zone, Ontological Anarchy, Poetic Terrorism.* Brooklyn: Autonomedia, 1985. Print.

Binkin, Martin, et al. *Blacks and the Military.* Washington: Brookings Institute, 1982. Print.

The Black Bloc Papers. Comp. David and X of the Green Anarchist Collective. Ed. Mike A., Melissa, and Lady. Baltimore: Black Clover, 2002. Print.

Black, Bob. *The Abolition of Work and Other Essays.* Port Townsend, WA: Loompanics, 1986. Print.

"The Black Mood: More Militant, More Hopeful, More Determined." *Time* 6 Apr. 1970.Web. 30 Apr. 2007.

Black Panther 14 Sept. 1968: 6. Print.

———. 26 Oct. 1968: 14, 17. Print.

———. 4 Jan. 1969: 3. Print.

———. 17 Feb. 1970: 15. Print.

———. 15 Mar. 1970. Print.

———. 19 May 1970: 7. Print.

The Black Panther Party. Speech by John Hulett. Interview with Stokely Carmichael. Report from Lowndes County. New York: Merit Publishers, 1966. Print. Box 2, folder 1. Bay Area Black Panther Party Collection. California Ethnic and Multicultural Archives. Davidson Library, U of California, Santa Barbara.

Black Vanguard 1.5 (Aug. 1965). Print. Box 1. Underground Newspapers Collection. Bentley Historical Library, U of Michigan, Ann Arbor.

"Black Workers Uprising." *Inner City Voice* 1.8 (June 1968): 1+. Print.

Blood Brother. "The Black Fascist Funnies Presents: The Rise and Fall of Mickey Mouse." *Black Panther* 23 Aug. 1969: 5. Print.

Bloom, Allan. *The Closing of the American Mind.* New York: Simon & Schuster, 1987. Print.

Boggs, Grace Lee. *Living for Change: An Autobiography.* Minneapolis: U of Minnesota P, 1998. Print.

Bontemps, Arna, ed. *American Negro Poetry.* New York: Hill and Wang, 1963. Print.

Bracey, John, ed. "At the Point of Production." *Radical America* 5.2 (Mar.–Apr. 1971): 63–79. Print.

Bracey, John H., Jr., and Sharon Harley, eds. *The Black Power Movement, Part 3: Papers of the Revolutionary Action Movement, 1962–1966.* Microform. Bethesda: University Publications of America, 2002.

Breitman, George, Paul Le Blanc, and Alan Wald. *Trotskyism in the United States: Historical Essays and Reconsiderations.* Atlantic Highlands, NJ: Humanities, 1996. Print.

Brown, Elaine. *A Taste of Power: A Black Woman's Story.* New York: Pantheon, 1992. Print.

Brown, Lloyd. *Amiri Baraka.* Boston: Twayne, 1980. Print.

Brownmiller, Susan. *In Our Time: Memoir of a Revolution.* New York: Dial, 1999. Print.

Bryant, Jerry H. *"Born in a Mighty Bad Land": The Violent Man in African American Folklore and Fiction.* Bloomington: Indiana UP, 2003. Print.

Buechler, Steven M. *Social Movements in Advanced Capitalism: The Political Economy and Cultural Construction of Social Activism.* New York: Oxford UP, 2000. Print.

Bufe, Chaz. *Listen Anarchist!* Tucson: See Sharp Press, 1998. Print.

Bullins, Ed. *Death List. Four Dynamite Plays.* New York: Morrow, 1972. *Black Drama.* Alexander Street Press, 2005. Web. 2 May 2007.

Butler, Octavia. *Kindred.* 1979. Boston: Beacon Press, 1988. Print.

———. *Parable of the Sower.* New York: Aspect, 1993. Print.

———. *Parable of the Talents.* New York: Seven Stories Press, 1998. Print.

Byington, Margaret Frances. *Homestead: The Households of a Mill Town.* New York: Charities Publication Committee, 1910. Print.

Call, Lewis. *Postmodern Anarchism.* Lanham: Lexington, 2002. Print.

Campbell, Slick [Albert]. "Let Freedom Ring" *DRUM* 1.5 ([1968?]): 4. Print. Box 6, folder 6-24. Kenneth V. and Sheila M. Cockrel Collection. Walter P. Reuther Library of Labor and Urban Affairs, Wayne State U, Detroit.

Carter, Susan B. "Unemployment Rate by Age, Sex, Race, and Hispanic Origin: 1947–2000." Table. *Historical Statistics of the United States: Millennial Edition Online.* Ed. Susan B. Carter, et al. 2007. Web. 8 Jan. 2007.

CBS News. *Face the Nation, 1966: The Collected Transcripts from the CBS Radio and Television Broadcasts.* Vol. 9. New York: Holt, 1972. Print.

Çelik, Zeynep, and Leila Kinney. "Ethnography and Exhibitionism at the Expositions Universelles." *Assemblage* 13 (Dec. 1990): 34–59. Print.

Chomsky, Noam. Interview with Paul Jay. *Real News Network.* 20 Oct. 2008. Web. 10 Oct. 2010.

Chretien, Todd. "Why I'm Not Voting for Barack Obama." *Socialist Worker* 683 (22 Oct. 2008). Web. 10 Oct. 2010.

Churchill, Ward, and Jim Vander Wall. *Agents of Repression: The FBI's Secret Wars against the Black Panther Party and the American Indian Movement.* Cambridge, MA: South End, 2002. Print.

———. *The COINTELPRO Papers: Documents from the FBI's Secret Wars against Dissidents in the United States.* Cambridge, MA: South End, 2002. Print.

Cleaver, Eldridge. "On the Ideology of the Black Panther Party." *The Black Panther* 6 June 1970: 12–15. Print.

———. *Soul on Ice.* New York: Delta, 1968. Print.

Cleaver, Kathleen Neal. "Back to Africa: The Evolution of the International Section of the Black Panther Party." *The Black Panther Party Reconsidered.* Ed. Charles E. Jones. Baltimore: Black Classic, 1998. 211–54. Print.

———. "Women, Power, and Revolution." *Liberation, Imagination, and the Black Panther Party.* Ed. Kathleen Cleaver and George Katsiaficas. New York: Routledge, 2001. 123–27. Print.

Clegg, Claude Andrew III. *An Original Man: The Life and Times of Elijah Muhammad.* New York: St. Martin's, 1997. Print.

"Coal Miner Fights Deportation." *Militant* 14 Nov. 1980: 12–13. Print.

Cockburn, Alexander, Jeffrey St. Clair, and Allan Sekula. *5 Days that Shook the World: Seattle and Beyond.* London: Verso, 2000. Print.

Cockrel, Kenneth V. "From Repression to Revolution." *Radical America* 5.2 (Mar.–Apr. 1971): 81–91. Print.

Cohen, Mark Nathan. *Health and the Rise of Civilization.* New Haven: Yale UP, 1989. Print.

Cole, Nancy. "Marroquín Denied Asylum." *Militant* 12 Jan. 1979: 8. Print.

Coleman, James. "The Silent Majority and the War." *Workers' Power: International Socialist Biweekly* 21 (11–24 Sept. 1970): 7. Print.

"College Study." Gallup Poll (1 Nov. 1970–30 Nov. 1970). *Gallup Brain.* Web. 14 May 2008.

"Confidential Communication for Internal Use Only." Detroit: League of Revolutionary Black Workers, n.d. Print. Box 6, folder 6-23. Kenneth V. and Sheila M. Cockrel Collection. Walter P. Reuther Library of Labor and Urban Affairs, Wayne State U, Detroit.

Cotter, Holland. "Putting Primitive to Rest." Rev. of "African and Oceanic Art from the Barbier-Mueller Museum, Geneva." *New York Times.* 5 June 2009: C25. Print.

The Couple in the Cage. Ed. Daisy Wright. Perf. Guillermo Gómez-Peña and Coco Fusco. Video Data Bank, 2000. Film.

Courtright, John A. "Rhetoric of the Gun: An Analysis of the Rhetorical Modifications of the Black Panther Party." *Journal of Black Studies* 4.3 (Mar. 1974): 249–67. Print.

Cowie, Jefferson. *Beyond the Ruins: The Meanings of Industrialization.* Ithaca: ILR Press, 2003. Print.

Crawford, Margo Natalie. "Black Light on the *Wall of Respect.*" *New Thoughts on the Black Arts Movement.* Ed. Lisa Gail Collins and Margo Natalie Crawford. New Brunswick: Rutgers UP, 2006. 23–42. Print.

———. "Productive Rites of 'Passing': Keorapetse Kgositsile and the Black Arts Movement: How Did It Come about That All of a Sudden Africans Became Negroes?" *Black Renaissance/Renaissance Noire* 7.3 (2007): 112–20. Web.

CrimethInc. Ex-Workers Collective. *A Revolutionary Vindication of Refusal, Marginality and Subculture.* 2006. *Zine Library.* Web. 16 Feb. 2007.

CrimethInc. Workers' Collective. *Days of War, Nights of Love: Crimethink for Beginners.* Olympia: CrimethInc. Free Press, 2001. Print.

Crowe, Kenneth C. *Collision: How the Rank and File Took Back the Teamsters.* New York: Scribner's Sons, 1993. Print.

Cunnigen, Donald. "The Republic of New Africa in Mississippi." *Black Power: In the Belly of the Beast.* Ed. Judson L. Jeffries. Urbana: U of Illinois P, 2006. 93–115. Print.

Curran, Giorel. *21st Century Dissent: Anarchism, Anti-Globalization and Environmentalism.* New York: Palgrave, 2006. Print.

Dan Georgakas Collection. Walter P. Reuther Library of Labor and Urban Affairs, Wayne State U, Detroit. Print.

Danton, Marilyn. "Protective Legislation and the ERA." *Workers' Power* 23 (9–22 Oct. 1970): 3–4. Print.

Debord, Guy. *Society of the Spectacle.* New York: Zone, 1994. Print.

DeFilippo, Bernard. *Hoodoo, Voodoo, and Conjure: The Novels of Ishmael Reed.* Ann Arbor: UMI, 1989. Print.

Deloria, Philip. *Playing Indian.* New Haven: Yale UP, 1998. Print.

DeNavas-Walt, Carmen, Bernadette D. Proctor, and Jessica Smith. *Income, Poverty, and Health Insurance Coverage in the United States: 2006.* U.S. Census Bureau. Washington: GPO, 2007. Print.

Denby, Charles [Matthew Ward]. *Indignant Heart: A Black Worker's Journal.* Boston: South End, 1978. Print.

DePastino, Todd A. "The Strange Career of the American Hobo." *Community in the American West*. Ed. Stephen Tchudi. Reno: Nevada Humanities Committee, 1999. 337–58. Print.

Detroit Revolutionary Movements Collection. Walter P. Reuther Library of Labor and Urban Affairs, Wayne State U, Detroit. Print.

DeVries, Arnold. *Primitive Man and His Food*. Chicago: Higgins, 1952. Print.

Dillard, Angela D. *Faith in the City: Preaching Radical Social Change in Detroit*. Ann Arbor: U of Michigan P, 2007. Print.

Dobbs, Farrell. *Teamster Bureaucracy*. New York: Monad, 1977. Print.

———. *Teamster Politics*. New York: Monad, 1975. Print.

———. *Teamster Power*. New York: Monad, 1973. Print.

———. *Teamster Rebellion*. New York: Pathfinder, 1972. Print.

Donaldson, Jeff. "The Rise, Fall, and Legacy of the *Wall of Respect* Movement." *International Review of African American Art* 15.1 (1998): 22–26. Print.

Donovan, Colin, and Qwo-Li Driskill. *Answers for White People on Appropriation, Hair and Anti-Racist Struggle*. N.p: Planting Seeds Community Awareness Project, [2007?]. *Zine Library*. 12 Jan. 2008. Web. 23 Mar. 2008.

Doss, Erika. "Revolutionary Art Is a Tool for Liberation: Emory Douglas and Protest Aesthetics at the *Black Panther*." *Liberation, Imagination, and the Black Panther Party: A New Look at the Panthers and their Legacy*. Ed. Kathleen Cleaver and George Katsiaficas. New York: Routledge, 2001. 175–87. Print.

DRUM 1.5 ([1968?]). Print. Box 6, folder 6-24. Kenneth V. and Sheila M. Cockrel Collection. Walter P. Reuther Library of Labor and Urban Affairs, Wayne State U, Detroit.

——— 2.18 ([1969?]). Print. Box 6, folder 6-24. Kenneth V. and Sheila M. Cockrel Collection. Walter P. Reuther Library of Labor and Urban Affairs, Wayne State U, Detroit.

——— 3.3 ([1970?]). Print. Box 6, folder 6-24. Kenneth V. and Sheila M. Cockrel Collection. Walter P. Reuther Library of Labor and Urban Affairs, Wayne State U, Detroit.

"DRUM Demands" N.p.: n.p., n.d. Handbill. Box 1, folder 1-1. Detroit Revolutionary Movements Collection. Walter P. Reuther Library of Labor and Urban Affairs, Wayne State U, Detroit.

"DRUM's Program" N.p.: n.p., n.d. Handbill. Box 1, folder 1-1. Detroit Revolutionary Movements Collection. Walter P. Reuther Library of Labor and Urban Affairs, Wayne State U, Detroit.

Duncombe, Stephen. *Notes from Underground: Zines and the Politics of Alternative Culture*. London: Verso, 1997. Print.

Durante, Jimmy, and Jack Kofoed. *Night Clubs.* New York: Knopf, 1931. Print.

Earth First Journal! Web. 28 Feb. 2008.

"Economic and Financial Indicators." *Economist* 26 Apr. 2008: 119–20. Print.

Elbaum, Max. *Revolution in the Air: Sixties Radicals Turn to Lenin, Mao, and Che.* London: Verso, 2002. Print.

Elkins, Stanley M. *Slavery: A Problem in American Institutional and Intellectual Life.* Chicago: U of Chicago P, 1969. Print.

Ellison, Ralph. *Shadow and Act.* New York: Random House, 1964. Print.

ELRUM 1.2 ([1968?]). Print. Box 6, folder 6-27. Kenneth V. and Sheila M. Cockrel Collection. Walter P. Reuther Library of Labor and Urban Affairs, Wayne State U, Detroit.

———— 3.1 ([1970?]). Print. Box 6, folder 6-27. Kenneth V. and Sheila M. Cockrel Collection. Walter P. Reuther Library of Labor and Urban Affairs, Wayne State U, Detroit.

———— [3.2?] ([1970?]). Print. Box 6, folder 6-27. Kenneth V. and Sheila M. Cockrel Collection. Walter P. Reuther Library of Labor and Urban Affairs, Wayne State U, Detroit.

———— 3.3 (Jan. 1971). Print. Box 6, folder 6-27. Kenneth V. and Sheila M. Cockrel Collection. Walter P. Reuther Library of Labor and Urban Affairs, Wayne State U, Detroit.

———— 3.5 ([1971?]). Print. Box 6, Folder 6-27. Kenneth V. and Sheila M. Cockrel Collection. Walter P. Reuther Library of Labor and Urban Affairs, Wayne State U, Detroit.

————. n.d. Print. Box 6, folder 6-27. Kenneth V. and Sheila M. Cockrel Collection. Walter P. Reuther Library of Labor and Urban Affairs, Wayne State U, Detroit.

"ELRUM Is Asking All Concerned Black Workers to Meet and Support Us and the Black Sisters in Dept. 76." Handbill. N.p.: n.p., n.d. Box 3, folder 3-12. Dan Georgakas Collection. Walter P. Reuther Library of Labor and Urban Affairs, Wayne State U, Detroit.

Emerson, Ralph Waldo and Edward Waldo Emerson. *The Complete Works of Ralph Waldo Emerson.* Boston: Houghton, Mifflin, 1904. Print.

Engels, Friedrich. "On Social Relations in Russia." *The Marx-Engels Reader.* Ed. Robert C. Tucker. 2nd ed. New York: Norton, 1978. 665–75. Print.

————. *Socialism, Utopian and Scientific.* Trans. Edward Aveling. Chicago: Charles H. Kerr, 1907. Print.

"Equal Opportunity My Ass." *Eldon Avenue Revolutionary Union Movement* 2.2: 2. Print. Box 6, folder 6-27. Kenneth V. and Sheila M. Cockrel

Collection. Walter P. Reuther Library of Labor and Urban Affairs, Wayne State U, Detroit.

Ervin, Lorenzo Komboa. *Anarchism and the Black Revolution.* 2nd ed. *Infoshop. org.* 1993. Web. 18 Mar. 2008.

———. "Anarchism + Black Revolution = New Autonomous Politics." Seattle: Black Autonomy Collective, n.d. Web. 9 May 2008.

Evasion. Atlanta: CrimethInc., 2003. Print.

F., Ken, Will F., and Cliff H. "Resolution on Working Class Perspective." N.p.: n.p. [1969?]. Print. Box 1. International Socialists Issuances, 1967–1976. Hoover Institution Archives. Stanford U, Stanford.

Fanon, Frantz. *Black Skin, White Masks.* Trans. Charles Lam Markmann. New York: Grove, 1967. Print.

———. *The Wretched of the Earth.* New York: Grove, 2004. Print.

"Favorable Report Near on 2-Year NRA as Opposition Lags." *New York Times* 24 May 1935: 1. Print.

Federal Bureau of Investigation. Tap Logs. 21 Mar. 1969. Print. Huey P. Newton Foundation Records. Department of Special Collections and University Archives. Green Library, Stanford U, Stanford.

Feeley, Dianne. Telephone interview. 8 Aug. 2007.

Feral Forager. N.p.: n.p. [2005?]. *Zine Library.* 6 Nov. 2005. Web. 4 Feb. 2008.

Ferguson, Sarah. "Better Homes and Squatters: New York's Outlaw Home-steaders Earn the Right to Stay." *The Village Voice* 27 Aug. 2002. Web. 23 Mar. 2008.

Ferrell, Jeff. *Tearing Down the Streets: Adventures in Urban Anarchy.* New York: Palgrave, 2001. Print.

Fields, A. Belden. *Trotskyism and Maoism: Theory and Practice in the United States.* New York: Praeger, 1988. Print.

"Fight for Workers' Power." *IS Bulletin* 1 (1 Sept. 1970). Print. Box 1. International Socialists Issuances, 1967–1976. Hoover Institution Archives. Stanford U, Stanford.

Finkel, David. E-mail to the author. 20 Nov. 2007.

———. Telephone interview. 21 Aug. 2007.

Fisk, Milton. *Socialism from Below in the United States.* Cleveland: Hera, 1977. Print.

———. Personal communication. 27 Aug. 2007.

Flam, Jack D., and Miriam Deutch. *Primitivism and Twentieth-Century Art: A Documentary History.* Berkeley: U of California P, 2003. Print.

Foner, Philip S., ed. *The Black Panthers Speak.* Philadelphia: Lippincott, 1970. Print.

————. *Organized Labor and the Black Worker 1619–1981.* New York: International, 1982. Print.

Freedom Road Socialist Organization. "2008 Presidential Elections: Defeat McCain." June 2008. *www.frso.org.* Web. 10 Oct. 2010.

Fujita, Kuniko. *Black Worker's [sic] Struggles in Detroit's Auto Industry, 1935–1975.* Saratoga, California: Century Twenty One, 1980. Print.

Fuller, Hoyt W. "Towards a Black Aesthetic." *The Black Aesthetic.* Ed. Addison Gayle. Garden City: Anchor, 1972. 3–11. Print.

Fulton, DoVeanna. *Speaking Power: Black Feminist Orality in Women's Narratives of Slavery.* Albany: State U of New York P, 2006. Print.

Garrett, Jimmy. *We Own the Night. Black: An Anthology of Afro-American Writing.* Ed. LeRoi Jones and Larry Neal. New York: Morrow, 1969. 527–40. Print.

The General Policy Statement and Labor Program of the League of Revolutionary Black Workers. Highland Park, MI: n.p., [1970?]. Print. Box 4, folder 4-12. Dan Georgakas Collection. Walter P. Reuther Library of Labor and Urban Affairs, Wayne State U, Detroit.

Georgakas, Dan, and Marvin Surkin. *Detroit: I Do Mind Dying: A Study in Urban Revolution.* New York: St. Martin's, 1975. Print.

Geschwender, James A. *Class, Race, and Worker Insurgency: The League of Revolutionary Black Workers.* Cambridge: Cambridge UP, 1977. Print.

————. "The League of Revolutionary Black Workers: Problems Confronting Marxist-Leninist Organizations." *The Journal of Ethnic Studies* 2.3 (Fall 1974): 1–23. Print.

Geschwender, James A., and Judson L. Jeffries. "The League of Revolutionary Black Workers." *Black Power: In the Belly of the Beast.* Ed. Judson L. Jeffries. Urbana: U of Illinois P, 2006. 135–62. Print.

The Ghetto Garden: D.I.Y. Country Trash Livin'. Boone, North Carolina: n.p. [2005?]. *Zine Library.* 6 Nov. 2005. Web. 4 Feb. 2008.

Glasper, Ian. *The Day the Country Died: A History of Anarcho Punk 1980 to 1984.* London: Cherry Red, 2006. Print.

"G.M. Joins Campaign to Provide More Jobs for Negroes in Detroit." *New York Times* 10 Nov. 1967: 38. Print.

Godesky, Jason. "A Pirate's Life for Me." *The Anthropik Network.* July 2006. Web. 8 Mar. 2008.

————. "Thesis #21: Civilization Makes Us Sick." *The Anthropik Network.* 2 Jan. 2006. Web. 26 Mar. 2008.

Goldman, Emma. *Living My Life: An Autobiography of Emma Goldman.* Salt Lake City: G.M. Smith, 1931. Print.

Goldman, Russell. "Rhetoric or Revolution?: Obama Rev's Fiery Language." *ABCNews.com*. ABC News, 21 March 2008. Web. 18 Dec. 2009.

Gordon, Jane Ann. *Why They Couldn't Wait: A Critique of the Black-Jewish Conflict Over Community Control in Ocean-Hill Brownsville, 1967–1971*. New York: Routledge, 2001. Print.

"Gray Panthers' History." *Gray Panthers: Age and Youth in Action*. N.d. Web. 2 Jan. 2007.

Green Anarchy and the Wild Roots Collective. *Back to Basics Volume Three: Rewilding*. N.p.: n.p., 2004. *The Green Anarchist Info/Shop*. Web. 24 Mar. 2008.

Green, Andy. "Folk Legend Pete Seeger: 'I Feel Optimistic.'" *Rolling Stone* 27 Feb. 2008. Web. 10 Oct. 2010.

Greene, Linda. "The Black Revolutionary Woman." *Black Panther* 28 Sept. 1968: 11. Print.

Guérin, Daniel. *Anarchism; from Theory to Practice*. New York: Monthly Review, 1970. Print.

Guy, Jasmine. *Afeni Shakur: Evolution of a Revolutionary*. New York: Atria, 2004. Print.

Haenfler, Ross. *Straight Edge: Clean-Living Youth, Hardcore Punk, and Social Change*. New Brunswick, NJ: Rutgers UP, 2006. Print.

"Hail James Johnson." *DRUM* 3.[n.v.] ([July 1970?]): 1–4. Print. Box 6, folder 6-24. Kenneth V. and Sheila M. Cockrel Collection. Walter P. Reuther Library of Labor and Urban Affairs, Wayne State U, Detroit.

Haley, Alex. *Roots*. 1974. New York: Vanguard Books, 2004. Print.

Hall, Stuart. "Gramsci's Relevance for the Study of Race and Ethnicity." *Critical Dialogues in Cultural Studies*. Ed. David Morley and Kuan-Hsing Chen. London: Routledge, 1996. 411–40. Print.

Hamlin, Mike. *Fight on to Victory! Detroit's League Speaks*. Detroit: Radical Education Project, 1970. Print.

——. Interview with Ahmad Muhammad. 27 Sept. 1999. *The Black Power Movement, Part 3: Papers of the Revolutionary Action Movement*. Ed. John H. Bracey and Sharon Harley. Microform. Bethesda: University Publications of America, 2001. Reel 9.

"Hands off the Panthers." *Workers' Power* 25 (6–26 Nov. 1970): 2. Print.

Hardt, Michael, and Antonio Negri. *Empire*. Cambridge: Harvard UP, 2000. Print.

Harrison, Linda. "On Nationalism." *The Black Panthers Speak*. Ed. Philip S. Foner. Philadelphia: Lippincott, 1970. 151–54. Print.

Haskins, James. *Profiles in Black Power*. New York: Doubleday, 1972. Print.

Hayden, Casey, and Mary King. "Feminism and the Civil Rights Movement." 1964–1965. *Freedom Song: A Personal Story of the Civil Rights Movement.* By Mary King. New York: Morrow, 1987. 568–69. Print.

Hayden, Tom, Barbara Ehrenreich, Bill Fletcher, Jr., and Danny Glover. "Progressives for Obama." *The Nation* 7 Apr. 2008. Web. 9 Oct. 2010.

Haywood, Harry. *Black Bolshevik: Autobiography of an Afro-American Communist.* Chicago: Liberator Press, 1978. Print.

Headland, Thomas. *The Tasaday Controversy: Assessing the Evidence.* Washington, DC: American Anthropological Assoc., 1992. Print.

Headland, Thomas N., and Lawrence A. Reid. "Hunter-Gatherers and Their Neighbors from Prehistory to the Present." *Current Anthropology* 30 (1989): 43–66. Print.

Healey, Dorothy Ray and Maurice Isserman. *California Red: A Life in the American Communist Party.* New York: Oxford UP, 1990. Print.

Hebdige, Dick. *Subculture: The Meaning of Style.* London: Routledge, 2002. Print.

Heglar, Charles J. *The Slave Narrative: Slave Marriage and the Narratives of Henry Bibb and Ellen Craft.* Westport, CT: Greenwood Press, 2001. Print.

Heinberg, Richard. "The Primitivist Critique of Civilization." *Primitivism.* June 1995. Web. 24 Mar. 2008.

Hemley, Robin. *Invented Eden: The Elusive, Disputed History of the Tasaday.* Lincoln: U of Nebraska P, 2006. Print.

Henry, Joseph. "A *MELUS* Interview: Ishmael Reed." *MELUS* 11.1 (Spring 1984): 81–93. Print.

Hirsch, Barry T., and David A. Macpherson. "Union Membership and Coverage Database from the Current Population Survey: Note." *Industrial and Labor Relations Review* 56.2 (Jan. 2003): 349–54. Print.

Hoffman, Abbie. *The Autobiography of Abbie Hoffman.* New York: Four Walls Eight Windows, 2000. Print.

Hopkinson, Nalo. *Brown Girl in the Ring.* New York: Warner, 1998. Print.

Hopkinson, Nalo, and Alondra Nelson. "Making the Impossible Possible: An Interview with Nalo Hopkinson." *Social Text* 71 (Summer 2002): 97–113. Print.

"How Membership Has Changed." *UAW Solidarity* 12.6 (June 1969): 11. Print.

Hudlin, Reginald, et al. "Bride of the Panther: Part One." *Black Panther* #14. Marvel Comics, 2006. Print.

Huey P. Newton Foundation Records. Dept. of Special Collections and University Archives. Green Library, Stanford U, Stanford.

Hufbauer, Gary Clyde, and Jeffrey J. Schott. *NAFTA Revisited: Achievements and Challenges*. Washington, DC: Institute for International Economics, 2005. Print.

Hughes, Langston. *The Big Sea: An Autobiography*. 1940. New York: Thunder's Mouth, 1986. Print.

Huxley, Aldous. *Brave New World*. Cutchogue, New York: Buccaneer Books, 1946. Print.

Independent Socialist 19 (May 1970). Print.

Inner City Voice 2.1 (Oct. 1969). Print.

International Socialists Issuances, 1967–1976. Hoover Institution Archives. Stanford U, Stanford. Print.

Jacobs, Harriet. *Incidents in the Life of a Slave Girl*. 1861. Mineola, NY: Dover, 2001. Print.

Jacobs, Lawrence R. and Robert Y. Shapiro. *Politicians Don't Pander: Political Manipulation and the Loss of Democratic Responsiveness*. Chicago: U of Chicago P, 2000. Print.

Jacoby, Scott. "To the National Committee. *IS Bulletin* 6 (1 Mar. 1971). Print. Box 1. International Socialists Issuances, 1967–1976. Hoover Institution Archives. Stanford U, Stanford.

JanMohamed, Abdul R. "The Economy of Manichean Allegory: The Function of Racial Difference in Colonialist Literature." *Critical Inquiry* 12.1 (Autumn 1985): 59–87. Print.

Jayko, Liz. "Socialist to GE: 'Stop Right-Wing Harassment.'" *Militant* 19 Jan. 1979: 8. Print.

Jemie, Onwuchekwa, ed. *Yo Mama!: New Raps, Toasts, Dozens, Jokes, and Children's Rhymes from Urban Black America*. Philadelphia: Temple UP, 2003. Print.

Jenkins, D. "Brooklyn." *Black Panther* 6 June 1970: 2. Print.

Jennings, Regina. "Why I Joined the Party: An Africana Womanist Reflection." *The Black Panther Party Reconsidered*. Ed. Charles E. Jones. Baltimore: Black Classic, 1998. 257–66. Print.

Jensen, Derrick. *Endgame, Volume I: The Problem of Civilization*. New York: Seven Stories, 2006. Print.

Johnson, Charles. *Oxherding Tale*. 1982. New York: Scribner, 2005. Print.

Johnson, Helene. *This Waiting for Love: Helene Johnson, Poet of the Harlem Renaissance*. Ed. Verner D. Mitchell. U of Massachusetts P, 2000. Print.

Jones, LeRoi, and Larry Neal, ed. *Black Fire: An Anthology of Afro-American Writing*. New York: Morrow, 1969. Print.

Joseph, Peniel E. *Waiting 'Til the Midnight Hour: A Narrative History of Black Power in America.* New York: Holt, 2006. Print.

Jules-Rosette, Bennetta. *Josephine Baker in Art and Life.* Urbana: U of Illinois P, 2007. Print.

J. W. "Document on Industrialization." *IS Bulletin: Documents of the National Committee Meeting, January 1971* (1 Mar. 1971). Print. Box 1. International Socialists Issuances, 1967–1976. Hoover Institution Archives. Stanford U, Stanford.

Karenga, Ron. "Black Cultural Nationalism." *The Black Aesthetic.* Ed. Addison Gayle, Jr. Garden City: Anchor, 1972. 31–37. Print.

Karg, Elissa. Telephone interview. 8 Aug. 2007.

Kasson, John. *Civilizing the Machine: Technology and Republican Values in America, 1776–1990.* New York: Grossman, 1976. Print.

Kelley, Robin D. G. *Hammer and Hoe: Alabama Communists During the Great Depression.* U of North Carolina P, 1990. Print.

Kenan, Randall. "An Interview with Octavia E. Butler." *Callaloo* 14.2 (Spring 1991): 495–504. Print.

Kenner, Martin. Letter to Elaine Brown. 20 March 1971. Series 2, box 12, folder 1. Huey P. Newton Foundation Records. Department of Special Collections and University Archives. Green Library, Stanford U, Stanford.

Kenneth V. and Sheila M. Cockrel Collection. Walter P. Reuther Library of Labor and Urban Affairs, Wayne State U, Detroit.

Kent, Roy. "Rockford Store Owner Intimidates Small Children." *Black Panther* 25 July 1970: 12. Print.

Knapp, James. "Primitivism and the Modern." *boundary 2* 15.1 (Autumn 1986/Winter 1987): 365–79. Print.

Kornbluh, Joyce L., ed. *Rebel Voices: An I.W.W. Anthology.* Ann Arbor: U of Michigan P, 1964. Print.

Kromer, Tom. "The Economy: Prices Up, Wages, Jobs Down." *Workers' Power* 27 (11 Dec.–14 Jan. 1971): 4–5. Print.

Kure, Nils. *Living with Leopards.* Cape Town, South Africa: Sunbird Publishing, 2003. Print.

Labadie Special Collections Library, U of Michigan, Ann Arbor.

La Botz, Dan. *In Search of the Revolution: The Autobiography of an American Radical of the Generation of 1968.* Unpublished memoir, 2007. Print.

Lacey, Henry C. *To Raise, Destroy, and Create: The Poetry, Drama, and Fiction of Imamu Amiri Baraka (LeRoi Jones).* Troy, New York: Whitston, 1981. Print.

LaHaye, Tim and Jerry B. Jenkins. *Left Behind: A Novel of the Earth's Last Days.* Wheaton, Illinois: Tyndale House, 1995. Print.

Lakoff, George. *Don't Think of an Elephant!: Know Your Values and Frame the Debate: The Essential Guide for Progressives.* White River Junction, Vermont: Chelsea Green, 2004. Print.

———. *Metaphors We Live By.* Chicago: U of Chicago P, 1980. Print.

Lamanna, Giulianna. "Let's Get Primitive." *The Fabulous Forager.* 29 Apr. 2008. Web. 11 May 2008.

Lawrence, A. H. *Duke Ellington and His World.* New York: Routledge, 2001. Print.

Lazerow, Jama and Yohuru Williams. "The Black Panthers and Historical Scholarship: Why Now?" *In Search of the Black Panther Party: New Perspectives on a Revolutionary Movement.* Ed. Jama Lazerow and Yohuru Williams. Durham: Duke UP, 2006. 1–12. Print.

LeBlanc-Ernest, Angela D. " 'The Most Qualified Person to Handle the Job': Black Panther Party Women, 1966–1982." *The Black Panther Party Reconsidered.* Ed. Charles E. Jones. Baltimore: Black Classic, 1998. 305–34. Print.

Le Blanc, Paul. Telephone interview. 23 and 25 Aug. 2007.

———. "Trotskyism in the United States: The First Fifty Years." *Trotskyism in the United States: Historical Essays and Reconsiderations.* Ed. George Breitman, Paul Le Blanc, and Alan Wald. New Jersey: Humanities, 1996. 3–87. Print.

Lee, Don L. *Directionscore: Selected and New Poems.* Detroit: Broadside, 1971. Print.

Lee, Edward. *Whoever Heard of Bongo Drums on the Picket Line.* Pamphlet. [Detroit]: n.p., n.d. Print. Labadie Special Collections Library, U of Michigan, Ann Arbor.

Lee, Richard. *The !Kung San: Men, Women, and Work in a Foraging Society.* Cambridge: Cambridge UP, 1979. Print.

Lee, Richard B. and Irven DeVore, eds. *Man the Hunter.* Chicago: Aldine, 1968. Print.

Lee, Stan, et al. *The Fantastic Four #52–56. 44 Years of Fantastic Four.* DVD-Rom. Collector's Edition. Graphic Imaging Technology [Marvel Comics], 2005.

Lefever, Harry G. *Undaunted by the Fight: Spelman College and the Civil Rights Movement, 1957–1967.* Macon: Mercer, 2005. Print.

Lemke, Sieglinde. *Primitivist Modernism: Black Culture and the Origins of Transatlantic Modernism.* Oxford: Oxford UP, 1998. Print.

"Lessons of Our First Two and a Half Years in New York Telephone." N.p.: n.p. [1972]. Print. Box 3. International Socialists Issuances, 1967–1976. Hoover Institution Archives. Stanford U, Stanford.

"Let's Get Down: How Can You Get Any Respect When You Haven't Had Any Yet!!!" Handbill. [c. 1969–1972]. Box 6, folder 6-26. Kenneth V. and Sheila M. Cockrel Collection. Walter P. Reuther Library of Labor and Urban Affairs, Wayne State U, Detroit.

"Letter Written by a Racist to Sister Frances Carter of the Conn. 9, Recently Released from Prison." *Black Panther* 19 July. 1970: 4. Print.

Lévi-Strauss, Claude. "The Concept of Primitiveness." *Man the Hunter.* Ed. Richard B. Lee and Irven DeVore. Chicago: Aldine, 1968. 349–352. Print

Lindsay, Vachel. *The Congo and Other Poems.* New York: Macmillan, 1914. Print.

Lindsey, Robert. "Algerians Seize 1-Million Ransom." *New York Times* 2 Aug. 1972: 1+. Print.

Littmann, William. "The Production of Goodwill: The Origins and Development of the Factory Tour in America." *Perspectives in Vernacular Architecture* 9 (2003): 71–84. Print.

Locke, Alain. *The Negro and His Music.* 1936. New York: Arno, 1968. Print.

Longfellow, Henry Wadsworth. *The Complete Poetical Works of Henry Wadsworth Longfellow.* London: Routledge, 1871. Print.

Lott, Eric. *Love and Theft: Blackface Minstrelsy and the American Working Class.* New York: Oxford UP, 1993. Print.

Lovejoy, Arthur O., and George Boas. *Primitivism and Related Ideas in Antiquity.* New York: Octagon, 1965. Print.

Lynd, Alice, and Staughton Lynd, eds. *Rank and File: Personal Histories by Working-Class Organizers.* Boston: Beacon, 1973. Print.

Mackenzie, Brian. "Telephone Strike Hung Up." *Workers' Power* 29 (29 Jan.–11 Feb. 1971): 14–16. Print.

———. "Socialists in Industry." *IS Bulletin* 16 (1 Feb. 1972). Print. Box 1. International Socialists Issuances, 1967–1976. Hoover Institution Archives. Stanford U, Stanford.

Madhubuti, Haki R. *Groundwork: New and Selected Poems of Don L. Lee/ Haki R. Madhubuti from 1966–1996.* Chicago: Third World, 1996. Print.

Madison Foster Papers. Bentley Historical Library, U of Michigan, Ann Arbor.

Manes, Christopher. *Green Rage: Radical Environmentalism and the Unmaking of Civilization.* Boston: Little, 1990. Print.

Mao, Douglas and Rebecca L. Walkowitz, eds. *Bad Modernisms.* Durham: Duke UP, 2006. Print.

Marchand, Roland. *Creating the Corporate Soul: The Rise of Public Relations and Corporate Imagery in American Big Business.* Berkeley: U of California P, 1998. Print.

Martineau, Harriet. "A Manchester Strike." *Illustrations of Political Economy: Selected Tales.* Ed. Deborah Anna Logan. Peterborough, Ontario: Broadview, 2004. 137–216. Print.

Martinez, Elizabeth. "The WTO: Where Was the Color in Seattle?" *Color Lines* 3.1 (Spring 2000): 11–12. Print.

Marx, Karl. *The Communist Manifesto.* 1848. Ed. Frederic L. Bender. New York: Norton, 1988. Print.

———. "Critique of the Gotha Program." *The Marx-Engels Reader.* Ed. Robert C. Tucker. 2nd ed. New York: Norton, 1978. 525–41. Print.

———. *The Eighteenth Brumaire of Louis Bonaparte.*1852. New York: International, 2004. Print.

Marx, Leo. *The Machine in the Garden: Technology and the Pastoral Ideal in America.* New York: Oxford UP, 1964. Print.

Mast, Robert H, ed. *Detroit Lives.* Philadelphia: Temple UP, 1994. Print.

Matthews, Tracye. "'No One Ever Asks, What a Man's Role in the Revolution Is': Gender and the Politics of the Black Panther Party, 1966–1971." *The Black Panther Party Reconsidered.* Ed. Charles E. Jones. Baltimore: Black Classic, 1998. 267–304. Print.

Mayfield, Julian. "You Touch My Black Aesthetic and I'll Touch Yours." *The Black Aesthetic.* Ed. Addison Gayle, Jr. Garden City: Doubleday, 1971. 24–31. Print.

Mayhew, Henry and George Cruikshank. *1815, or, The Adventures of Mr. and Mrs. Sandboys, Their Son and Daughter, Who Came Up to London to Enjoy Themselves and to See the Great Exhibition.* New York: Stringer and Townsend, 1851. Print.

McCarthy, Cormac. *The Road.* New York: Knopf, 2007. Print.

McClintock, Anne. *Imperial Leather: Race, Gender and Sexuality in the Colonial Contest.* New York: Routledge, 1995. Print.

McDonough, Tom. *Guy Debord and the Situationist International: Texts and Documents.* Cambridge: MIT Press, 2002. Print.

Meyer, Philip, survey director. *The People beyond 12th Street: A Survey of Attitudes of Detroit Negroes after the Riot of 1967.* Detroit: Detroit Urban League, 1967. Print.

Miah, Malik. "Socialists and Barack Obama." *Against the Current* 135 (Aug./Sept. 2008). Web. 10 Oct. 2010.

Milton Genecin Papers. Hoover Institution Archives. Stanford U, Stanford.

Mitchell, Angelyn. "Not Enough of the Past: Feminist Revisions of Slavery in Octavia E. Butler's *Kindred*." *MELUS* 26.3 (Autumn 2001): 51–75. Print.

Moody, Kim. *Workers in a Lean World: Unions in the International Economy*. London: Verso, 1997. Print.

Morgan, Edward P. "Media Culture and the Public Memory of the Black Panther Party." *In Search of the Black Panther Party: New Perspectives on a Revolutionary Movement*. Ed. Jama Lazerow and Yohuru Williams. Durham: Duke UP, 2006. 324–73. Print.

Morrison, Toni. *Beloved*. 1987. New York: Plume, 1988. Print.

Mos Def, and Talib Kweli. *Black Star*. Rawkus, 1998. CD.

Moses, Wilson Jeremiah. *Afrotopia: The Roots of African American Popular History*. Cambridge: Cambridge UP, 1998. Print.

Moylan, Tom, ed. *Dark Horizons: Science Fiction and the Dystopian Imagination*. New York: Routledge, 2003. Print.

Neal, Larry. "The Black Arts Movement." *The Black Aesthetic*. Ed. Addison Gayle. Garden City, New York: Doubleday, 1971. 272–90. Print.

Nelson, Alondra. " 'Making the Impossible Possible': An Interview with Nalo Hopkinson." *Social Text* 20.2 (2002): 97–113. Print.

Newton, Huey. "In Defense of Self-Defense." *Black Panther* 4 May 1968: 6–7. Print.

———. *The Genius of Huey P. Newton, Minister of Defense, Black Panther Party*. San Francisco: Ministry of Information, Black Panther Party, 1970. Print.

Newton, Huey P. with J. Herman Blake. *Revolutionary Suicide*. New York: Writers and Readers, 1995. Print.

Ngozi-Brown, Scot. "The Us Organization, Maulana Karenga, and Conflict with the Black Panther Party: A Critique of Sectarian Influences on Historical Discourse." *Journal of Black Studies* 28.2 (Nov. 1997): 157–70. Print.

Nicholls, William L. II, and Earl R. Babbie. *Oakland in Transition: A Summary of the 701 Household Survey*. Berkeley: Survey Research Center of UC Berkeley, 1969. Print.

"19 Year Old Sister Murdered by Fascist K.C. Pigs." *Black Panther* 23 Aug. 1969: 21. Print.

Njeri, Akua. *My Life with the Black Panther Party*. St Petersburg, Florida: Burning Spear, 1991. Print.

North, Michael. "Modernism's African Mask: The Stein-Picasso Collaboration." *Prehistories of the Future: The Primitivist Project and the Culture of Modernism*. Ed. Elazar Barkan and Ronald Bush. Stanford: Stanford UP, 1995. 270–89. Print.

Northrup, Herbert R. *The Negro in the Automobile Industry.* The Racial Policies of American Industry 1. Philadelphia: U of Pennsylvania P, 1968. Print.

Nye, David. *American Technological Sublime.* Cambridge: MIT P, 1994. Print.

Obama, Barack. "A More Perfect Union." National Constitution Center, Philadelphia. 18 Mar. 2008. Speech.

"Obama's Speech on Climate Change." *New York Times.* New York Times, 22 Sept. 2009. Web. 22 Dec. 2009.

Ogar, Ted. "To Start Off '69: New Range of Pension Benefits." *UAW Solidarity* 12.1 (Jan. 1969): 3. Print.

Ogbar, Jeffrey O. G. *Black Power: Radical Politics and African American Identity.* Baltimore: Johns Hopkins UP, 2004. Print.

————. "Brown Power to Brown People: Radical Ethnic Nationalism, the Black Panthers, and Latino Radicalism, 1967–1973." *In Search of the Black Panther Party: New Perspectives on a Revolutionary Movement.* Ed. Jama Lazerow and Yohuru Williams. Durham: Duke UP, 2006. 252–86. Print.

O'Hara, Craig. *The Philosophy of Punk: More than Noise!!* Edinburgh: AK, 1999. Print.

Olney, James. " 'I Was Born': Slave Narratives, their Status as Autobiography and as Literature." *Slave Narrative.* Ed. Charles T. Davis and Henry Louis Gates, Jr. New York: Oxford UP, 1985. 148–75. Print.

Olsen, Jack. *Last Man Standing: The Tragedy and Triumph of Geronimo Pratt.* New York: Anchor, 2000. Print.

O'Neale, Sondra A. "Ishmael Reed's Fitful Flight to Canada: Liberation for Some, Good Reading for All." *Callaloo* 4 (Oct. 1978): 174–77. Print.

O'Neill, Eugene. *The Hairy Ape, Anna Christie, The First Man.* New York: Boni and Liveright, 1922. Print.

Opening of the Liverpool and Manchester Railroad. Edinburgh: Blackwood, 1830. Print.

"An Open Letter to Black Artists." *Inner-City Voice* 3.2 (Apr. 1971): 6–7. Print.

Orwell, George. *Nineteen Eighty-Four.* 1949. New York: Harcourt Brace, 1983. Print.

————. *Shooting an Elephant, and Other Essays.* London: Secker and Warburg, 1950. Print.

"Our Thing Is DRUM." [By George Jones]. *The General Policy Statement and Labor Program of the League of Revolutionary Black Workers.* Highland Park, MI: n.p. [1970?]. Print. Box 4, folder 4-12. Dan Georgakas Collection. Walter P. Reuther Library of Labor and Urban Affairs, Wayne State U, Detroit.

The Overall Program of the League of Revolutionary Black Workers. Detroit: League of Revolutionary Black Workers, 1970. Print. Box 1. Madison Foster Papers. Bentley Historical Library, U of Michigan, Ann Arbor.

P., Mike, and James M. "The 1972 Convention and Beyond." *IS Bulletin* 35 (20 Dec. 1972). Print. Box 1. International Socialists Issuances, 1967–1976. Hoover Institution Archives. Stanford U, Stanford.

Panter-Brick, Catherine, Robert Layton, and P. Rowley-Conwy, eds. *Hunter-Gatherers: An Interdisciplinary Perspective*. Cambridge: Cambridge UP, 2001. Print.

"Panther Is Executed." *The Pittsburgh Courier* 4 Sept. 1926: 12. Print.

Pardun, Robert. *Prairie Radical: A Journey through the Sixties*. Los Gatos, California: Shire, 2001. Print.

Parke, Richard H. "Westport Urged to Bar Industry." *New York Times* 14 Feb. 1962: 41. Print.

Payne, Roz. "WACing Off: Gossip, Sex, Race, and Politics in the World of FBI Special Case Agent William A. Cohendet." *In Search of the Black Panther Party: New Perspectives on a Revolutionary Movement*. Ed. Jama Lazerow and Yohuru Williams. Durham: Duke UP, 2006. 158–80. Print.

Pierce, Wayne. "Racism in Auto." *Workers' Power: International Socialist Biweekly* 21 (11–24 Sept. 1970): 5. Print.

The Pink Phink. Dir. Fritz Freeleng and Hawley Pratt. DePatie-Freeleng Enterprises, 1964. Film.

Podair, Jerald. *The Strike that Changed New York: Blacks, Whites, and the Ocean Hill–Brownsville Crisis*. New Haven: Yale UP, 2002. Print.

Pope, Debby. Telephone interview. 2 Sept. 2007.

Porter, Emily. *Tracker of Plants*. Web. 7 Feb. 2010.

Potassium, Hannah. *Power Machine: A Lengthy Discourse on the Nature of Squatting*. Emeryville, California: n.p. [2006]. Print.

Powers, Richard Gid. *Broken: The Troubled Past and Uncertain Future of the FBI*. New York: Free Press, 2004. Print.

Price, David. *Before the Bulldozer: The Nambiquara Indians and the World Bank*. Cabin John, MD: Seven Locks, 1989. Print.

Price, Wayne. "Letter to a YSA Member." *IS Bulletin* 10 (1 Aug. 1971). Print. Box 1. International Socialists Issuances, 1967–1976. Hoover Institution Archives. Stanford U, Stanford.

Prieur, Ran. *Crash!* Ed. Green Anarchist Infoshop. N.p.: Creative Commons, 2006. Print.

Prince, Mary. *The History of Mary Prince: A West Indian Slave*. 1831. London: Penguin, 2000. Print.

Pritchett, Wendell E. *Brownsville, Brooklyn: Blacks, Jews, and the Changing Face of the Ghetto*. Chicago: U of Chicago P, 2002. Print.

Purkis, Jonathan, and James Bowen, eds. *Changing Anarchism: Anarchist Theory and Practice in a Global Age*. Manchester: Manchester UP, 2004. Print.

"The Radioactive Runway with Molly Strand." [2008]. *Urban Scout*. Web. 11 May 2008.

Rameau, Max. *Take Back the Land: Gentrification and the Umoja Village Shantytown*. Miami: Nia Interactive Press, 2008. Print.

Rampersad, Arnold, ed. *The Oxford Anthology of African-American Poetry*. Oxford: Oxford UP, 2006. Print.

Raskin, A. H. "Labor: A New 'Era of Bad Feeling'?" *New York Times* 5 Jul. 1959: SM8. Print.

"The Real Deal on the 'Special Conference.'" *Eldon Ave. Revolutionary Union Movement*. N.p.: n.p., n.d. Print. Kenneth V. and Sheila M. Cockrel Collection. Walter P. Reuther Library of Labor and Urban Affairs, Wayne State U, Detroit.

Reed, Ishmael. *Flight to Canada*. New York: Random, 1976. Print.

Reed, T. V. *The Art of Protest: Culture and Activism from the Civil Rights Movement to the Streets of Seattle*. Minneapolis: U of Minnesota P, 2005. Print.

———. *Fifteen Jugglers, Five Believers: Literary Politics and the Poetics of American Social Movements*. Berkeley: U of California P, 1992. Print.

Reid-Pharr, Robert. *Once You Go Black: Choice, Desire, and the Black American Intellectual*. New York: New York UP, 2007. Print.

"Report on the Militant's Circulation in 1973." Print. Box 9. Milton Genecin Papers. Hoover Institution Archives. Stanford U, Stanford.

"Report on the 1974 Spring Sales Campaign." 14 June 1974. Print. Box 9. Milton Genecin Papers. Hoover Institution Archives. Stanford U, Stanford.

Rewild.info: The Free Field Guide to Rewilding that Anyone Can Edit. 15 Aug. 2007. Web. 13 Mar. 2008.

Rhodes, Colin. "Review: *The Sleep of Reason: Primitivism in Modern Art and Aesthetics, 1725–1907*, by Frances Connelly." *Burlington Magazine* 137.1110: 628. Print.

Rhodes, Jane. *Framing the Black Panthers: The Spectacular Rise of a Black Power Icon*. New York: The New Press, 2007. Print.

Riker, William. *The Art of Political Manipulation*. New Haven: Yale UP, 1986. Print.

Ritterband, Paul. "Ethnic Power and the Public Schools: The New York City School Strike of 1968." *American Sociological Association* 47.2 (Spring 1974): 251–67. Print.

Robinson, Candi. "Message to Revolutionary Women." *Black Panther* 9 Aug. 1969: 23. Print.

Robinson, Cedric. *Black Marxism: The Making of the Black Radical Tradition.* Chapel Hill: U of North Carolina P, 2000. Print.

Roediger, David. *The Wages of Whiteness: Race and the Making of the American Working Class.* London: Verso, 1999. Print.

Rojas, Fabio. *From Black Power to Black Studies: How a Radical Social Movement Became an Academic Discipline.* Baltimore: Johns Hopkins U Press, 2007. Print.

Rose, Phyllis. *Jazz Cleopatra: Josephine Baker in her Time.* New York: Doubleday, 1989. Print.

Rowthorn, Robert and Ramana Ramaswamy. "Deindustrialization—Its Causes and Implications." *International Monetary Fund.* 1997. Web. 20 Mar. 2008.

Rushdy, Ahsraf. *Neo-Slave Narratives: Studies in the Social Logic of a Literary Form.* New York: Oxford UP, 1999. Print.

Rydell, Robert W. *All the World's a Fair: Visions of Empire at American International Expositions, 1876–1916.* Chicago: U of Chicago P, 1984. Print.

Sackett, S. J. Rev. of *Black Fire: An Anthology of Afro-American Writing,* ed. LeRoi Jones and Larry Neal. *Negro American Literature Forum* 8.3 (Autumn 1974): 252–53. Print.

Sahlins, Marshall. "The Original Affluent Society." *Stone Age Economics.* Chicago: Aldine-Atherton, 1972. 1–40. Print.

Salaam, Kalamu Ya. "A Primer of the Black Arts Movement." *Black Renaissance/Renaissance Noire* 4.2/3 (Summer 2002): 40–58. *LexisNexis* Web. 19 Jan. 2010.

"Salute to a Black Patriot." *Spear* 26 Mar. 1971. Print. Box 1. Madison Foster Papers. Bentley Historical Library, U of Michigan, Ann Arbor.

Sanchez, Sonia. *Home Coming.* Detroit: Broadside, 1969. Print.

Sanders, Mark A. "The Ballad, the Hero, and the Ride: A Reading of Sterling A. Brown's *The Last Ride of Wild Bill.*" *The Furious Flowering of African American Poetry.* Ed. Joanne V. Gabbin. Charlottesville: UP of Virginia, 1999. 118–34. Print.

Saunders, Charles. "Why Blacks Should Read (and Write) Science Fiction." *Dark Matter: A Century of Speculative Fiction from the African Diaspora.* Ed. Sheree R. Thomas. New York: Time Warner, 2000. 398–404. Print.

Sauti 1.9 (Sept. 1969). Print.

Sauti: The Inner-City Voice 2.2 (Nov. 1969). Print.

Scarce, Rik. *Eco-Warriors: Understanding the Radical Environmental Movement.* Updated ed. Walnut Creek, California: Left Coast, 2006. Print.

Seale, Bobby. *Seize the Time: The Story of the Black Panther Party and Huey P. Newton.* New York: Random House, 1970. Print.

Segal, David R., and Mady Wechsler Segal. "America's Military Population." *Population Bulletin* 59.4 (Dec. 2004). Washington: Population Reference Bureau, 2004. Print.

Self, Robert O. *American Babylon: Race and the Struggle for Postwar Oakland.* Princeton: Princeton UP, 2003. Print.

Sell, Mike. *Avant-Garde Performance and the Limits of Criticism: Approaching the Living Theatre, Happenings/Fluxus, and the Black Arts Movement.* Ann Arbor: The U of Michigan P, 2005. Print.

Shadle, Mark Francis. *Mumbo Jumbo Gumbo Works: The Kaleidoscopic Fiction of Ishmael Reed.* Ann Arbor: UMI, 1984. Print.

Shakur, Afeni. "Housing Conditions: Capitalism and Our Children." *Black Panther* 6 June 1970: 2. Print.

Shakur, Assata. *Assata: An Autobiography.* 1987. Chicago: Lawrence Hill, 2001. Print.

Shames, Stephen. *The Black Panthers: Photographs.* New York: Aperture, 2006. Print.

Sheppard, Barry. *The Party: The Socialist Workers Party, 1960–1988.* Vol. 1. Chippendale, Australia: Resistance, 2005. Print.

"A Short Missive to Anarchists of Color on Primitivism, Ideology and Options." *Illvox: Setting Fire to the Master's House.* 19 Sept. 2007. Web. 9 May 2007.

Simmons, Roscoe. "The Week." *Chicago Defender* 2 Aug. 1924: A1. Print.

Sinclair, Upton. *The Jungle.* 1906. New York: Barnes and Noble, 2003. Print.

Singer, Stu. "Young Workers Discuss Iran: A Different View." *Militant* 8 Feb. 1980: 5. Print.

Singh, Nikhil Pal. "The Black Panthers and the 'Undeveloped Country' of the Left." *The Black Panther Party Reconsidered.* Ed. Charles E. Jones. Baltimore: Black Classic, 1998. 57–108. Print.

Smethurst, James Edward. "The Black Arts Movement and Historically Black Colleges and Universities." *New Thoughts on the Black Arts Movement.* Ed. Lisa Gail Collins and Margo Natalie Crawford. New Brunswick, Rutgers UP, 2006. 75–91. Print.

———. *The Black Arts Movement: Literary Nationalism in the 1960s and 1970s.* Chapel Hill: The U of North Carolina P, 2005. Print.

Smith, David. "Amiri Baraka and the Black Arts of Black Art." *boundary 2* 15 (Autumn 1986): 235–54. Print.

Smith, David Lionel. "The Black Arts Movement and its Critics." *American Literary History* 3.1 (Spring 1991): 93–110. Print.

Snoop Dogg featuring The Game. "Gang Bangin' 101." *The Blue Carpet Treatment*. Geffen, 2006. CD.

Sobek, Matthew. "Occupations." *Historical Statistics of the United States, Earliest Times to the Present: Millennial Edition*. Ed. Susan B. Carter, et al. New York: Cambridge, 2006. Web. 7 Feb. 2010.

Sollers, Werner. *Amiri Baraka/LeRoi Jones: The Quest for a 'Populist Modernism.'* New York: Columbia UP, 1978. Print.

South End 23 Jan. 1969. Print. Box 4, folder 4-26. Detroit Revolutionary Movements Collection. Walter P. Reuther Library of Labor and Urban Affairs, Wayne State U, Detroit.

———. 28 Feb. 1969: 4. Print.

———. 26 Mar. 1971. Print. Box 1. Madison Foster Papers. Bentley Historical Library, U of Michigan, Ann Arbor.

Spaulding, A. Timothy. *Re-Forming the Past: History, the Fantastic, and the Postmodern Slave Narrative*. Columbus: The Ohio State UP, 2005. Print.

Spellman, A. B. "Big Bushy Afros." *The International Review of African American Art: The Art of Political Struggle and Cultural Revolution of the 1960s and 70s* 15.1 (1998): 53. Print.

Stacy, Kate. Telephone interview. 5 Sept. 2007.

Stark, Louis. "Shattering of Labor Front Quiet Spurs Drive for Restrictive Laws." *New York Times* 8 Apr. 1947: 1. Print.

Starling, Marion Wilson. The Slave Narrative: Its Place in American History. Washington, DC: Howard UP, 1981. Print.

Stepto, Robert. *From Behind the Veil: A Study of Afro-American Narrative*. Urbana: U of Illinois P, 1979. Print.

Stidger, William. *Henry Ford: The Man and His Motives*. New York: George H. Doran, 1923. Print.

Stiglitz, Joseph. *Globalization and its Discontents*. New York: Norton, 2002. Print.

Stone, Ben. *Memoirs of a Radical Rank and Filer*. New York: Prometheus, 1986. Print.

Stovall, Tyler Edward. *Paris Noir: African Americans in the City of Light*. Boston: Houghton Mifflin, 1996. Print.

Styron, William. *The Confessions of Nat Turner*. 1967. New York: Modern Library, 1994. Print.

Sullivan, Joseph F. "Panther, Trooper Slain in Shoot-Out; Woman Sought in Killing of Officers Here Captured." *New York Times* 3 May 1973: 89. Print.

Swearingen, M. Wesley. *FBI Secrets: An Agent's Exposé.* Boston: South End, 1995. Print.

Szántó, András, ed. *What Orwell Didn't Know: Propaganda and the New Face of American Politics.* New York: Public Affairs, 2007. Print.

Tabor, Ron. "Tasks and Perspectives (Draft), 4/2/72." *IS Bulletin* 21–22 (April 1972). Print. Box 2. International Socialists Issuances, 1967–1976. Hoover Institution Archives. Stanford U, Stanford.

Taylor, John. Statement to Dan Georgakas. 25 Aug. 1972. Print. Box 3, folder 3-17. Dan Georgakas Collection. Walter P. Reuther Library of Labor and Urban Affairs, Wayne State U, Detroit.

Thomas, Sheree, ed. *Dark Matter: A Century of Speculative Fiction from the African Diaspora.* New York: Time Warner, 2000. Print.

Thompson, Frank. Telephone interview. 20 Sept. 2007.

Thompson, Heather Ann. *Whose Detroit? Politics, Labor, and Race in a Modern American City.* Ithaca: Cornell UP, 2001. Print.

Thompson, Wendy. Telephone interview. 23 Aug. 2007.

"Tom of the Month." *Sauti* [The Inner-City Voice] 1.9 (Sept. 1969): 17. Print. Labadie Special Collections Library, U of Michigan, Ann Arbor.

Torgovnick, Marianna. *Gone Primitive: Savage Intellects, Modern Lives.* Chicago: U of Chicago P, 1990. Print.

Torres, J., writer. *Black Panther: Coming to America, Part 2 of 2.* Cover art by Liam Sharp. Pencil by Ryan Bodenheim. Ink by Walden Wong. Color by Jennifer Schellinger. Letters by Paul Tutrone. New York: Marvel, 2003. Print. Vol. 2, No. 58 of *Black Panther.*

"To the Point of Production: An Interview with John Watson of the League of Revolutionary Black Workers." Boston: New England Free Press [c. 1969]. Print.

Tripp, Luke. "D.R.U.M.—Vanguard of the Black Revolution: Dodge Revolutionary Union Movement States History, Purpose and Aims." *South End* 23 Jan. 1969: 1–5. Print.

Tucker, Kevin. "Prepare for the Best, Train for the Worst: Getting Ready for the Collapse." *Species Traitor: An Insurrectionary Anarcho Primitivist Journal* 4 (Summer 2005): 72–81. Print.

Ture, Kwame [Stokely Carmichael] and Charles V. Hamilton. *Black Power: The Politics of Liberation.* New York: Vintage, 1992. Print.

28 Days Later. Dir. Danny Boyle. DNA Films, 2003. Film.

"The 2008 Elections." *Solidarity.* May 2008. Web. 10 Oct. 2010.

2012. Dir. Roland Emmerich. Columbia Pictures, 2009. Film.>

Underground Newspapers Collection. Bentley Historical Library. U of Michigan, Ann Arbor.

United Auto Workers International Executive Board. Letter to members. 10 Mar. 1969. Print. Box 4, folder 4-25. Detroit Revolutionary Movements Collection. Walter P. Reuther Library of Labor and Urban Affairs, Wayne State U, Detroit.

"United National Caucus Meets in Detroit." *Workers' Power* 46 (26 Nov.–9 Dec. 1971): 3. Print.

United States. Commission on Civil Rights. *Hearings Before the United States Commission on Civil Rights: Hearings Held in Detroit, Michigan December 14, 1960 and December 15, 1960.* Washington: GPO, 1961. Print.

United States. Cong. House. Committee on Internal Security. *Black Panther Party, Part One: Investigation of Kansas City Chapter; National Organization Data.* Hearing, 4, 5, 6, and 10 Mar. 1970. 91st Cong., 2nd sess. Washington: GPO, 1970. Print.

United States. Cong. House. Committee on Internal Security. *Black Panther Party, Part Three: Investigation of Activities in Detroit, Mich.; Philadelphia, Pa.; and Indianapolis, Ind.* Hearing, 21–24 July 1970. 91st Cong., 2nd sess. Washington: GPO, 1970. Print.

United States Dept. of Labor. "Union Members in 2007." Washington, DC: Bureau of Labor Statistics, 2008. Print.

Urban Scout. *The Adventures of Urban Scout: A Hunter-Gatherer Wannabe.* Web. 28 Mar. 2008.

Van Deburg, William L. *New Day in Babylon: The Black Power Movement and American Culture, 1965–1975.* Chicago: U of Chicago P, 1992. Print.

Van Savage, Rick. "Squatting the Lower East Side." Kick It Over 35 (Summer 1995) Flag.blackened.net. Web. 23 Mar. 2008.

Varon, Jeremy. *Bringing the War Home: The Weather Underground, the Red Army, and Revolutionary Violence in the Sixties and Seventies.* Berkeley: U of California P, 2004. Print.

Veney, Bethany. *The Narrative of Bethany Veney: A Slave Woman.* 1889. Collected Black Women's Narratives. Intro. Anthony G. Barthelemy. New York: Oxford UP, 1988. Print.

Veviaka, Rose. "New York Operators—Join CWA, to Change It." *Workers' Power* 39 (Aug. 1971): 3. Print.

———. "Traffic Trouble." *Workers' Power* 29 (29 Jan.–11 Feb. 1971): 16. Print.

The Wailers. "Concrete Jungle." By Bob Marley. *Catch a Fire.* Island Records, 1973. LP.

Walcott, Derek. *Ti-Jean and His Brothers*. 1957. *Black Drama*. Alexander Street, 2002. Web. 28 Apr. 2008.

Walker, Margaret. *Jubilee*. 1966. New York: Mariner Books, 1999. Print.

Wallace, Michele. *Black Macho and the Myth of the Superwoman*. 1978. London: Verso, 1990. Print.

Weixlmann, Joe. "African American Deconstruction of the Novel in the Work of Ishmael Reed and Clarence Major." *MELUS* 17.4 (Winter 1991–1992): 57–79. Print.

West, Kanye. "Crack Music." *Late Registration*. Roc-a-Fella, 2005. CD.

Whatley, Warren C. "African-American Strikebreaking from the Civil War to the New Deal." *Social Science History* 17.4 (Winter 1993): 525–58. Print.

White, Deborah Gray. *Too Heavy a Load: Black Women in Defense of Themselves, 1894–1994*. New York: Norton, 1999. Print.

White, Michelle-Lee, et al. "Afrotech and Outer Spaces." *Art Journal* 60.3 (Autumn 2001): 90–104. Print.

Whitman, Walt. "To a Locomotive in Winter." *Leaves of Grass*. 1855. Oxford: Oxford UP, 1998. 358. Print.

"Who Is James Johnson?" *Spear* n.d. Print. Box 1. Madison Foster Papers. Bentley Historical Library, U of Michigan, Ann Arbor.

"Why Cuba Has Jobs for All." *Militant* 23 May 1980: 26. Print.

Widick, B. J. *Detroit: City of Race and Class Violence*. Detroit: Wayne State UP, 1989. Print.

Wilentz, Sean. "Confounding Fathers: The Tea Party's Cold War Roots." *New Yorker* 18 Oct. 2010: 32–39.

Wilkins, Roy, and Ramsey Clark, chairmen. *Search and Destroy: A Report*. Commission of Inquiry into the Black Panthers and the Police. New York: Metropolitan Applied Research Center, 1973. Print.

Williams, Duncan. "From Trotsky's Archives: Founding the International Left Opposition." *International Socialist Review* (May 1980): 8. Print.

Williams, Randy. "Urban Guerrillas." *Black Panther* 6 June 1970: 5. Print.

Williams, Sherley Anne. *Dessa Rose*. Thorndike, Maine: Thorndike, 1986. Print.

Winterhalder, Bruce. "The Behavioral Ecology of Hunter-Gatherers." *Hunter-Gatherers: An Interdisciplinary Perspective*. Ed. Catherine Panter-Brick, Robert Layton, and P. Rowley-Conwy. Cambridge: Cambridge UP, 2001. 12–38. Print.

Wohlforth, Tim. *The Prophet's Children: Travels on the American Left*. New Jersey: Humanities, 1994. Print.

Woodard, Komozi. *A Nation within a Nation: Amiri Baraka (LeRoi Jones) and Black Power Politics*. Chapel Hill: U of North Carolina P, 1999. Print.

————. "Imamu Baraka, the Newark Congress of African People, and Black Power Politics." *Black Power: In the Belly of the Beast.* Ed. Judson L. Jeffries. Urbana: U of Illinois P, 2006. 43–67. Print.

Wood, Ean. *The Josephine Baker Story.* London: Sanctuary, 2000. Print.

"Wright's 'Audacity to Hope' Sermon." *New York Times.* New York Times, 30 Apr. 2008. Web. 18 Dec. 2009.

X, Malcolm, as told to Alex Haley. *The Autobiography of Malcolm X.* New York: Grove, 1966. Print.

Yaroslavsky, E. *History of Anarchism in Russia.* New York: International, 1973. Print.

Yates, Michael D. *Naming the System: Inequality and Work in the Global Economy.* New York: Monthly Review, 2003. Print.

Yoruba-English/English-Yoruba Concise Dictionary. New York: Hippocrene, 1996. Print.

Young, Lowell. *The 1928 and 1930 Comintern Resolutions on the Black National Question in the United States.* Washington, DC: Revolutionary Review Press, 1975. Print.

Young, Nigel. *An Infantile Disorder?: The Crisis and Decline of the New Left.* London: Routledge, 1977. Print.

Young, Paul. "Mission Impossible: Globalization and the Great Exhibition." *Britain, the Empire, and the World at the Great Exhibition of 1851.* Ed. Jeffrey A. Auerbach and Peter H. Hoffenberg. Hampshire, England: Ashgate, 2008. 3–26. Print.

Young, Robert J. C. *Colonial Desire: Hybridity in Theory, Culture and Race.* London: Routledge, 1995. Print.

Zerzan, John. "Elements of Refusal." *Against Civilization: Readings and Reflections.* 1999. Ed. John Zerzan. Los Angeles: Feral House, 2005. 68–73. Print.

————. *Future Primitive and Other Essays.* Brooklyn: Autonomedia, 1994. Print.

————. Interview with John Filiss. N.d. *Primitivism.com.* Web. 29 Feb. 2008.

Zimmerman, Michael E., et al., eds. *Environmental Philosophy: From Animal Rights to Radical Ecology.* 4th ed. Upper Saddle River, NJ: Pearson, 2005. Print.

Index